DROHOBYCZ, DROHOBYCZ

AND OTHER STORIES

True Tales from the Holocaust and Life After

Drohobycz, Drohobycz . . .

FOR DR. LEOPOLD LUSTIG

The house was built by my great-grandmother Gitl, a midwife and a healer, who earned very good money. When she died, Jews and non-Jews placed hundreds of candles on her grave. The front of the house was plastered and corniced. It had a gate for my great-grandfather's carts and buggies. There was a well in the backyard. We were proud of it, because the water was very good. Imcio, the water-carrier, carried bucketfuls upstairs. Running water was installed in 1933. My great-grandfather Shloyme Erdman had thick curly hair and a long beard, and was called Shloyme the Goat. His brother was called Berl the Goat and his nephew Lipe the Goat because that curly hair ran in the family. My great-grandfather was a horse and buggy dealer. His deals usually ended in a net loss. Once he bought a mare that had its tail fastened on with pitched thread. After that my great-grandmother would give him pocket money for beer and beg him not to make any more deals. He suffered from uremia. They would place him on the kitchen table while the entire family stood around and watched as Doctor Tepper pushed a catheter into his penis. He died a year after my great-grandmother.

They had two sons. Icek went to America in 1905 and Jakub right after the Great War. And three daughters. Hanna married Josek Sternbach, who used to travel to Hungary and Romania for southern fruit for three seasons of the year, and in the winter lay sick in bed. They had no children because he neglected his gonorrhea on those long trips. They kept cats and he lay in bed with those cats. Hanna gave me money for chocolates. My great-grandmother also adored me. I was the only male descendant in her dynasty. In the evening, everyone sat in the kitchen under a lamp that could be pulled up and down. Before dark I would sneak into the kitchen and push the lamp all the way up to the ceiling. They had to call me to pull it down because even as a child I was already the tallest in the family. "Give me ten groszy and I'll put it down," I'd say. Yetka, the youngest, the prettiest, and vain, married a butcher, Szymon Fleischer, who promised her jewels and everything her heart desired, and then couldn't keep up and got into debt. One morning the maid went up to the attic to fetch the laundry and found him hanging between the shirts. Their daughter, Mania, was just a few years older than me. Yetka was married off to Arie Mańczyk, a widower who had a cheap ready-made clothing store on the main street in Lublin. Back then, everybody went to Truskawiec, a health resort near Drohobycz, and arranged marriages. Everybody wanted to dupe everybody, so the woman was always beautiful and had a big dowry, and the man had a terrific business, and then it would turn out that neither the one nor the other was true, just like in horse trading. My grandmother Pesia, who was the oldest, was going out with a law student, but my great-grandmother forced her to marry a proper man, a furrier, Eisig Grauman, who was fifteen years older than she was, and Pesia poisoned everybody's life after that. It was because of her that our family perished. We wanted to flee in 1941, but Pesia was against it. I try to forgive her, but I can't.

One room on the ground floor was occupied by Judge Drozdowski, whom the Soviets deported to Siberia. Before him another judge had lived in that room, Fruchtman. He was the illegitimate son of the maid and of a Jew from Stryj, who adopted him. Judge Fruchtman, who got baptized in order to become a judge, moved out after he married Singer's daughter, who had herself baptized to become the judge's wife. She was deported to Siberia, and he was found along with others under a pile of coal behind the courthouse. Mr. Weissber, a *cetlfirer*, a messenger, lived next door. If a woman needed lace, she went to Mr. Roth's shop, and if he didn't have the right kind just then, he would say, "I can have it for you the day after tomorrow." Then Mr. Weissber would come with a slip of paper and write down "Two yards of lace." He went from store to store and wrote down everything that had run short in Drohobycz, and then he traveled to Lwów taking letters, receipts and money orders at the same time. He would come back at night exhausted, and received three percent for that. He had a wife, Yachcia, and two very talented sons, who were communists from the time they were in their mother's belly. Leybko did time in Bereza and disappeared when the Soviets liberated him in 1939. Izio became an officer in the Soviet Army, and then in the Security Forces after the war. On the other side of the ground floor lived Mrs. Mermelstein, a widow, with one son and two daughters. Next to them the Jolleses, a young couple. He had a business in the small market square selling salmon and herring whose odor always trailed after him. On the first floor, also, lived Hanna with Josek and the cats, and Yetka with Mania before she married Mańczyk, and then again later when Mańczyk made her a widow for a second time. In the cellar, to the right, Mr. Schnepf had a beer bottling plant. The Münzers, who had a textile store in the main square, lived right above. On the second floor lived my grandmother Pesia with my grandfather whose life she was poisoning. Next to her, in separate rooms but with a common kitchen, lived my three aunts: Tonia, the pianist, with her old Bösendorfer grand piano and the Playel spinet; Regina and Klara, the youngest, sweet and beautiful with whom I was in love. Sofas, couches, folding beds stood everywhere. My parents and I occupied a room with a partition, above the main gate. Our maid Fesia, and Chéri, our black-and-white chihuahua, slept on a folding cot in the kitchen. The tenants changed. Our next door neighbors were in turn the Margulieses, the Habermans, and the Josefsbergs. When Jonasz Haberman who was a jeweller, bought his own house, my grandmother Pesia graciously allowed us to have one of their rooms. We paid the rent like everyone else and God forbid if father fell behind. The Gestapo took Haberman off the street, right after the pogroms, along with his father-in-law, Josl Herschman, a watch-maker. Mr. Herschman was a bearded Jew, and Jonasz Haberman a secular one, but he had a long Jewish nose. Neither came back.

Regina also left for Lublin. Arie Mańczyk arranged a match for her with a divorced man, owner of a prosperous junk yard, Adam Mandelkern who was really well off. Their son, Mareczek, was born three years before the war. I used to visit them during my vacations. Klara married Mayer Goldstein who was sent to her from Lublin by Mandelkern. Mayer studied at a merchant marine academy at Civita Vecchia in Italy. Sons of affluent families were sent there be-cause as sailors they could find their way to Palestine. Two young men from Drohobycz, Jakub Fiternik and Jakub Altschuler, studied there too. They used to come home for vacation in beautiful uni-forms, Italian in cut. Some young people would also go to Italy to study medicine when Jews were no longer admitted to medical schools in Poland. Those who could went to Prague, Budapest, Bucharest, Belgrade; the wealthier ones to France and, before the *Anschluss,* to Vienna. A renowed pianist, Yasha Fuhrman, fell in love with Klara, but my grandmother Pesia absolutely refused to let her marry some *klezmer.* She wanted her to marry Yosek Segal, a *Strassen-engineer* from a good family. *Strassen-engineers* were those who didn't study anywhere, just strolled along the streets with noth-ing to do. But that didn't pan out because a match was made for Yosek with a richer girl, Nusia Schnapp, the daughter of a sawmill owner. And then Mayer arrived, a refugee from Lublin, handsome and with nowhere to go, so they got married. Tonia left at that time for Lwów and married Jakub Rauchfleisch, who was an attorney, but worked as a proofreader for a Jewish newspaper.

Arie Mańczyk managed to die of a heart attack in 1938, and Yetka returned with Mania from Lublin. The Germans made Lublin *Judenrein* first, as a gift to Governor Frank. Grandmother Pesia received a short letter from Mandelkern, who was in Maj-danek, telling her that Regina and Mareczek were gone. He put a hundred dollars into the letter, and the money arrived. Josek Stern-bach went to Bronica with the handicapped, and Hanna in the first transport to Bełżec. Yetka in the second. Mania and Klara were taken to Bronica with everyone from the roof-tiling plant. Rauch-fleisch hid Tonia in a suburb of Lwów with his two sisters. He was supposed to join them but was caught and killed in the Janowska Street camp. Iza Haberman, Jonasz's widow, bought a house for a certain Pole on Borysławska Street and hid there in a cellar with her son Alex, her mother, the watchmaker Herschman's widow, and her sister Adela. Mrs. Mermelstein went with her children to Bełżec. So did the Münzers, the Jolleses, the Josefsbergs, as well as the Alt-bachs. Słowacki Street 17 was a two-story house like most buildings in Drohobycz.

Behind our property stood Mr. Lang's orchard and house. He was a Jewish Pole, a veteran of Piłsudski's Legions, and had the Cross of Valor. Such crosses were owned also by Semmel, a barber, Mr. Le-ichter, the owner of the movie-theater "Art," and by Mr. Bernfeld, who lived off his wife's dowry. On November 11, Independence Day, they paraded in their uniforms and the Poles chanted, "Jew-boy soldiers!" Carpenter Wang was also one of the Jewish veterans. He had ended up inadvertently in Haller's anti-Semitic army. Gen-eral Haller comes to Drohobycz, and out steps Mr. Wang in a blue uniform. Mr. Lang, a cavalry man, owned a livery shipping business with Belgian horses for transporting heavy furniture. When the Germans came, he became an *ordner* and afterwards was marched off to the cemetery with the other *ordners*. His son Kuba served as a messenger, but wore stiff cavalry boots like his father. He tried to run away as they led him to the train, but couldn't run far in those boots.

The neighboring buildings were shabby and wooden. On one side lived the cobbler, Sztuka, a Russian, a former White Guard of-ficer whose wife spoke only Russian and every evening played the mandolin. He was a cobbler because he had to make a living some-how. The wooden house on the other side was carefully renovated a short time before the war, and a young rabbi, Yeruchim, handsome, with a black beard, moved in there. His wife went around in a wig, his children I remember as if in a dream. They received money from her family in Costa Rica and lived off that. When the Germans came, he had to shave off his beard, and my father got him a job in the flour mill to save him. The rabbi had sold everything, keeping for himself only a ritual circumcision knife with an ornamental silver handle and a Hebrew inscription. He always carried it with him and said, if they were taken, he would kill his family and himself with that knife.

I also knew each family on Podwale Street, right behind Słowacki, Jews all of them, except for the house in which Mr. Załucki, who ran a brothel, kept his prostitutes. There was also a Jewish brothel— Mr. Lipowicz's, next to the Europejski Hotel, with billiards and a club with dancers. A family business, Mrs. Lipowicz was the madam. In our house, too, there was a brothel later on the first floor—for Germans. One Polish girl and one Ukrainian, just a small enterprise. And on Borysławska Street, opposite the camp, Mrs. Kwaśniewski, the doctor's wife, and her daughter, Dusia, serviced the SS men. Gabriel and Günther liked to go there.

Mickiewicz Street was longer than Słowacki. Suchestov's villa stood where Mickiewicz Street ended and Ivan Franko began. Suchestov owned pumps supplying the refineries with water from the mountain streams. He rode around in a limousine, played the saxophone and paid my aunt Tonia to accompany him on the piano. He married his secretary, Jeanette, a beautiful German Jewish woman who was considerably younger than he was. He adored her and let her do anything she wanted. So Jeanette traveled to the Riviera by herself, where she met Prince Radziwiłł, a well-known profligate. Radziwiłł fell in love, and even wanted to marry her, but his family cut off his funds, and Jeanette supported him with Suchestov's money. Which he gambled away. And since, at the same time, King Edward was romancing Mrs. Simpson, all the newspapers wrote that Windsor and Simpson . . . , and that Radziwiłł and Suchestov . . . , and newsboys shouted, *Suches-tov, tuches-tov, mazel-tov!* Newspapers made fortunes on that. In the end, Edward had to give up the throne and Radziwiłł had to give up Jeanette, and she came back to Drohobycz. Old Suchestov forgave her, because what else could he do? A practical Jew, what would he have gained by not forgiving her? Their son, Edzio, younger than I, was unusually intelligent and well-read. Tonia taught him to play the piano. The Bolsheviks took everything away from them, and ordered them, as class enemies, to move outside of town. Jeanette became a singer, nothing special, but she had a pleasant voice and she was still very attractive, so one of the more influential Bolsheviks took care of her, and that's why they weren't deported. When the Germans came, Jeanette, a qualified stenographer whose first language was German, became the secretary to Herr Höchtsmann, the new director of the oil refinery, and was again a part of the most privileged class.

My paternal grandfather, Moses, leased a flour mill. The mill went bankrupt in 1929, and Grandfather died during a typhus epidemic. Father's brother, Shmuel, also died. His other brother, Salomon, married the beautiful Ruchcia Hirschhorn. Their Mania, my age, was as fast and as nimble as a squirrel—it was like chasing a wind, or a shadow. After Grandfather's death, Grandma Ratse continued to sell flour for some time, but it was hard on her, and her heart stopped in her sleep. Father and Mother ran a grocery—a sack of white flour, a sack of rye, a sack of buckwheat, of pearl barley, and a sack of sugar—a stall in the small market square. The goods were displayed in front of the stall, on top of bricks. The real stores with "cinnamon" panelling were located in the main square. The stalls along the street in the so-called small market square didn't resemble them in any way, but Father and Mother dressed elegantly when they strolled along Mickiewicz Street, our Corso, on Saturday or Sunday. Father had a double-breasted grey coat like King Edward's, his hair combed with a part like King Edward's, and glasses like those worn by the intelligentsia. His head inclined toward her, Father earnestly counted something out to her on his fingers. In her high heels, she seemed slightly taller than him, especially in her

Wallis Simpson hat which didn't quite cover her Wallis Simpson
perm, in a dark suit, probably navy-blue, in a skirt tapered at the
bottom to emphasize her Wallis Simpson figure, along with a scarf,
most likely silk, and a brooch, most likely gold. They were the same
age as Edward and Wallis Simpson, and looking at that photo,
someone might think that the King of England and his lady had
visited Drohobycz. No one in Drohobycz knew about Eddie's and
his flame's Nazi leanings. Everything my parents wore was custom
made. Only peasants wore ready-made clothes. They went to Mr.
Wegner's fabric store where Doctor Kupferberg had bought his English king woolens, and Father chose the same. Mr. Wegner was surprised, "Can you afford it?" "I like it and that's what I want to
have." Don't let them get you, that's how he was.

They sent me to school a year early because I was big, and already in
first grade I heard, "You lousy Jew." And because I was big and
didn't let them get me, they went to complain that I was beating
them up, and they were believed and I wasn't. Mr. Dumin tugged
the orthodox boys by their side-locks and called them "stinking
kikes." In third grade Mr. Komarnicki, Komarnyćki in Ukrainian,
was our teacher. Each letter had to look exactly like his. For each de-
viation we got caned on our backsides while the class recited, "This
is a good hiding for Polish writing." I didn't want give in, so I
kicked him and dodged out from under the cane. Father went over
and Komarnicki told him that everyone else . . . But Father said,
"Everyone else doesn't concern me, just don't you dare touch my
Poldzio! I'll go to the school inspector!" Father was wonderful.
Once in that school, a teacher had struck a boy with his fist and
killed him. Komarnicki left me alone but never gave me a good
grade. Even later, after he retired and saw me with Grandma Pesia
in the street—he lived at Wójtowska Góra and was passing our way
with his cane—he stopped, the old son-of-a bitch, and says to
Grandma Pesia, "He was the worst student in the school." And Pesia, of course, immediately told my parents. She was a nasty Jewess,

that grandmother of mine! In fourth grade, Mr. Malawski, a civilized man, didn't beat us. But the higher the grade, the more repeaters there were, peasant sons, older and stronger, who beat us up and destroyed our homework.

In King Jagiełło Public Secondary school, our history teacher, Marian Krokier from Lwów, found anti-Jewish quotations everywhere in history. Math was taught by a Ukrainian anti-Semite, Krawczyszyn, who afterwards zealously served the Germans. Physics was taught by Smolnicki, a patriot, the leader of the boy scouts troop—Catholic boys only—and later the head of the *Arbeitsamt*. Our Latin teacher, Wojtunik from the Poznań region, said, as soon as he came, "Keep quiet, Yids, new times are coming." And indeed they were. You could see that in the newspapers. A senior scout and a lyceum student, Andrzej Chciuk, was the main hawker of *Mały Dziennik* and *Rycerz Niepokalanej*. Before Christmas, Chciuk and his scouts sold academic fish. "Don't buy from the Jews. Buy academic fish, the profit goes to our students!" So the students could beat up Jews at the universities. On fences, they plastered Colonel Koc's call to boycott Jews. "Polmin," the state oil refinery, the largest, three thousand people, did not employ Jews. Its workers lived in their own settlement and bused their children to school. The sons of refinery officials, Jankowski, Kozłowski, Denasiewicz, were in my class. All Nazis. As were the sons of the foreman, Kuś, two morons, they later turned *Volksdeutsch* and I saw them on the street on Sundays wearing brown SA shirts and daggers, the dad and his sons. Seremak, another "patriot," served in the Kripo and caught Jews. The son of Major Pitak was in my class too. Major Pitak, as army representative, was in charge of fuel deliveries—fuel which turned out to be in short supply when the tanks and airplanes most needed it. A lyceum graduate, Wolk, a Ukrainian from Wójtowska Góra, was friends with Chciuk. He had a brown birthmark on his forehead and wore a black uniform later on.

Bruno Schulz painted Piłsudski and Mościcki for the May 3 and November 11 holidays. He also designed the school banner: on one side King Jagiełło and "God and Fatherland"; on the other Our Lady of Ostra Brama and "Mother Queen of the Polish Crown, pray for us." The text came of course from Kaniowski, the principal. The Society of the Religious Library at Lwów was commissioned by the committee headed by Major Pitak to make the banner—for 1,250 zloty!—and it was consecrated in a Catholic rite on May 18. After the speeches, in which everybody spoke about Polish military victories as if it were the banner of cavalry, it was placed in a glass cabinet to "ponder the unknown future." That's how it was written in the yearbook of 1939.

In the first year of gymnasium, Schulz taught us cabinetry. He walked between the tables, measured, and showed how to slide the plane—lightly, with feeling. He had a perfect hand. In second year he taught glasswork. He wore grey suits, light grey in spring and summer, dark grey in fall and winter. He walked sloping toward the walls, obliquely, almost sidelong, with his head lowered, making way for everybody. Sometimes he took part in Sunday afternoon readings at the private Jewish gymnasium named after Leon Sternbach. He didn't read, he improvised. Nobody read his *Cinnamon Shops* or *Sanatorium Under the Sign of the Hourglass,* because they were too difficult, but everybody listened to him carefully. The historian, Mayer Bałaban, once spoke there, too. Mother would always send me there as well as to the theater and the concerts. She never skimped on those. In third grade we had metal shop, but Schulz took a leave of absence, and an anti-Semite, Hoffman, replaced him. Stupnicki taught biology and a senior-class introduction to philosophy. He wore a stiffly starched collar with a bow tie and said "h" instead of "r," just like Schulz. He could draw every plant and every insect perfectly on the blackboard. He tried to instill admiration and respect for life in us. He painted landscapes, his watercolors hung in the hallways. His red-haired daughter, bearing no resemblance to him, took piano lessons from our Tonia, and his wife, much younger than he, seduced senior students. Afterwards, both wife and daughter hosted the Gestapo men, and he walked around town with an astounded look, until one day he joined the

Jews who were being led to the train. German was taught by Anatol Scherman, a doctor of philosophy from Stanisławów. We, the Jewish boys, boycotted German, and he couldn't understand why. Why blame the language? But when they were shoving him onto a train, he said he was ashamed that he taught German, spat into a German's face and saved himself the rest of the trip. Doctor of Philosophy Bernard Mantel, who taught us French, was taken in a truck to Bronica.

There were twice as many Jews as Poles in Drohobycz, but we were only about one fifth in our school, and every day we walked a gauntlet of hits and kicks. Complaints were heard, but no one was punished. I didn't let them get me. Once I got Jankowski in the stomach. "You son of a Jewish bitch!" he screamed. And I, "Just keep my mother out of it!" I pulled my bike wrench out of my pocket and smacked him. A cry went up: "Thug!" "A blunt instrument!" "The tribunal!" The tribunal consisted of Kaniowski, the principal, an ex-National Democratic senator; the anti-Semitic priest Gościński; and Rabbi Schreyer, who had ever fewer students because ever fewer Jews were admitted to the gymnasium, told my father that I behaved like a *shaygets* and that I was endangering other Jews, and none of the Jewish boys or teachers wanted to testify on my behalf. Krawczyszyn and Smolnicki failed me in math and physics, so that I wouldn't pass to the next grade, and Kaniowski failed me in conduct, so that no school would admit me, and they announced that I had nothing to come back for next year. My life wasn't worth living, but it was they who had nothing to come back for. When the new school year began, the gymnasium of King Jagiełło and Our Lady became a Bolshevik teachers' college, and I was admitted to the *desatiletka* which had replaced the hard-to-get-into Jewish private school.

I had sensed danger for a long time. Especially when refugees started to arrive. Milek Heimberg's uncle came with his wife, two children and four suitcases. They didn't unpack the suitcases and left for Palestine. Then came my father's cousin, Rafael, with his wife, Thea, a Jewish woman from Erfurt. Their ten-year-old Lola knew all the German classics. Rafael's sister, Bronia, also came back with her husband, Jakub, who was a representative of the "Salamander" shoe factory in Erfurt. Everything was taken away from them. Refugees from Vienna came. Kuba Lang's uncle Beno, grey, bald, with vacant eyes, sat for hours in the park called Abbazzia, opposite our house. In the evening young couples necked there, and in the daytime canoes floated on the pond. He sat alone, so I joined him.

"I saw terrible things there," he said.

"Where?"

"In their eyes, in their mouths . . . "

"But what? Like what?"

"They will murder us?"

"Whom do you mean, 'us'?"

"All of us. They'll come and murder. But nobody listens, nobody believes."

I listened and believed, and I told about it at home. "Never mind him, he's nuts," they said. But I was afraid, I knew.

New times were coming, Wojtunik knew what he was saying. Young physicians at a national conference in Poznań passed a motion on *"numerus nullus for Jews at all medical departments, and numerus nullus for Jewish professors and doctoral candidates at all medical departments and hospital wards . . . regarding the present status as an insult to the dignity of the Polish nation."*

At the general assembly of the National Association of Polish Physicians, *"the Aryan clause was passed unanimously with four abstentions, and subsequently the overwhelmingly Jewish district organizations of Lwów and Kraków were dissolved to be replaced by purely Polish ones . . . This is the unquestionable contribution of the National Democratic Movement, which carries on the arduous, daily tasks of setting forth the Jewish question as the most urgent and requiring a radical solution."* That was Przegląd Katolicki of November 28, 1937.

Przegląd Katolicki of January 2, 1938: *"The proposed law that Jews be deprived of their rights and forced into ghettos has already taken shape in the consciousness of the legitimate masters of this land, and it will be realized. It is true that the presently existing legislation hinders creating special legislation for the Jews, but laws can be changed by legally empowered authorities . . . Wishing each other a happy New Year, let's not forget to introduce anti-Jewish laws in the Republic."*

Mały Dziennik of November 21, 1938. *"The most recent political incidents and events have proven that the only solution to the Jewish question is a complete removal of Jews from Christian societies . . . Of course, the Jewish emigrants would be allowed to take away a very small sum in cash while their property and businesses would be taken over by the state."* The views of Engineer J. Holewiński, in a questionnaire *"Towards Nationalization of Polish Life."*

Mały Dziennik of November 25, 1938: *Considering the worldwide increase, not excluding Poland, in the understanding of the importance of indigenous peoples striving to secure their political, economic, and spiritual independence, in connection with the hitherto overwhelming dominance in those areas of the Jewish element that desires to control all the aspects of national life, on November 20, 1938, the General Assembly of the POZTS, fully appreciating the heroic struggle of the Polish Nation to free itself from under the fourth [Jewish] conquest, passed the motion to dissolve POZTS since it would taint the honor of the Polish sports organization if it remained a member of the Association, which, due to the prevalence of the Jewish element, is Polish only in name . . . The clubs united in the former POZTS further decide not to join any organization which would have any contact with Jews.* POZTS, or the Poznań Regional Association of Table Tennis, was right. In Poland, Ping-Pong was a Jewish sport. Ping-Pong and chess, sports so private that it was difficult to prevent anyone from participating.

Mały Dziennik of December 12, 1938: *"An attorney from Lublin, rep. Stoch, not a member of the OZN parliamentary circle, has prepared a bill which aims to abridge Jewish rights."*

January 6, 1939: *"Until we remove Jews from Poland completely, we need to demand separate clinics for Jews, or perhaps that Jews treat Jews only. We can accomplish that by a complete avoidance of Jewish doctors and demanding that insurance companies direct us only to Poles."* The views of Dr. Jan Witkowski in *"Towards Nationalization of Polish Life."*

January 12, 1939: *"Dentistry Rises to Fight Jews."* Out of one hundred and sixty last-year students at the Dental School, there are *"as many as thirty-five Jews!"* But in the third year only twenty-five, in the second, sixteen, and in the first, eight. And *"a comforting fact: not a single Jew among the eighteen professors of the Academy."* And so: *"we have to continue fighting tirelessly until the final victory,"* writes Mr. Platon Luszpiński in the questionnaire *"Towards Nationalization of Polish Life."*

January 14, 1939, a very disturbing front-page news in *Mały Dziennik:* *"The Jew Frankfurter was, after all, nominated Justice of the Supreme Court"* of the United States. So perhaps it wasn't only the *"nationalization of Polish life"* at stake.

January 20, 1939: *"The Second Anti-Jewish Bill"* was sent to the OZN Parliamentary Club. *"The bill consists of twenty-two articles, most of which concern depriving all Jews of Polish citizenship."* Its far-sighted Article 13: *"Within a month of implementing the law all Jews should report the value of all their property to the revenue offices. After the deadline, property that hasn't been reported is by law no longer the property of a Jew but becomes the property of the state."*

January 26, 1939: *"Minister Ribbentrop in Warsaw."* In the picture: a frown, tightly-drawn lips, a uniform. Under the picture: *"One of the most trusted associates of Chancellor Hitler."* And the details: *"At the Central Railway Station in Warsaw, decorated with German and Polish flags, the German guest was welcomed by the Minister of Foreign Affairs, Col. Józef Beck, accompanied by top ministerial officials, all the officials of the German Embassy, the Ambassador of the Kingdom of Italy, as well as many other diplomatic and government representatives."* And next to the implacable face of Hitler's trusted associate, in large lettering: *"Revoke the citizenship of six hundred thousand Jews. A significant parliamentary motion."*

And in *Readers' Opinions:* *"Fighting Jews at every step is the slogan of our times. Never before has there been for us a more opportune inter-*

national situation which would allow us to cast off the Jewish yoke. The nation is ready for that." January 29/30, a reader from Kraków, M. Kaczyński: *"The only argument that can force Jews to leave us once and for all, is depriving them of their civil rights."* On February 6, Doctor R. Sz. from Kraków: *"One wonders if some time from now the compulsory seizure of Jewish businesses, real estate, factories etc. for the benefit of the state won't be indispensable, as it is taking place in Austria and Germany."* March 5, 1939, M. Smerczyński from Stryj: *"Deprive them of citizenship and confiscate their property for the benefit of the State Treasury."*

Przegląd Katolicki, March 5, 1939, I. K. Jastrzębiec in correspondence from Berlin: *"For several months German society has been absorbed by the superbly prepared exhibition 'The Eternal Jew.' It was organized in Munich. Next it was moved to Berlin where every day it draws crowds of people who before the accumulated facts are strangely quiet, as if speechless . . . with some terrible implacability in their faces. It's enough to look into those eyes, hard and merciless, to be convinced of unwavering resolve of the nation . . . This hatred is justified . . . From among the images, warnings, statistical graphs, photo montages and calls for defense against the Jewish polyp rises the direct, rigorous structure of recent German social solutions that are justified by necessity . . . Growing for centuries in the life-giving womb of the German mother-country, the Jewish tumor, the blind and deaf protozoan of perverted instincts and fanaticism . . . of crippled existence with no roots and future, knows only one commandment: parasitical existence at the expense of worthy nations . . . What right—it was asked—does the Jewish nation-dwarf have to exist in Germany? . . . No negotiating with Jews, only a firm either-or, said Hitler. Those Führer's words, emblazoned in big letters in each exhibition room, are the leading slogan of the show, just as the whole exhibition is undeniably a symptomatic signum temporis . . . By what right? Who are these people who have encircled the globe with the black serpent of caftans? . . . One reads with horror the files from the ritual murder trials, displayed in several glass cases."*

Przegląd Katolicki, April 30, 1939—a discussion of the article from *Goniec Warszawski* written by *"a poet, Z. Pietrkiewicz"* who "*quotes several passages from the despicable poems by Słonimski, Tuwim, Wittlin . . . There's no point in deceiving ourselves, everybody knows whom we are dealing with. Polish citizenship gets revoked for such poems. Our nationalistic youth was jailed in Bereza, but not the most vile saboteurs, thugs clearly worthy of the gallows, like Tuwim, Słonimski, Wittlin and the whole legion of pacifists from Stern to Wat to Alberti. By God, where was censorship back then? . . . We demand that all the books of the above-mentioned poets be confiscated as hostile to the state.*"

Przegląd Katolicki, June 4, 1939: "*Aryan theaters should be prohibited from staging Jewish plays, adaptations and translations,*" and "*Jewish studios, Jewish movie directors and actors should be strictly prohibited from making movies with Polish national or patriotic content.*" Also, "*Jewish appropriation of Aryan names, mainly Polish, should be strictly forbidden.*"

Mały Dziennik, August 18, 1939: "*The Association of the Polish Architects (SARP) in Łódź, 102 Piotrowska Street, mailed letters to its Jewish members, notifying them that their names had been removed from the membership list. In the letter, the Association of Polish Architects refers to the resolution of the general assembly which took place in June and passed the Aryan clause for the Association. The resolution was approved by supervisory authorities in Warsaw.*"

The Franciscan monthly *Rycerz Niepokalanej* of August 1939: "*Our nation inherited vast masses of Jewry as the legacy of the partitions . . . And this Jewry has harmed us every step of the way. It eats into the body of the nation like cancer . . . Nevertheless, Poland has rebuilt all her towns and villages . . . And how much better off we would be if all the towns and their riches were in purely Polish hands!*" The humble Franciscans of Niepokalanów.

In 1938, "Betar" won the regional soccer championship against "Junak." The spectators pulled out knives after the match. There were wounded on both sides because we had our own scum too. Such as Fischel, who was built like the wrestler Zbyszko Cyganiewicz and loved to beat anti-Semites. "Junak" recruited Gierula from the Lwów "Pogoń" and Makomacki from Warsaw. "Polmin" provided funds and fake jobs, and in 1939, "Junak" won not only the regional but the national championship as well. Schulz placed an announcement in the *Drohobycko-Boryslawski Głos* that he was withdrawing from the Jewish community. He didn't get baptized, but he didn't want to be a Jew. He knew.

The Jews were very happy that the Germans didn't take our town, and they welcomed the rag-tag Soviet army with real joy, and I stopped having nightmares and started to breathe normally. Drohobycz became even more crowded because Jews drifted over from the German side. A detachment of the NKVD, with the scales of justice on their sleeves, arrived from Russia. They took over our house and most of our furniture—"What do you need so much for?" They housed us at the Borysławskis, Ukrainian half-peasants, in a lean-to where chickens were kept before. Father, who was an expert on flour, became a warehouseman in a flour mill, so we had enough to eat and we could even help the Borysławskis. This is how it went:

The *natchalnik* came and said, "I need one hundred kilograms of flour."

"Please sign for it," Father said.

"But I don't want to sign for it," he said, "I want you just to give it to me."

"But it isn't mine, or yours, it belongs to the state."

"Then you don't understand our system. If you give it to me, then you'll be able to take some too. That way you will live and so will I. And if you don't, I will take it at night, and later we'll do the inventory, and you'll go to jail. It's as simple as that."

Tarnawski, a mechanic who always worked in the mill, saw the *natchalnik* and Father steal, so he got to it as well.

A few Jewish boys joined the militia, but it was mainly the Ukrainians. Mostly Russians and Ukrainians arrived in NKVD uniforms, but you could see Poles and Jews among them too. Hesio Josefsberg came back with tuberculosis from Bereza and became the propaganda chief at the town hall. Schillinger's daughter, a notorious Communist, who sat in jail each May Day before the war, married a Ukrainian illiterate who became a deputy to the Supreme Soviet. "With us, Jew or not a Jew, *odin hui,* same fuck," the Soviets used to say, to the joy of the Jews who had never before experienced such equality. And the anti-Semites couldn't forgive us because what they hated most was equality with the Jews.

Schulz now taught mathematics and drafting. We went in two shifts to the overcrowded school, lower grades in the morning, higher in the afternoon. The overloaded power station would cut off electricity and we would often have classes by candlelight. And when we ran out of candles, we'd yell, "Professor Schulz, Professor Schulz, tell us a story." He told us *Gulliver's Travels,* verbatim, or made up stories about gnomes and other eerie creatures that lived in dark corners and crevices, in a different reality hidden from our eyes. We couldn't repeat those stories because only he could tell them like that, and we didn't quite understand them, but we listened spellbound. We'd put a kopeck under a fuse so that the light would go out. "Tell us a story, Professor, tell us a story." He was never angry, never raised his voice, a silken man, too silken. I walked him home in the dark carrying his briefcase. He didn't paint Stalin or any other Bolshevik portraits. They came ready-made from the town hall. He designed the inscriptions for May 1 and November 7, but the text also came ready-made, from Hesio Josefsberg.

When the arrests began, Hesio retreated from the town hall to the library which he had established in the former Jewish Old Age Home. This was one of the best buildings made of clinker bricks from the Drohobycz brick and roof-tiling plant, just like the courthouse. First they took away planos, then people. Trotskyists, Zionists, Bundists, Petlurites, Piłsudski Legionnaires, National Democrats —"same fuck." Our cousin, Lipe Erdman, was deported for selling a kilo of sugar on the sly. Doctor Adlersberg, Doctor Nacht and Doctor Pachtman were taken for no reason. Also Judge Fruchtman, Mrs. Kobryń, who taught Ukrainian in our school, Judge Drozdowski and Doctor Kwaśniewski, the county epidemiologist.

"With these bandits you want to escape? With those thieves? At least the Germans are cultured people," Grandma Pesia reasoned. The train was standing at the railway station, and I knew we should be fleeing, and Father wanted to, but Pesia: "What? With this rabble?! With this stench?!" And she convinced my mother, and the train left. But the stench remained. It didn't dissipate. On the contrary, more and more of it came out from under the coal, which the Soviets dumped behind the courthouse as they were fleeing. Ukrainians with tridents on their sleeves drove out the Jews to dig it up. Peasants in sheepskin caps with pitchforks and axes gathered and screamed, "The Jews killed our people!" Doctor Adlersberg, Doctor Nacht, Doctor Pachtman, Judge Fruchtman were dug up, but to the Ukrainians all the victims were Christians, and all the NKVD men who murdered them were Jews. They stabbed and hacked to death those who were digging the victims up, and hundreds of other Jews. They led them out as if to work, but the mob was waiting there with hatchets, pitchforks and crowbars. They beat Jews in the streets, plundered houses, ripped off watches and rings, tore off earrings. The Germans let them do it. The Borysławskis hid us in a cellar. Later, we returned to our building on Słowacki Street, but we shared our apartment with a bookkeeper, Leon Herschman, and his wife and daughter who had moved in before us. Next to us, the Frommers with their three children lived together with the Hauptmans. The Hauptmans and Frommers were refugees from Schodnica where Ukrainians had murdered most of the Jews. Mr. Hauptman, a disabled veteran of the previous war, walked on a wooden leg and didn't have children. The other apartments were taken by Poles.

Besides Yosl Herschman and Jonasz Haberman, the Germans arrested fifty other Jews, mostly refugees from Vienna. On July 12, they shot half of them in the nearby woods. A Viennese, Landau, was one of those who did the shooting, and he described it in his diary. Two weeks later, the Ukrainians reported that they had found a grave of twenty-four Ukrainians who had been murdered by Russians and Jews. The Germans went to verify that. A Ukrainian clergyman thanked them for coming and invited them to participate in the funeral. "The most degrading thing is that Jewish documents were placed in their pockets," he said to Landau. Landau ordered that gasoline be poured over the papers and that they be burned.

Work was God, our lives depended on it. The *Arbeitsamt* was the temple. Güldener, a plainclothes Gestapo man, was the German high priest, Professor Smolnicki, the Polish one, and Herzig, a usurer and a black marketeer who dealt in foreign currencies, the Jewish one. Güldener controlled Smolnicki, while Smolnicki controlled Herzig, who knew best who had what. This way all three of them squeezed money out of the Jews. Herzig, elegantly dressed, cultured, went to Güldener for dinner with his wife and with gifts from "the grateful employees." His son, Izak, couldn't bear to watch it and escaped to the forest, where he was knifed to death by the Ukrainian nationalists. Güldener was an interesting man: the Jews built a hiding-place under his house, and he pretended he didn't know about it.

The former owner of the flour mill, Mr. Sasyk, a Ukrainian, returned with the Germans, wearing a Tirolean hat with a tassel, the *Volskdeutsche* liked to wear them. His younger brother, Michał, had a glass eye and carried a pistol. The Germans didn't give the mill back to Sasyk, but made him director. Tarnawski came to my father and said, "The system will be the same, we'll steal the same way, only now Mr. Sasyk will be the *natchalnik*." Through Tarnawski, Father also arranged for Uncle Salomon to be given a job in the warehouse, and I ran with reports between the mill and the *Landwirtschaftliche Zentralstelle,* where Krawczyszyn, my math professor, sat behind the desk. He knew how to shrink Jewish rations. He didn't even look at me or mutter, for him we no longer existed.

They started with the Jewish dogs. Fesia came and took our Chéri to the country. After a few days Chéri came back. She took him a second time, he came back again. The third time he didn't come back, and we didn't find out what had happened to him. Afterwards, they made the disabled assemble at the Old Age Home and took them away in trucks, "to gather acorns in the woods." Their clothes came back in the same trucks. Mayer worked in the Gestapo warehouse and he brought Uncle Yosek's jacket from there. We didn't tell Hanna, who believed that they had been taken to do light work. And later still, the Ukrainians would come and take letters to Bronica for a fee. Mr. Hauptman had hidden in the basement of the Old Age Home and didn't go to Bronica. They got him during the first general deportation, together with the Frommers, but he jumped off the train, with his wooden leg, and came back again. During the second deportation, they shot him in the street. During the second deportation, they shot six hundred people, and one hundred and eighty during the third. Michał Sasyk was seen with his pistol in the streets. With left eye made of glass, he didn't need to squint. Leon Herschman's wife and daughter were taken away. He hid in the toilet. Jurczak, a Kripo agent, looked in, saw him, closed the door and went on. With Tarnawski's aid, Father concealed Mr. Herschman in the mill. He slept in the office, and during the daytime, kept books. He was a very good bookkeeper. One morning Michał Sasyk came with a Gestapo man. "Take him," he said. Worobec, Sasyk's assistant director, walked up to Uncle Salomon and said he needed a diamond ring for his fiancée. "All right, I'll see what I can do." "You don't understand, I need it at once." Uncle brought him his wife's ring. Father knew things were bad in the mill, so he gave Herzig a gold twenty-dollar piece to place him in "Polmin" where Jews worked now—for nothing. He gave another twenty-dollar piece to Reitman, the agronomist, to give me a job in Hyrawka.

Gärtnereilager in Hyrawka, an agricultural camp with hothouses and greenhouses, was created by Helmrich so that the Gestapo and the Sipo would have fresh vegetables. And we would be safe. He lived in an unfinished house that belonged to Dörfler, an architect, on Sienkiewicz Street, opposite our former gymna-

sium. Fräulein Jordan, his secretary, also lived there with her mother
who was his housekeeper, and later Sylvia, a beautiful Jewish girl
from Vienna, moved there as a maid. The work on the house was
never finished, and the boys who were underfed were sent there.
When Musiek Weidman and I were insulating the attic for winter,
the older Mrs. Jordan brought us *eintopfsuppe* with meat, hot
sausage, and fruit cake. Helmrich's wife came to visit from Berlin,
bought Aryan papers, and took along Jewish girls dressed in
Ukrainian folk costumes to place them as maids in the households
of her Berlin friends. She also took Sylvia away. A handsome
Gestapo man, Sokal, fell in love with Irka Jankielewicz, the daughter of an engineer from the "Galicja" refinery. I was in love with her
when I was still a child. Everyone was in love with her. Her picture
was in a photographer's window on Mickiewicz street. Sokal sent
her with forged papers to his family and she survived there.

"Did he marry her?"

"No, he was sent to the front and killed."

Most of the young people worked in Hyrawka. There, Mania,
uncle Salomon's daughter, met Moszko Zukerberg from a well-to-
do family with a large estate near Drohobycz. The parents were
killed by Ukrainian peasants.

We repeatedly dug up the same beds, pulled weeds before they
grew, carried bricks from one place to another. Each cucumber and
each tomato went to *Zentralstelle*. Nobody stole, because no one
wanted it to come out that the *Gärtnerei* had more workers than
tomatoes. Helmrich as *Kreishauptman für Landwirtschaft* shielded
us, but a reliable and vigilant mathematician, Krawczyszyn, sat in
the *Zentralstelle*. Helmrich signed proper reports and requests prepared by the certified agronomist, Reitman, and an experienced administrator, Altman, a refugee from Vienna. Helmrich's wife took
both of Altman's daughters to Berlin. One day Günther galloped in
on a white horse, and behind him, on a bay horse, Marysia
Steczkowska, a dancer and a soloist with the song and dance ensem-
ble from our Soviet school. Everybody rushed to work, and I held
the horses while they were visiting.

Schulz was seen for weeks on end on the scaffolding in the hall of the *Arbeitsamt* lying on his back under the ceiling like Michelangelo and painting at Landau's command. He also painted in the *Reithalle*. He painted horses because Landau loved horses. It was Landau who made Jews build the *Reithalle,* which he himself had designed. Who drafted the plans? Most likely Schulz. Jews from the countryside attended to Landau's horses. The Germans called him "Der Judengeneral." He was born in Vienna as the bastard son of a Viennese woman, Maria Maier, and Paul Stipkovich, a baker from Hungary. Landau got his family name from a Jew who married his mother and died a few years later. Raised in boarding-schools, he took part in Nazi brawls early on. Stocky, strong as a horse, he beat people with relish. It was he who trained the black uniformed Ukrainian police in Drohobycz. Mr. Fliegner, a Jew over fifty, stopped digging twice in half an hour. Landau saw that from the balcony where he was sunbathing with his future second wife, so he picked up a rifle and shot him. In the same way, he shot Dorcia Sternbach, Wisia Zuckerman, and the Oher girl, whose first name I no longer remember. Wisia was a pianist, our Tonia's student. We buried them in one grave in the new cemetery. When twenty Jews didn't show up for work out of fear, Landau ordered twenty to be shot, pointing at them himself with his finger, *"Du, du und du!"* Poles and Ukrainians from shovel brigade *Baudienst* dug the large graves in the Bronica forest before mass executions there. After small-scale, spontaneous *Aktions,* just a few Jewish people from Hyrawka would be sent to the new Jewish cemetery, I and some country Jews who were used to the shovel. The old cemetery, packed beyond capacity, had been already closed before the war, and the Germans demolished it. The new one was three kilometers away from town, and only one kilometer from Hyrawka. We also buried people in common graves, but women and men separately.

Jews trembled at the sight of Landau, but he was kindly disposed toward Schulz, toward his talent. He had him make his portraits and talked to him during the sessions. About aesthetics, of course. Unfortunately, he later had to burn all those interesting portraits. And Günther's Jew was Hauptman, an artist-cabinetmaker, who created phenomenal marquetries, mosaics, panoramas of Drohobycz from various types of wood. Günther had a broad face, pock-marked from adolescent acne, and rough workman's hands. Landau and Günther were the same age and competed in everything. When Landau noticed that Günther was sending the marquetries to the Reich, he called Günther's Jew aside and shot him in the nape of the neck. And for that, Günther shot Schulz. Ignaz Kriegel saw Schulz lying on the sidewalk near the Judenrat. Ignaz's father worked in the Judenrat, so Ignaz ran there to hide. Schulz lay on his back, in a dark grey suit, his face splattered with blood. I saw him already at the cemetery, without shoes, without a jacket, in dark grey pin-striped pants and a white striped shirt. His skull was opened on one side, and there was blood in his mouth. Hauptman lay next to him, also without shoes or jacket. His skull wasn't as badly smashed. He had red hair. They were lying by the wall to the right of the entrance, and we buried them there in one grave.

Every two weeks I got a pass from Hyrawka to visit my parents. Once Mother made me stop by the ghetto and take Grandma Pesia a loaf of bread. By then only a few people remained in the ghetto. When I entered, Grandma and Grandpa were sitting on the bed next to each other, holding hands, in complete harmony as never before. And I never saw them again. One afternoon I came from Hyrawka and didn't find Mother or Father. It was getting dark, and they weren't there. I sat on their bed, afraid to move. Suddenly, I heard footsteps on the stairs. I opened the door—it was them. That was the happiest moment in my life, and we decided never to part again. Father gave a twenty-dollar piece to Tomaka, a Pole, who was the supervisor in "Nafta," and I became a metalworker with the letter "R"—*Rüstungsbetrieb,* war industry—which saved lives. Everybody could see that I didn't know how to do anything, so I helped Mr. Leber, a craftsman, to forge iron candlesticks. The Germans liked such things, they said they were "*germanisch.*" He made me hold the wedge while he embossed them, although he would have done it more easily without my help, because my hand kept slipping and he had to correct the work all the time.

In May, Hildebrand came from Lwów for inspection. In June, he came to close down the sewing shops. He called it the *Frauenaktion*. The majority of the one hundred and seventy people taken to Bronica were young girls, as well as eighteen children, twelve of them orphans. He said to the mother of two children that she could keep one, she could make the choice. Anitka Einfuss handed her father a jacket. "I won't need it anymore, and you can buy yourself bread with it." In July, Hildebrand became commandant of the camps in Drohobycz and Borysław. He moved to Drohobycz with his wife and children and closed down Hyrawka. Mr. Reitman abandoned his seriously sick wife and two sons and escaped with his Aryan lover. Those who had money escaped to the refinery, those who didn't to the roof-tile plant. The strongest, the fittest. Helmrich also recommended whomever he could. Klara with Mayer, Yetka's daughter, Mania, and our cousin Rafael with Thea and Lola went to the roof-tile plant. And Heda Lantner—slim, elegant, educated, a refugee from Kraków, whom all of us admired. The roof-tile plant was surrounded by barbed wire and watch towers. No one could escape from there. On August 25, at four in the morning, they were driven out of the barracks. Hildebrand came at eight. He looked and looked, and then ordered them to be taken to the Drohobycz jail. Six hundred people—they had barely enough standing room in the cells. In the afternoon, he came with Gabriel and they turned everybody out into the corridors to select eighty skilled workmen. Hildebrand walked in front of the lines to take a good look at those who knew that their "last little hour had struck." *"Das letzte Stündlein"*—that's how he said it in court. He told a girl who was crying, "You're too weak to work, I'll send you to the *Himmelkommando*." Mayer found himself among the chosen, and became an *ordner* and a sonofabitch. At the last minute, Mr. Altman kept Thea back, saying that she spoke and wrote German so beautifully and that she would be of use in the offices, but Rafael and Lola went. And Mr. Altman went, he couldn't help himself. The Ukrainian black police took them in trucks to the Bronica woods. They made them undress and brought back their clothes—to the warehouse. The Jewish girls, who scrubbed their floors and cleaned their boots when they came back drunk from Bronica, heard them bragging how they had raped Heda Lantner before they shot her. Among them were Dumycz, Farynowicz, Fedkiewicz, Hrzaj, Kolinko, Kossar, Magur, Mak, Tempko, and Wolk.

Hildebrand had space made for the skilled workers in the refinery, that is, he had those who weren't indispensable removed. The list was prepared by the Jewish *Arbeitseinsatzleiter,* Weintraub, together with Supervisor Kuś, who had changed his name to Kuss, and it was he who ordered me to be taken out. Imek Feingold asked them to leave his wife who was young and strong enough to work. Hildebrand raised his sluggish eyelids. "If you want to be with her, you can cross over to the other side." Imek turned out to be a man and went over. We stood on the other side and we knew that the black police were waiting behind the gate. Suddenly Supervisor Tomaka rushes in. "Is Lustig here somewhere?" He pretends not to know me. "To the director! Right this minute!" I run upstairs with Tomaka, and he shoves me into the toilet and locks the door. "Be quiet here, fucker." He got another twenty from my father. Father always saved me. But I could do nothing for him.

Several small camps remained, for oil, but for Hildebrand they were still too large. We would be surrounded by the Wehrmacht and sorted out by Krause, a plainclothes Gestapo man, blond with a parting on the side, forty years old like Hildebrand. "*Seit doch vernünftig,* be reasonable, sooner or later, what's the difference?"— he would persuade us, mildly, as if we were children. He sorted out Zlatkis, a poor boy with no one to buy him out. They stood him up at the fence, and Zlatkis who didn't look like much was devilishly nimble. He jumped up, slipped over the fence and was gone. The

Wehrmacht man took aim, but too late. At the next selection, Krause sorted him out again.

"So he came back?"

"Where could he have gone? With no money, with a Jewish accent, Jewish nose?"

Again he sprang up and jumped over, but this time Rindfuss, a civilian in a Tirolean *janker,* had an eye on him. He immediately ran up to the fence, climbed a crosspiece, and shot. "*Seit doch vernünftig,*" said Krause.

Father moved over to the "Nafta" refinery where Dietemayer managed the warehouses. For me, he found a place in the boiler shop. I crawled into the cisterns and held the rivets with tongs while the real boilermaker did the riveting. Dietemayer also took on my mother and Uncle Salomon at the warehouse, and found a spot for Ruchcia and Mania in the Dereżyca refinery, where his friend, Larsen, a Dutchman, was the manager. Dietemayer, a German from Reutlingen near Stuttgart, was in love with Ada Teicher, a married woman, who was the daughter of the former director of "Nafta," Wiszniowicer. Dietemayer knew that during the *Frauenaktion* my mother was hiding with several other women under the tarpaulins in the warehouse.

We lived in the camp on Borysławska 6 with the Ernsts, seven people in one room with a balcony. I slept with Lusiek and his younger brother Izio on one mattress. After work, we sat on the balcony and smoked hand-rolled cigarettes. We saw Mrs. Sobel walking with a bundle toward the intersection of Garncarska Street, where the main section of the camp was. Suddenly, Hildebrand appeared from around the corner, she stopped to let him pass. Hildebrand took out his pistol, fired and walked on. We also saw Wolk approach the Garncarska gate in a black uniform, with an automatic. In a backyard apartment lived the Hauptmans, the brother and the sister-in-law of the dead cabinetmaker, and the Suchestovs below us.

Suchestov was dying of throat cancer, Jeanette sat with him in the evenings. Gabriel, a Viennese SS man with a thick red nose, came to see who was already *arbeitsuntauglich,* and Suchestov was lying mute and unable to move. "Either you'll do something with him or I will have to," said Gabriel loyally, because she was after all Höchstmann's secretary. Suchestov couldn't talk, but he wrote a farewell letter to her and to Edzio, and that same night she gave him potassium cyanide. She obtained permission to carry him to the cemetery in a cart. I went with them to bury him. The driver helped me. Edzio had tuberculosis and couldn't do much. It was a cold grey afternoon, like the time I buried Schulz, but we buried Suchestov in the main pathway alongside his family. A young Jew with sidelocks emerged from the tipped-over tombstones and said a prayer because we didn't know how. My mother was angry with me, because outside the camp they could finish you off, whether you had papers, or not.

After work, I stopped by to see Salek Welzer who studied medicine in Italy before the war. His mother says, "Salek has hidden because they're looking for him to unload potatoes." In comes Wilek Ornstein, an *ordner,* former hockey-player for "Betar." I had run around with his younger brother, Mundek. "Where's Salek?" "I don't know," says Mrs. Welzer, and he hits her in the face, and raises his fist again, but I grabbed his arm from behind and twisted it. People came running so he went off. The next morning, Schönbach comes to the *appellplatz.* A Silesian, fists like hooves, signet ring with a skull and crossbones. Wilek points at me. Schönbach hits me with that signet ring and crushes my nose. That amused him. He ordered a *lauspromenade,* louse road, to be shaved down the middle of my scalp, so that they could keep an eye on me, and walked away satisfied. He must have been in an exceptionally good mood, because they shot you for much lesser offenses.

Fredzio W. went to secondary school with me. His mother died before the war. His father, a pipe-fitter by trade, muscular as a bull and incapable of speaking in a human way in any language, became one of the most dreaded *ordners.* When the Germans had taken away most of the Jews and didn't need so many *ordners,* they led them in formation to the cemetery and said, "We swore to you that, in recognition of your good services, you wouldn't be taken away, so we are going to kill you on the spot." Later the *ordners'* new commandant brought Fredzio his father's cap. "If you want to, you can put it on." And Fredzio put it on and became an *ordner.* Alek Madfes, also from my gymnasium, talented, from a well-to-do family, his father was in the oil business, became an *ordner* after they had taken his parents away. And Mićko R.—the best soccer player in "Betar"—they took his wife, he turned his own relatives in. And Lonek Felsen, the goal-keeper whose wife, Erka Unickel, as beautiful as Ava Gardner, perished in Bronica. All strong, fit, in athletic condition.

There were specialists among them. Bross and Baustein knew how to find children who had been hidden and blackmail their parents. Bross had a furniture store before the war; Baustein had been a sergeant in the Austrian army in the previous war. Handsome Bronek Dauerman, black hair and blue eyes, a butcher who knew his trade, hit where it hurt the most. Poliwka, a snitch with watery eyes, watched where someone was hiding and informed Mensinger, brought in from Lwów by Hildebrand. Meszko Weiss, a pre-war street urchin, headed the *Raubkommando* and searched wealthy homes. They killed Imek Grunfeld's parents and he went around bloated with hunger, so he joined Weiss.

And the intelligentsia. Yoel Holzman, an attorney, he took our Yetka to *Sammelstelle.* Nemlich, a refugee from the west, who taught us geography in the Soviet school. A first-rate young violinist, Galotti, whose father was an Italian Jew and mother a Polish gentile, became the first commandant of the ghetto police. They didn't consider themselves Jewish. Maciek Ruhrberg, a young lawyer, unsuccessful before the war because there were too many lawyers in Drohobycz. His father-in-law, Doctor Rosenblatt, became chairman of the Judenrat and Maciek handled extortions. Educated, speaking good Polish and German, they had better access and took more. After he had robbed enough, Maciek bought himself Aryan papers and fled to Warsaw. He sported a beard and paraded there, elegant as an English lord. But the Gestapo, who had their snitches from Drohobycz in Warsaw, brought him back, beat him until he returned everything, and shot him by the fence.

Nobody else, though, enriched himself as much as Engineer Weintraub. He prepared the lists for Hildebrand—who was indispensable and who wasn't—and he was the lord over life and death. He had his experts who knew who had dollars and valuables, because he wasn't from Drohobycz himself, he had drifted to us. Small piggy eyes, fat face, he ate and drank with Hildebrand and Mensinger.

"So they ate and drank with Jews?"

"Why not? They got rich off them."

Baumgarten, Weintraub's main confidant and supplier, drank with him and the SS men. He supplied them with gold and the best boots from the artisan bootmaker, Freilich. Baumgarten had a lover, Giza Bachman, former secretary to an attorney. She knew how to blackmail people, and his son specialized in servicing beautiful married women. They believed that the world belonged to sons-of-bitches, and, indeed, it did. One of the Wiesenthal brothers—they owned a perfumery on Mickiewicz Street—was with us on Borysławska with his wife and little son. They had money. During a selection in the court, Minkus pulled their boy out. Mr. Wiesenthal says, "If our son is going, my wife and I want to go, too." Baumgarten, who had been bribed, approached Minkus, "Herr Scharführer, we need this Jew, could you make an exception?" Minkus, with his red, drunkard's face, foamed at the mouth and put the barrel of the gun to Baumgarten's temple, *"Saujude, du sollst nicht frech werden!"* And afterwards they drank together again.

Sobotta, a barber from Opole—a baker's son, thirty years old, tall, dark hair parted in the middle, an aquiline nose, strikingly handsome with elegant high boots from Freilich—beat his victims and trampled them. Only after he grew tired, did he shoot. He beat seventeen-year-old Mundzio Weitz to death because he wasn't wearing the Jewish armband. And Izio Eisenstab because he didn't take off his yarmulke before him. And a ten-year-old boy because he was peeing against a wall.

Mensinger, a twenty-two-year-old *Volksdeutsch* from Yugoslavia, raised as a Lutheran, attended church regularly and sang in the choir. After finishing sixth grade, he worked as a helper in his father's bakery. "*Mensinger, du bist ein Held*"—"Mensinger, you are a hero"—Hildebrand said after Mensinger and Semmer shot eighty children in the Borysław slaughterhouse. Previously, he served in Lwów at the notorious camp on Janowska Street. Short, thin, he had a metal tooth and smiled all the time. Hildebrand was the son of a court bill collector from the vicinity of Bremen. A store clerk, later an office manager, also a Lutheran, never smiled—a pale, stony face. But he liked emotional scenes, such as the ones with Anitka Einfuss, Imek Feingold, and the mother who had to choose between her two children. This idea with the mother has also been attributed to others, but in Hildebrand's case it is in the records.

A young engineer, Medias, suggested an escape to Hungary. He was taking his mother and sister along. Engineer Priop, Wilek Gärtner with his parents, Iśko Rosenrauch with Rita from Tarnopol, a prewar *unterweltnik* Sussman, and Henio Margulies were also going with him. Mr. Gärtner, who came from Schodnica, knew many people in the area and he was the one who found Edek Papierkowski. "Ah, a decent *goy,* completely trustworthy!" Engineer Priop knew him too. Mr. Gärtner, Medias and I met Papierkowski in Mrażnica. Over forty yet strong and fit, he brought us flat breads baked on hot furnace pipes. He was in a good mood. We paid him an advance and agreed to meet in the evening by the bridge over the ravine. "I'll flash my light three times on the other side, you'll cross the bridge, and we're off to Hungary." I had a small German Walther with six bullets, which Rita had bought for our group. Sussman had his own Belgian FN. We see three lights, we're walking—Henio Margulies and I in front, then the Gärtners, Sussman and Priop. We were more than halfway across the bridge when suddenly shots from all sides! We jumped into the ravine. Henio, Priop, and I were already close to the other side, so it wasn't that high. Mrs. Gärtner managed too.

Henio Margulies's father, who worked in the office of the refinery, had found out that a train from Hungary would carry back a few empty cistern cars. He bribed a worker so that one cistern wouldn't be shut. It was an appealing suggestion, and I wanted to go, but after what had happened on the bridge, my mother wouldn't let me, and Henio went alone. We waited to hear from him, but we didn't. The cistern in which he traveled was shut.

Uncle Salomon said that Moszko Zuckerberg knew a decent farmer in Litynia—a pious Jehovah's Witness, he would hide them. First Moszko went with his brother, and a smuggler brought a note from them that everything was fine. Then Ruchcia went with Mania and, again, a note that all was well. Uncle Salomon went last, no word came from him, only Mr. Benkendorf, a former fish wholesaler, showed up with a small package. He said that walking at night to his peasant in Litynia, he saw a naked body in the water and, on the bank, a blood-stained scarf. Father glanced at it, yes, it was his brother's scarf. Father didn't want to go there, but told Dietemayer. The Germans went to the farmer and found Ruchcia, Mania, and both Zuckerbergs—slaughtered and buried in the barn. They hanged him and his son in the market square. For hiding Jews.

First, the black Ukrainian uniforms disappeared, next, the plainclothes Gestapo and some SS men. Later Weintraub and Baumgarten. People leaked through fences. When the evacuation was ordered, Hildebrand opened the gates. "You want to go there? Who and what awaits you there? And all of you are needed in the western oil territories. Your fate is in your own hands, choose!" The *ordners* also assured us that it's Jasło, and Krosno, and jobs. Father had no more money left, so where could we go to, where could we hide? Mother tossed my pistol into an oil ditch and we went. In open boxcars, legs dangling, just as we used to go to summer camps in the past. An old German with a rifle didn't even watch. No one tried to escape. Only once, when the train stopped in Jasło, Miss Achsen, a light blonde, wearing knee boots, went to get water and didn't return.

We thought the worst was behind us. Instead of to Jasło and Krosno, they brought us to Plaszów. Goeth was waiting for us on horseback and, in silence, inspected the freight. Prisoners walked up for our baggage, and Father asked, *"Men harget du?"* "No, they don't kill any more." By that time, they had taken Goeth's license away, they had Auschwitz at hand. But the *ordners* and Kapos beat people with truncheons. Mrs. Hilewicz from Kraków, in a shapely suit and knee boots, goaded the women on with a riding whip: "Hurry on, you Venetian cunts, you're not in Drohobycz!" "Hurry on, pricks!" shouted Mr. Hilewicz, the boss of the men's camp. The jackals approached us before we entered the showers: "Give me what you have, I'll give you half of it back. If not, they'll take all of it." The people gave, and naturally didn't get anything back. And anyway everything went into the pockets of the Hilewiczes and Finkelstein, the main Kapo. In the end, Mother was taken to a sewing shop where they cleaned and mended blood-stained uniforms. Father and I lugged rocks from place to place in a quarry. Hostages from Kraków would come there in trucks, under a tarp, singing patriotic songs. On "Prick Hill" they were ordered to undress and a *Scharführer* fired from an automatic. A dentist came with a glass jar collecting bridges and caps, and we brought Jewish furniture from the warehouse. An SS man poured on gasoline, the fire burned for three, for four hours. If someone from among the hostages turned out to be circumcised, they didn't shoot him but took him to the camp. Kleiman, a young son-of-a-bitch, would position us by the barracks next to the ditch filled with shit. I stood in the first line of fives and shielded Father who could barely stand on his legs. Kleiman walked up and pushed him. "Straighten up, old geezer!" I pushed him off and he fell into the ditch with shit. Everybody was delighted, but Finkelstein came and dislocated my jaw with a single blow. Later he called me and told me to report to the kitchen on the following day. I did, but it turned out that Kleiman's cousin was the manager. "No, we don't need any more."

In the last transport, came those lured out of their hiding places by the news that there was no more killing, that workers really were needed. Jeanette also came with Edzio. An *SS-Arzt,* Doctor Blancke, was waiting for her on the platform. "*Wo ist das verückte Judenweib, Jeanette Suchestov?*" Jeanette stepped out, scared. "*Du bist meine Sekretärin!*" They selected out the old, the emaciated. Doctor Blancke did the sorting, the Jewish functionaries wrote down the names. A lot of the intelligentsia went then, classical music was playing from the loudspeakers. We were taken in trucks to Wieliczka, and the Hiléwiczes and Finkelstein to "Prick Hill"—the Germans had decided they had already stolen enough.

In Wieliczka, they immediately drove us to erect prefabricated barracks. They were in a big hurry. They also brought the Jews from Budzyń and Mielec, and the Jewish prisoners of war from 1939. *Lagerälteste,* Captain Stockman, maintained military discipline. The work was murderous. As soon as we had erected the barracks, heavy machines arrived, which we had to unload and transport under-ground into the salt mines in open elevators so that an evacuated airplane and rocket factory could be quickly reassembled there. The elevators were overcrowded, and every now and then a miner would shove someone into the shaft where he got crushed to a pulp. The miners knew the Germans would go and they didn't want the Jews to come back for what was theirs, naturally. They would bring bread and bacon fat. "You have something? I'll give you bread and some bacon for that." Father had his gold teeth taken out and we sold them for bread with bacon fat.

The women pulled wagons underground, but after work we talked to Mother across the barbed-wire fence. Suddenly they are taking the women away. Back to Płaszów, we were told. We knew it wasn't true, but Mother was still in good shape, and I believed she would survive. The next day we were ordered to disassemble every-thing and load it again onto the train cars. Father was growing weak. In exhaustion, I prayed to God for them to finally kill us. I tried to grasp Father's hand when they were shoving us into boxcars, but I couldn't. It was hot, the middle of the summer, the car was jammed, and we had only one bucket of water. We ate the bread the first day, no one knew if they would survive till tomorrow. We traveled about a week in a terrible stench because a lot of people got dysentery. They died, and in the dark you didn't know who was dead, or who was alive. In Flossenbürg, the half-alive were loaded onto wagons pulled and pushed by the living. I pushed the wagon onto which my father had been placed.

In Flossenbürg, German criminals with green triangles were the block elders and the Kapos. After years in the camps, they knew Yiddish and called out, *"Me wet de du bagrubn, me wet du kaddish nuch de zugn,"* to assure us that here would be the end of us. The *Lagerälteste* walked around with a rod and slashed till he drew blood. "This is my interpreter," he'd say. "If someone doesn't understand, it will translate." The SS men didn't come for fear of typhus, so he was the absolute ruler. Instead of blankets, we had paper sacks, which also served as coffins. The paper was sturdy. When you died, they pulled the drawstring over your head and off you went to the crematorium. They murdered people on the steep hundred steps, along which we carried rocks. An SS man or a Green Triangle kicked you down and that was it. Some boys sold themselves to them. They also had a brothel, for coupons, behind the canteen. The whores, female prisoners, sat there on the porch and laughed at us as we passed by. An SS doctor with a brush and a flask of red ink drew lines on the forehead. One meant you were fit for work, two, I don't know, and three—*untauglich,* finished. Father wasn't even able to stand up in front of the physician. He was sitting by the fence when they took me away. I asked people from Drohobycz to take care of him, and he lived until almost the end of November.

In Leitmeritz, in the Sudeten, we lugged beams and sacks with cement for the construction firm *BSA Hoch und Tiefbau.* In *Laufschritt,* running, because they were in more and more of a hurry. I was the tallest and carried the largest part of the beam. They laid one sack on everyone's back but two on mine, and I grew weaker and weaker. Suddenly, a transport from Warsaw arrives—Polish insurgents, as strong as horses. The moment they found out that Jews were here, they came to our barracks with boards, nails in some of them, and "Beat the Jews, we'll finish you off!" But they miscalculated, because we no longer feared anything, and we hit with what we could. Blood flowed and the SS watched. Then an SS man whistled, "*Alles in die baracken!*" The game was over.

They divided us into two transports: from A through M one way, from N through Z the other. This time, only thirty to a car. It was cold and we had to huddle together. The front line kept moving, and they didn't know what to do with us. It took them about a week to cover the four hundred kilometers from Leitmeritz to Dachau. They marched us through Dachau in broad daylight and the residents shouted, "*Saujuden*, finish them off!" Later, they said they didn't know anything. But in Dachau the camp itself was paradise. Thick soup, fresh bread with margarine, a slice of sausage, only two in a bunk and clean blankets. All the Kapos were political prisoners, and no one ever hit me there. I prayed that we would stay in Dachau, but their territories were shrinking and they brought transports from other camps, with their Kapo-thugs. The bunks got arranged into platforms, and again we were lying one on top of the other. And again the lice, and again our hell had followed us.

Augsburg was so badly bombed that our hearts were filled with joy. We didn't know if we'd survive, but we knew they were being finished. In Augsburg, Soviet prisoners of war stole and robbed. They'd throw a blanket on your head and take away shoes, bread, whatever you had, even bowls and spoons. They had intimate relationships with German criminals for whom they served as whores. And the Gypsies sold themselves too. They worked as barbers and shaved our genitals, so as not to leave a single hair, and they cut us on purpose—"*Ah, entschuldigen, Jude.*" And we had our own sons-of-bitches as well. The Friedman brothers from the Mielec transport sliced our bread more thinly and stole like ravens. Felczer, a Kapo from Sosnowiec, dished out nothing but water from the top of the cauldron, and whoever protested got hit on the head with a ladle.

The Greek Jews hated us for "Canada," the *kommando* which in Auschwitz sorted out the baggage of those sent to the gas, and gorged themselves, keeping others away. A camp was hatred. They couldn't do anything to the Germans, so they hated one another. Some people describe movingly noble characters. I didn't see any like that.

We got up before dawn, marched for an hour to the train, in a cold train, and rode the train another hour to the forest. We were building a tunnel. Messerschmidt or Heinkel wanted to assemble planes or rockets there. We got furunculosis, boils all over the body, but didn't report ourselves because the medical attendants were criminals and you couldn't tell what they would do. A new selection, everyone naked, and who turns up? This *malkhamuves* Blancke, and right away sends me to the other side. Onto the truck, it's over. We arrive—there are no barracks, only steps leading underground, to the grave. And underground we see platforms with naked bodies, you can't tell who's alive and who isn't. "This is the last station," said the *älteste,* a Polish Jew who graduated from a Czech medical school. This dying place in Kaufering had one advantage though: you didn't work there. I lay with Yasha Aronowicz from Vilna and his father. A transport with Russians arrived, but there was nothing to steal from us, and there were too damn many bowls and spoons from the dead. In the morning when the *Todeskommando* came to pick up the corpses, the thighs had been cut out. Typhus broke out, and they needed nurses, from among those who had already had typhus. Many volunteered because the sick weren't able to eat their soup and bread. I went too. I'll croak anyway, I thought, so at least I'll eat my fill. The sick died, and I fortified myself with their portions. I even fed the Aronowiczes. When I fell sick, they brought me water and saved bread for me.

I didn't die, so they sent me to the *Scheisskommando* to pour shit from the latrines over the fields. Already, American leaflets were lying there, written in German, Polish, Russian, Hungarian. They knew who was where. They knew everything. We passed SS barracks and doghouses with German shepherds. Bowls with scraps stood in front of the doghouses. I swung a fence slat, the dog ran into the doghouse, Yasha snatched the bowl, and we devoured everything. The SS man would come and see the empty bowl, happy that his dog had such a good appetite. Walking by the pigsties, we ate from the troughs. They saw we were still alive, so they took us to Urlach number 7 to cart rocks—like horses. I knew I wouldn't survive that, so I thought I'd rather croak without having to work. At the next selection, by that same Blancke, I hunched up and let my arms hang loose. They wanted to send us to Mauthausen and finish us off in the underground tunnels there, but the tracks had been bombed. They drove us back and forth until at last the bombs fell and the train started to burn. We broke into a car that had bread in it, and then we scattered over the fields. We spent the night in a barn, three Hungarian boys who spoke Yiddish and I. In the morning we heard shelling and heavy motors. We slid the roof tiles apart and saw tanks with white stars on them. I thought they were red Soviet stars that had faded. We ran out to them, and behind the tanks we saw infantrymen with black faces. Suddenly a red-haired man with a hooked nose leaned out from the turret. "*Ir zent Yidn?*" "*Yo, yo, mir zainen Yidn!*" He jumped off the tank, embraced us and started to cry.

They took us to a hospital, in Landsberg, where Hitler once did time and wrote *Mein Kampf*. There, they segregated us according to where we were from, and they wanted to put me on the train to the Soviet Union, together with the former Vlasov troops and Soviet prisoners of war. But on that day, a transport was leaving for Italy, headed by Franco Lancilotti, an acquaintance from Dachau. I ran up to him and said, "Save me, I don't want to go back to my fatherland." He told me to pretend I was a deaf-mute and I went south.

They kept us in Cinecittà near Rome, in the film studios, among stage-sets representing various eras. We looked like extras from crowd scenes, like a misunderstanding, a staging error, a reality that had emerged from beneath outward appearances. Like in

Schulz's stories, only much worse. Like extras fleeing, because they
see what is really playing. In the UNRRA office, I met Roman
Sasyk and Worobec. They sat and waited, everybody there was waiting for something. "Ah, Lustig, we're so glad you're alive!" "And
where's Michał?—I asked. "He didn't feel good, so he didn't come."
I told the clerk at the counter, a Jew, to write down their address,
but they didn't give it to him. They fled to Argentina—via the Vatican. Why via the Vatican? Because the Vatican was helping the persecuted—particularly those persecuted by Jews.

   Bricha—which means escape in Hebrew—sent me to Santa
Maria di Bagni, southernmost, closest to Palestine. There I came
across two men from Drohobycz who had left Russia with Berling's
Polish army and deserted in Germany. They carried canisters of
olive oil north as far as Milan, where it was worth three times as
much, and brought back a barrel of salted sardines, which they sold
by the piece in the square. I became their mule, I carried those canisters and barrels. Once, in Bari, we stopped by the Szapiros who
traded with the Polish Second Corps and always had the latest information on where to register and where to go. Two Jews from the
Second Corps brought gold coins called "piggies" in from Cairo.
They spoke to the Szapiros in Yiddish and I keep hearing, Lipe Erdman, Lipe Erdman. I ask who he is. "Ah, a sergeant with the Second
Corps, he runs the canteen in Matera." I go there, and yes, it's Lipe
the Goat, my cousin. That kilo of sugar for which he was deported
to Siberia saved his life. They accepted him into Anders' army because he had served with the Austrian artillery in the previous war.
He was over fifty, but they willingly took old Jews—so as not to
take the young ones. When I told him that his father was shot in
the street, that his wife and children were gassed in Bełżec, and
what happened to Drohobycz, he started to drink. And he didn't
stop. His friends and I would put him in a tub with cold water, but
he didn't want to sober up. We took him out to the movies to see
"For Whom the Bell Tolls" with Gary Cooper. Suddenly, a few rows
away, I see a brown spot on a forehead. Wolk! In an Anders army
uniform! Lipe says, "I know him, he comes to the canteen, a like-

able guy." We approach and I ask, "Do you remember me?" "Yes, from school," he says. "You were a Ukrainian SS man." "Oh no, the Germans drafted us and sent us to the Italian front, so I crossed over to the Allies. I fought the Germans." The Polish MP wrote down the report and took him away. I asked about him later. "Ah, he's gone now, sent away, he won't be seeing the light of day again."

I searched all the lists posted in all the Jewish committees and transit camps, but to no avail. Father hadn't a chance, but Mother was in good shape when we parted, she was tough, she could have made it. Suddenly someone tells me that Mrs. Hauptman is here. She was also taken from Wieliczka back then. Her camp was in Leuca, an hour away by truck. The woman I found in the room told me that she was in the hospital. "Where is the hospital?" "No, no, I have to warn her, because she's very weak." It was getting dark. I sat and waited, and my heart pounded like back then in Drohobycz, even though I already knew I would never hear those familiar footsteps again. Mrs. Hauptman's friend returned. Yes, she had been in Auschwitz with my mother, and then in Stutthof, but she didn't want to talk, because she didn't have good news for me.

Someone came from Munich and said a woman from Drohobycz was playing the piano there. I went with Szlamek Bajrach, a tailor from the Łódź ghetto, who had found out that his fiancée was alive. We went to Rome, to *Bricha,* to obtain passes for Germany, but they said they didn't help people go back. We hired a Yugoslav who knew the route across the Alps. Szlamek paid. He earned good money because people traded on the black market and had money, but nothing to put on. We stayed over at a mountaineer's house, and Szlamek sewed him a pair of pants in exchange for his hospitality. In Villach, in the French zone of Austria, everything was under *Bricha*'s control as well, but the man in charge of the camp turned out to be Mr. Tell from Stryj who used to deal in flour with my grandmother Ratse. His lover, an Australian woman from the Welfare Office arranged our passes to the American zone. We arrived in the transit camp in Salzburg and suddenly I see Felczer, the kapo from Kaufering, again wearing some kind of band, again a big shot.

"Felczer, do you remember Camp 4 and how you beat us with a ladle, you son-of-a-bitch! I want you to arrange a pass to Munich immediately!"

Yes, it was Tonia. She stayed with the Rauchfleisch sisters in the cellar, in the attic, in the closet, wherever it suited the landlord, and she paid him with the dollars she had received as a dowry from Grandmother Gitl, but apparently he demanded sexual favors too. She accompanied a group of Jewish actors on the piano, and I went with them from camp to camp. In Feldafing, I ran across Bercio Gutenplan. We're walking down the main street, and whom do we see? Weintraub! The same swinish face and the same Tirolean hat. Bercio bows, "Herr Engineer, Herr Engineer." I walk up. "Ah, Lustig, Lustig," he extends his hand to me, old friend. I kicked him straight in the balls. "You murderer!" A crowd gathered, the MP came, wrote up a report. They did nothing to him, he had witnesses—people from Drohobycz who did business with him. One was Bercio Gutenplan. The others were dead.

The DP's were to get American visas, but Congress haggled over the quotas. Tonia didn't want to wait and sailed for Palestine. I remained because they were giving scholarships to study medicine. My mother had wanted me to become a doctor. The medical school was in Erlangen. Our physiologist, professor Ranke, was a polite, sweet man. The students liked him and invited him to an international student ball. A Polish orchestra played. They called themselves "The Tigers of Buchenwald," and played very nicely. Ranke came with his wife, they are dancing. Suddenly, one of the musicians springs to his feet. "That son-of-a-bitch Ranke is here, that murderer!" It turned out that Professor Ranke conducted hypothermia experiments in Buchenwald and had hundreds of prisoners on his conscience. Schübl, another Nazi, was professor of pharmacology. Everybody knew him, but nobody said anything because the whole town were Nazis. The blockade of Berlin began, and I was afraid I'd get stuck there, so I finished dental school because the studies were shorter, and I sailed to America. The professor of pharmacology at Harvard was Otto Krayer, a German, who fled with his

Jewish wife before the war. He says, "What, Schübl was your professor? That Nazi bastard who wore a brown shirt?!" That's how I
got a scholarship to Harvard.

I came to New York in 1949, and I heard that Jeanette Suchestov
was alive. I called her, "Poldek from Drohobycz." She says, "Edzio
died in Mauthausen, I don't want to live any more." "Can I see
you?" She didn't want to. Thea, the mother of my little cousin, Lola,
also survived, but she fled to Australia. At the Hildebrand trial, she
testified before I did and immediately returned to Australia, so I
didn't see her either. The Helmrichs got divorced, and he came to
New York with Sylvia. At a party to honor Helmrich, I saw Wilek
Ornstein. I wanted to inform on him, I spoke to Mrs. Laufer. She
said she didn't remember. I also spoke to Kuba Gold and Stella
Wolfgang about Bross when we testified at the trial. "*S'past nisht far
dee goyim*,"—it's unseemly in front of the *goyim*. They didn't want
to. Wilek Ornstein was the main stoker of the crematorium in
Mauthausen and Bercio Gutenplan was his helper. Bercio said that
in Mauthausen, Wilek distributed food and helped many people.
Those were the last months, of course. Michał Jaeger from Borysław, who worked with them in the crematorium, said they had
burned many people from Drohobycz there. Michał Jaeger hanged
himself in 1961, in New Jersey.

Herzig survived in the hideout under Güldener's house with his
wife, Rabbi Awigdor and a few other people. After the war, he was a
money lender in Berlin. Attorney Holzman, who delivered my aunt
Yetka to her death, lived in Düsseldorf and sat on the supervisory
board of the synagogue. No one wanted to touch his case. Baumgarten also hid well—for money—with his wife, son, mistress, and
the stepdaughter that his wife had taken in. Baumgarten and Giza
Bachman were deported to Siberia, sent there by Izio Weisberr who
returned with the Soviet Army. They came back later as victims of
Stalinism. I met Baumgarten's son at the airport in Amsterdam *en
route* to a dental convention in Cologne. His mother was no longer

alive, we didn't mention his father. He gave me his visiting card with the UN emblem. In New York, I saw Mićko R.'s brother. He said Mićko got married again, lived in Toronto and was doing well. Nobody wanted to remember. Nobody wanted to tell on a Jew.

"Not one of them was ever tried?"

"Only one, Bronek Dauerman, in Poland. Someone fingered him, but he had money from his robberies, so he hired good lawyers who got him out on bail and he made a getaway to Germany."

I had a girlfriend in Bamberg whose mother was Jewish and father a German. She boasted that she had met someone rich and handsome from Drohobycz, a notable man, his name was Bronek. Dauerman, by any chance? Yes. I told her about Bronek Dauerman and asked where I could meet him. She didn't want to say and our friendship ended. I don't know what happened with Mayer and with Fredzio W. I didn't see them in Płaszów. But Fredzio's sister, very pretty, had survived and married a multi-millionaire in New York. They gave a lot of money to the Holocaust Museum. Agronomist Reitman also survived, his Aryan mistress saved him.

A few years ago, I flew to Wiesbaden as a consultant. I'm sitting in an open air café, and a couple at the next table is telling jokes in Polish. I start to laugh. "Where are you from?" they asked. "From Drohobycz." "My mother was from Drohobycz, and my uncle, he just died in London. He served in the Anders army, had an English pension, a veteran." "What was his name?" "Wolk." "Did he happen to have a brown birthmark on his forehead?" "He did." "Your uncle wore a completely different uniform before he joined Anders . . ."

I met one Ukrainian policeman here in Boston. I go over to the dental laboratory of Jakub Birnbaum, a DP who also studied in Germany, and he says, "Someone from your area works for me here, with a German diploma." I glance at him, he looks familiar. "Where are you from?" "From Czortków." "Didn't you come to Drohobycz?" "I did." They also had black uniforms but with red insets on the collars. An FBI agent came to see me, took a deposition, but a single witness wasn't enough.

Chciuk lived in Australia after the war and published innocent, nostalgic reminiscences of Drohobycz. And the Jewish castaways bought them like fish for the Sabbath. And he got a very moving reception from our Drohobycz survivors in Israel. Jews are such a foolish people!

Izio Weissber who did time for the cause of justice, fought the Germans for its sake, and thought he served it in the Polish security police—I saw him in Tel Aviv, he was a broken man. Iza Haberman's hiding place was on Borysławska, right opposite our camp! Their landlord would get drunk, and then they would tremble in fear. When he was in a good mood, he'd call one of the women to him. He also hid other Jews for money. A little boy who was with them later wrote about it. Iza's mother, Mrs. Herschman died right after arriving in Israel. Adela went to a mental institution. Iza never married again.

Eberhard and Donata Helmrichs are in the Avenue of the Righteous in Jerusalem. Izydor and Bronisława Wołosiański and Iwan Pysk from Drohobycz are there too. They sheltered several dozen Jews in the cellars—for nothing. I don't know how they did that or why. Maybe they felt that life wasn't worth living when they looked at Drohobycz?

From the International Tracing Center of the Red Cross I got a multi-lingual *Certificat d'Incarceration* stating that Isaak-Hermann Lustig, *österreichisch/polnisch,* born 11.3.1900 in *Drohobytsch,* brought to *Konz-Lager Flossenbürg* on August 4, 1944, from *KL-Krakau-Plaszów* as *Haeftling* number 15532, category (*raison pour l'incarceration*)—"*Jude,*" died on November 23, 1944, in *KL-Flossenbürg/Kommando Herzbruck.* Underneath, it was added that the death certificate would be sent, but it wasn't, most likely because there was none. And from the Stutthof Museum, I got a letter that "Otylia Lustig, born on 10.15.1906 in Drohobycz, arrested on 10.10.1941, arrived in KL Stutthof on 9.10.1944 from KL Auschwitz, assigned the number 81 881—died in the camp. The Museum has no further information on the above mentioned." I hear their footsteps in my dreams, I open the door, no one's there.

*

In October, 1950, Wilek Ornstein was waiting in Bremen for a boat to America, while Hildebrand washed the front windows of his brother-in-law's advertising company, and that's how they met. But Hildebrand knew how to find witnesses who testified that the conditions in Drohobycz and Borysław improved considerably when he became commandant. That the Jewish supervisors, especially Weintraub, could communicate with him much more easily than, for example, with Minkus, who was a drunkard and a brute. That the defendant took care to provide better conditions in the latrines and lavatories, and that he had warmer clothes from the warehouse issued to the workers. That it's no wonder that at Christmas, Weintraub gave a party on behalf of the grateful Jewish employees in honor of the defendant, and that he was presented with a Christmas tree and a holiday cake, which he accepted with some reluctance. The carpentry shop made the wife of the defendant a chest for her sewing kit, and a few toys for his little daughter. It was at Hildebrand's request that Witness H. (Helmrich—full names weren't given) moved the people to the refinery and the brickyard, also called the roof-tile plant, when the order came from Lwów to close down the Hyrawka camp. He was given charge of the camps because of his merchandising and commercial experience, and the court quoted as very important the testimony of Witness D. that "until the time of the *Aktions,* nothing bad was heard about Hildebrand." And the *Aktions* were ordered from Lwów. He looked with sympathy at the innocent people for whom "the last hour had struck," and he thought it was terrible, but he couldn't help it. Out of sympathy, he gave Feingold a choice of going with his wife, and he let the mother keep at least one child for as long as it was possible. He didn't conduct the *Aktions.* He came to the roof-tile plant as late as eight. Didn't do executions, either. Witness St. testified that from her hiding place on the second floor she saw Hildebrand return after the *Frauenaktion* and that he had blood on his boot. On the basis of life experience—*Lebenserfahrung*—the court ruled out the possibility that from the second floor anyone could see blood on a black boot. The witnesses asked for water, spoke with difficulty, especially in German—that didn't make a positive impression on the court. Witness Ko. first said, "I myself heard the order given by the defendant," and then, "I didn't hear the order to shoot," and then admitted, "I don't know whether the defendant was shooting." For the court, his statements were contradictory. The court showed sympathy, for "who can be an impartial witness of events in which one's closest relatives were murdered? That's far more than anyone can bear." The court's task, however, was to determine the objective truth. Hence it likewise gave no credence to the testimonies based on accounts of a Jewish *Arbeitskommando,* which had buried the eighty children shot in the Borysław slaughterhouse at Hildebrand's orders and in his presence. The members of such a *Kommando* would have been killed on the spot as dangerous witnesses, the court pronounced—presumably on the basis of some kind of experience. The court believed that the defendant "didn't want that," that he considered what went on as *unmenschlich,* yet the court admitted that saying to a girl "I'll send you to the *Himmelkommando*" indicates that sometimes he was too eager in carrying out the orders. The court rejected the fourteen points of the prosecution, but in four cases, found the defendant guilty of *Beihilfe zum Mord,* or aiding in the murder, though not from base—for instance racial—motives, and in one case, found him guilty of a homicide under the extenuating circumstances of the front line. The court sentenced the defendant to a total of eight years in prison, counting his pre-trial confinement, and denied him rights of citizenship for four years. The court pointed out approvingly that he demonstrated unusual composure during the prolonged and nerve-racking trial.

Landau, the aesthete, worked in Stuttgart after the war as interior decorator Rudolf Jaschke. In 1956, he started his own company. Only in 1958, when he wanted to get married for the third time, did it come to light that he was someone else, and he got arrested for false identity. His own diary was a reliable witness in his trial. Why didn't he burn it, I wonder? He got a life sentence in 1962, when he was already fifty-two years old.

Mensinger worked in Karlsruhe in a candy factory, first in production, then in distribution. There, in 1949, he met a woman whom he married in 1956, but somehow God didn't bless him with children. Arrested in March 1956, in Bremen, Hildebrand's native city—hardly accidental—he couldn't blame Lwów, so he told about Hildebrand. And the stupidity—or premeditated stupidity—of the court's deliberations from 1953 came out to light. Meanwhile, the earth had shrunk and in flew witnesses from every continent. Now they spoke English and Hebrew and nobody stuttered. Thea, with her excellent German, flew in from Australia. The court had to give a life sentence in each case. Hildebrand was already sixty-five, so it wasn't that much after all. After the war they quickly abolished the death penalty. Guess for whom? In all likelihood, Mensinger contributed also to bringing Sobotta to trial. In 1968, *Landgericht Stuttgart* sentenced him to two-and-a-half years for *Beihilfe zum Mord*. In 1971, in Munich, he was found guilty of three premeditated murders and sentenced to life imprisonment when he was fifty-nine, having lived thirty years with impunity. Which only proves that trying them once is not enough. What happened to Günther, no one knows. There was a rumor that someone saw a pock-marked mug like that in Brooklyn.

Helga was nine when a Quaker charitable organization took her and a hundred other Jewish children to Holland. Her father owned two textile mills near Erfurt. We met in Cambridge, Massachusetts. Our older son graduated with a degree in biochemistry and business administration, and became an executive at General Instruments. The younger one loved wood. As a young boy, he built a boat with his own hands, and we sailed it on the Charles River. He graduated from the School of Fine Arts and specialized in furniture design. He outfitted the interiors of corporate jets with precious wood. He had a hand and an eye like Schulz, but wood dust and the fumes from paint, varnish and glue irritate the respiratory tract and sometimes cause tumors. By rare chance he was cured, but was no longer allowed to work in wood. The older son got divorced, the younger isn't married. We have a black-and-white *shi-tzu,* a Chinese breed.

I remember Broncia Reich from Drohobycz, a poor widow who got up at five in the morning and delivered hot rolls in order to get her son through secondary school. She died in Russia, but I met her son here, in the university clinic, dying of cancer. He told me with pride that his son studied at MIT. I don't know if it's him, but when I looked at the Secretary of Labor who had the same name, the face seemed very similar.

I have never been back to Drohobycz, and I don't want to. Wilek Tepper flew there to say good-bye and laid a plaque on one of those large graves in Bronica. And what happened? In broad daylight, people came with a bulldozer looking for gold and unearthed the bones. After the war, the Old Age Home was turned into a library again. At the entrance, they set Pushkin on a pedestal made of Jewish tombstones. Pushkin in front, Hebrew letters in the back. I don't know what's there now, nor who sits on that Jewish base.

The house still stands, I have a photo. Newly painted, with all its cornices, as if nothing had happened. It can go to the devil. I don't want it.

Escape from Boryslaw

To Tamara Sokel-Diamant

The news got worse and worse. Father and Big Brother didn't eat, just smoked cigarettes. I heard them talking at night. Father would go and Big Brother would go, and we'd be left on our own. I started to cry. Father bent over my bed. "Don't cry, I won't leave you. It's for you that I live." I felt a warm drop on my cheek. We didn't know what kind of a world this was. Our parents had no idea what kind of place it was they had us born in.

The Russians blew up the oil wells. They also laid dynamite beneath the mineral wax quarry opposite our house. I saw fear in Mother's eyes as we hurriedly carried out our things. Sister held me tight by the hand. Father and Big Brother kept running back inside to salvage something else. Little Iziaszek ran back inside, too. He was nimble and wasn't afraid of anything. Night came, bright as day, Borysław was in flames. Mother bundled us up, Father looked for lodgings for us. I had a mother and a father, I cherished every moment with them.

The Germans ordered arm-bands to be worn, death for non-compliance with the order. But I still had a father and mother, a sister and both brothers. One evening, Big Brother didn't return from work. Mother cried, Father didn't speak to anyone. Over a thousand had been taken at work, the most able and the most fit. Weeping could be heard in all the houses. Those who worked were supposed to have been safe. When Father didn't return, I was afraid to cry.

Mother hid us in cellars and attics. She did what she could, but any little kid could betray us. Sister woke in the night and grabbed me by the hand, the Action had appeared in her dreams. Don't cry, Sister, it's just a bad dream. But Action followed Action, and we couldn't wake up from that dream. The people who suffocated to death in the cattle cars did not know that they were more fortunate than those who completed the journey. And God who watched all this was as helpless as we were.

Mother woke me at dawn to go into the village for bread. She dressed me in my best, and kissed me tenderly. I had light braids and light-blue eyes, so I wasn't afraid. When I was coming back, the Action was in full swing. I felt a terrible pain in my heart, but I withstood it. Why did I bear it? Why didn't I go with them?

Why did you send me off, Mother? Why did you make me stay here? I who didn't know how to get through a day without you, haven't seen you for months. I have cried all the tears out of my eyes and my heart aches all the time. I comfort myself only that you are better off than I am. That you're not afraid of anything, that nothing hurts you anymore. Not even the fact that you left me.

They kept them in the Colosseum. It took them five weeks to gather the transport. I stayed at the washer-woman's. I gave her the gold Mother had sewn into my clothes. The washer-woman said that perhaps it might be possible to get them out, but Sister came down with erysipelas. Mother couldn't leave her. Only Iziaszek got out, he was such a nimble little boy.

We slipped through empty, narrow streets, sneaked into lifeless houses, ate what was left in cellars. We were afraid of light and of people. The rats warned us when someone drew near. I didn't have the strength and I didn't want to hide, I had to because of Iziaszek. Sister was more fortunate, she had gone with Mother and wasn't seeing that bad dream any more.

Two children, a sister and a brother, are walking down a road and they can't get over their wonder . . . and then all at once a murderer blocks their path. "Jews!" he shouted, "Jews!" He was small, no bigger than Iziaszek, but he knew that that word kills. We ran, but the word ran after us—"Jews! Jews!" A policeman ran out from around the corner. I didn't have the strength, I didn't want to run, I wanted to lie down, to burrow into the earth and never get up again, but Iziaszek wouldn't let me. He dragged me by the hand— "Run!" We passed the abandoned oil well. "Hide in the *heitz,* and I'll deflect him," Iziaszek shouted, "Don't worry about me, he won't catch me, I'm nimble . . ." There was a cupboard in the *heitz,* I hid inside it, closed my eyes. When I opened them again, no one was there.

I leave the *heitz* and walk. "Where are you going?" the voice inside me asks. My little brother had given his life for me, but I don't know about that yet. I go to look for him. Again, I come upon murderers. Little ones, smaller than me. "Jew!" they shouted, "Jew!" I took the ring off my finger, flashed it in front of them and threw it far into the sand. They rushed in that direction, and I disappeared.

Barracks stood on Pilsudski Street. They were surrounded by a tall stockade fence, the windows were boarded up, and above the gate a sign, "*Jüdisches Arbeitslager.*" A German with a rifle was standing there, and I didn't have the letter "R." I turned quickly into the courtyard on the other side where no one was standing guard. The murderers' helpers lived there. I went in and asked whether they had seen Iziaszek, but they didn't want to talk to me. They moved away, they pretended not to see me. In the end, Dr. Reiter said that he had seen him at the Police Station. "Can one bring him something to eat?" I asked. "Oh, he doesn't need anything in there," said Dr. Reiter. "And what's he doing there at the police station?" I asked. "He's repairing bicycles for them," said Dr. Reiter, "He's nimble, there's no need to worry about him."

I climbed into the attic, curled up. I dreamt about our house— my parents, Iziaszek, everyone for whom I longed. I wanted that dream to last as long as possible, but somebody's scream awoke me. I jumped up, looked out into the courtyard, but nothing was happening down there. The moon was shining as normal above Borysław. That had been my own scream.

I slept in the attic, during the day I stole into the kitchen for food. People pretended not to see me. I was sitting on the steps with a bowl of soup when suddenly the *Lagerführer* and three *ordners* appeared. It was too late to run. "A new *lager* guard is coming," he said. "For harboring illegals—death." Maks Heimberg came up to me and hit me with his cane. "What are you doing here, kid?" I jumped up and ran into the bushes.

The new *lagerwache* was made up of Germans, Ukrainians and Volksdeutsche. I didn't hide from them, I walked up close, I looked them straight in the eye. They thought I was legal. They gave me gloves to stitch up, socks to darn. I wormed my way into the kitchen as a helper, and slept there by the stove. Sometimes, I thought about setting everything on fire and escaping into the forest, but how would I have managed in the forest?

The potatoes and beets in the kitchen started to sprout. Spring was approaching. One rainy evening, the column returned from work, but people weren't dispersing. They formed groups and conferred with each other. I figured out that a deportation was coming, and my hands shook as I poured the soup.

Every night, someone slipped out. We heard shots and the moans of those who had been hit. Flaks, the manager, had a hiding place prepared in the forest. In order to placate everyone, he agreed to take the orphans with him. We left in the middle of night, in snow mixed with rain. We got drenched while we waited, because we had to sneak up to the fence one by one. It was difficult to climb over the fence in soaking wet clothes. Our feet sank into the earth as we ran across the ploughed field. In the forest, we stepped into a cold brook, the water washed our traces away.

The bunker was covered with logs through which the rain dripped. We stood ankle-deep in mud. We froze on the wet bunks. The children whimpered. Don't cry, children, we're Jews. We have gotten through so much already, we'll get through this cold grave. And from below this earth, soaked with Jewish tears, we will hear the trumpets of the Messiah.

We cooked stale barley and rotten beans. We baked pancakes out of mouldy rye. The smoke from the stove stung our eyes. We slept by day, we went outside by night. Contrary to the cave-men whom much less had threatened.

Rucia Ginsberg asked if we wouldn't have to be afraid in the next world. She wanted to be a bird. "If I were a bird, I would fly away from here, very far away, and I wouldn't be afraid anymore. And if one can't fly away anywhere, it's still better to die as a bird than as a human being. I'd dig out a hole with my own little beak, I'd cover myself with my wings." She made up a song like that for herself.

I couldn't look these children in the eye. I'll go into town, I'll bring them bread. I slipped out of the dugout when everyone was asleep. The flowers were already smiling in the meadows. The birds were singing to God. Thanking him that they were birds. Children played in the yards, they were not afraid of anything.

Maks Heimberg was standing in front of the barracks. "Come over here! Come over here!" he called just as I was about to turn into the courtyard on the opposite side. "What do you want from me? You don't even see me," I gave him a hint, but he pretended he didn't get it. Suddenly I saw Mensinger coming out from behind him. "This time, you're not going to get away, you spoiled brat! This time, you'll go, you'll go," Mensinger laughed.

They shoved me inside, took down my name, but there was no one in the barracks. I ran from room to room. Deathly silence everywhere. Maybe, they've already killed me, I thought. But if they had killed me, then it wouldn't be empty around me, it would be full. I ran out to the latrine, no one was keeping guard. I went up to the fence, no one was watching. I climbed up as fast as I could, no one was shooting. I crawled over to the other side, and caught up with a passing wagon. The driver didn't even look around.

I didn't tell any one in the bunker about my adventure. Next morning, as usual, I washed the dishes and tidied up, and when everyone had fallen asleep, I lifted the flap. I needed air. And life which awoke every morning. The brook was talking to the pine trees, the birds were chattering. I knew those voices well from the times when we came here with Father and Mother. Long, long ago, when we walked on the earth like people. The forest had stayed the same and spoke with the same voice, but something had happened to the people, their voices sounded different now. Suddenly hoof-beats rang out, a herd of horses came running, the roof of the dugout rumbled with hoofs. Where are these horses from? I wondered, opening my eyes wide. It wasn't horses, but people in hob-nailed boots. Their screams—*Raus! Raus!*—had not been known in the forest before.

They stood us at the wall outside the barracks and Hildebrand issued the verdicts. Without a word, with a flick of his horsewhip—in this or in that direction. Hundreds of people stood at that wall, and hundreds left—in one direction. Going into the washroom I drew a stool up to the window and looked out into the courtyard. Little Rucia Ginsberg was standing in a group of children at the wall. When I came back, they weren't there any more.

We broke the earth up and counted the days. The earth was hard. We broke it up with pickaxes and rolled it away in wheelbarrows. It put up a resistance, a greater one from day to day, we knew that we wouldn't manage. On the eighth day, shots awoke us. The barracks was surrounded—a deportation. Mensinger stood on the gate and shot at everyone he saw. We ran up and down the corridor, there was nowhere to run. All of a sudden everyone started to squeeze into one door. I squeezed in with the others. A hideout was there which you entered through the stove. About forty people went in, we had to breathe sparingly. We heard the Germans coming in and going out—*Raus! Raus!* We were starting to think that they wouldn't find us, when suddenly there was the sound of breaking boards and Schönbach shone his flashlight into our eyes.

They pulled people out of the latrine pit. They ripped them out of featherbeds. The feathers scattered like snow. They lit the stoves, we heard terrifying screams. A little girl ran out with burns all over her body, and a woman in a burning dress with a child in her arms. The child didn't make a sound.

Trucks took away the badly beaten and the burned, and we walked in fours. Hildebrand announced: death for stepping out of

line. People looked out of their windows, came out of their houses
when they led us through Borysłav. They looked at us as if we were
criminals.

There was nowhere to run, but a voice said to me, "Run." A
truck drove by. The little burned girl was still screaming. By her
side, I noticed the terrified face of Dr. Reiter. "No, I'm not going
anywhere," I said to the girl walking beside me, and I gave her my
bundle. We were passing a shop. The shopkeeper came out to have
a better look. She was so taken by the sight that she didn't notice me
run into the shop. She came back in only after the procession had
passed. "A Jew has escaped! A Jew!" she started screaming and
pushed me out into the street. A German rode up on a bike. "*Jüdin!*
Verfluchte Jüdin!" shouted the shopkeeper. "*Was . . . ? Bist du Jüdin
. . .*" the German looked me in the eye, surprised. "*Shchozhe? Ne
rozumeyu,*" I replied in Ukrainian. He waved his hand and rode on.

I ran to the meadows. Girls were tending cows and singing
wistful Ukrainian songs. "Do you know any farmer who needs a
cowherd?" I asked. "We'll find out, come tomorrow," they said. Tomorrow was a long way off. It grew dark and rain started to fall. The
cows went into the barns. I squatted under a bush, the wet earth
wouldn't let me lie down. Not one star shone, not one dog barked,
only darkness and deafening silence, as if there was no one left on
earth, neither man nor God.

The landlord was a policeman. "Where's your *Maty?*" he asked.
"It's eight months since she died." "And your *Bat'ko?*" "He disappeared without a trace." The landlord had a pretty young wife. He
brought her dresses, rings, earrings. He didn't take much care of the
farm, but he was well off. He harnessed the horse and rode off, and
came back with a wagon full of dresses, curtains, pots, tablecloths,
pillows. The landlord's wife picked out the best for herself and took
the rest to market. At the Ukrainian policeman's, I was safe, but I
was afraid of those rings, earrings and dresses because I thought I
recognized them, and I was nauseous when I cleaned the landlord's
stinking boots.

The first fifteen hundred taken from work, they shot in the

neighboring forest. Those from the Colosseum they transported to Bełżec. No one returned from there either. Whoever they caught later, they took to the slaughterhouse. They had a pit full of lime there. Every cowherd in the area, every housewife, knew about that. I mended worn-out gloves, darned threadbare socks, wiped blood off boots. God certainly made a mistake when He had me born here, but why did He torment me like this? Can God do such things? Who's, actually, the landlord of this world? I tended cows under God's great blue sky with girls who sang beautifully, and who were surprised that I didn't sing.

I herded cows through mud and stepped on glass with my bare foot. My foot swelled, and kept me from sleeping. At night, I heard a distant rumble, like a storm coming. "Get up, Zosia, the Russians are coming" shouted the landlady. "Phew, phew, it's going to be bad," said the landlord. I got up indifferently, to keep up appearances. "I'll go pick some grass for milking," I said, and walked out, limping, into the road where wagons were rushing, one behind the other. I boarded a wagon, my heart was beating hard.

I've made it! I've made it! I didn't give in to death. I'm going to dance, to sing! I'm going to jump for joy! I'll go back to my home, snuggle up to Father, to Mother. I'll hug Sister and Big Brother. I'll take Iziaszek into my arms. Dear ones, how much I've longed for you! How much I've wanted to see you! How bad it's been with me. How long this terrible dream has been . . . My heart beat until it ached. I didn't know who would return. I didn't know who would not return. I didn't know that no one would return.

In the hospital, I met a girl who had been bought out of the slaughterhouse. She told me that they had made them walk along a plank above a pit bubbling with quicklime. The plank wobbled, people fell in. Those who didn't fall got a bullet. They tried not to fall. They tried to walk as long as possible even after the shot. They tried to get another bullet so as not to fall in alive. Usually, however, they fell in alive and the quicklime kept moving. Her mother went and her younger sister. And our Iziaszek. They all remained there under the slaughterhouse in the middle of Borysłav. I didn't cry, I didn't have the tears. Ever since then, my eyes have been dry. So much worse. They burn like quicklime.

The landlord's wife found me. She found out that I am Jewish. She wanted me to go and testify that her husband had saved me. I didn't say anything, I couldn't find the voice, but when she took out a ring to give me, I howled.

"Run, get out of here," ordered the voice. I ran away to Wał-brzych. I met people who worked in *"Bricha,"* which meant "flight." I had a fine Aryan appearance, I travelled to Katowice for money. An Aryan appearance was still very important, especially in trains. I wrapped myself up with money and bandages. I trans-ported hundreds of thousands, millions, sometimes. We took Jews across the border, we needed a lot of money. For the guards.

When I landed here, the young man who received refugees held out his arms to me. I stayed in his arms. God wanted to repair the wrong, and I was born a second time—when I placed my feet on this ground; when I gave birth to my children here.

My son became a doctor. That's not a profession, it's a calling. We helped him because doctors didn't earn much. My older daugh-ter, a social worker, looked after orphans and orphaned parents. That's also not a profession, you have to have a heart for it, which she did. Two of her schoolmates perished. Chaim, who fell in the Sinai, had been an only child. His parents had met in Auschwitz, his mother was forty years old when she gave birth to him. Our daughter talked to her each Saturday. Dov finished Technion and went into the air force. He was with us for Sabbath evening before the accident. I asked him, "Dov, why the air force?" "Oh, I felt guilty that I was studying while others were serving." Our youngest daughter chose literature. Of course, that isn't a profession either.

I have five grandchildren. Nobody loves them like I do.

Without a Trace

FOR CHARLENE

> *. . . unfortunate little town, Jews on the thresholds, like corpses, I think to myself: whatever is going to happen to you . . .*

Isaak Babel

My father's oldest sister married her uncle, who had come for her from America. Then, in turn, the rest of them left. They could have brought my father over, too, by himself, but he didn't want to be parted from us. On my birthday, he took me down to the river, and I asked him whether America was over there on the other side and why they didn't want us there. My father's students stole away to Palestine. But only those who were single could go there, too, for those with small children it was out of the question.

We lived on Mickiewicz Street, the most beautiful one in Horochów, planted with tall, spreading chestnut trees. Our house stood in a garden. A flower bed and a hedge in front, fruit trees at the back. The district sub-prefect used to come over, and the priest and a Ukrainian *batyushka* with long grey hair; Professors Różycki and Stachura; Doctors Grosfeld and Daniłowski; Dentist Janiuk; Jewish teachers from the Tarbut. There was singing in Polish, in Yiddish, in Ukrainian. Tyjusia who was four years older than me played the piano. We both had music, French and German lessons, but I didn't want to learn. When our rooms were being painted, I took a brush and painted over the keyboard. I ran across gardens with boys, climbed apple and pear trees, jumped over hedges. When Father asked me what I wanted for my birthday, I said, a penknife. And I never parted with that penknife. I still carry a penknife in my handbag today, I don't leave the house without a penknife.

On my birthdays, Danusia Kobryń, a very good student, came over, and Hela Szubert, who had a beautiful voice; light blonde Zina Niebożyńska; two sisters, Ita and Lula Berger, and my best friend Tova, with golden-hair and blue eyes like an angel, always smiling or ready to smile, even later when she was very hungry. There wasn't a more beautiful child and everyone stared at her.

I didn't like private lessons, but I very much liked school: a large, noisy building with a crowd of children, games in the playground, excursions to Mirków and Chołojów—*where the stream flows slowly, May sows its flowers, the field daisy grows, and above her rustle the groves* . . . Later, I hid in those forests and groves.

My father had studied in Basel and Heidelberg. None of his sisters were educated, everything was sacrificed for him. He could read and write French, German, Polish, Russian, Ukrainian and Hebrew; he knew Greek and Latin, and had books in all these languages in his library. Rare, old editions with silver and gold letters. He collected books and would travel a very long way for them, and people would bring them to him, because they knew that he paid well. At our house, before any of us touched a book, we washed our hands the way you do for prayers or before eating. My father was the only one who took a book off the shelf, and only he put it back; no one else had the right to do so. The library could only be cleaned during his presence, so as not to disturb anything. We didn't have money or valuables, those books were our silver and gold.

Like his students from Horochów, Ostróg, Łokacze, Torczyn, Kamionka Strumiłowa, my father travelled to Lwów by train. Professor Różycki or Professor Stachura, both of whom had cars, drove him to the station in Boroczyce. Father's students gathered at our house on Saturdays and Sundays, and shut themselves up in his study with him. Every so often, one of them disappeared, and then a letter would come from Palestine which would be read at the meeting.

My father had dark, wavy hair parted in the middle and longer than most other men's, a thin face and a prominent nose, glasses with a thin gold frame, and ever-serious eyes—even when he was smiling. Tyja looked very much like him. In a photograph with Father and Mother, she is wearing a red, polka-dot dress with a big lace collar. Everything is black and white in the photograph, but I remember that dress. My mother's hair was lighter, and smooth, pulled back into a knot which you can't see in the photograph. Around her neck, she has a colorful Ukrainian kerchief which is black in the photograph and the pattern doesn't show. Her face is round like mine, the same round eyes and small nose. People think that it's me in the past. Father has lowered his eyelids as though he is reading something, Tyja is deep in thought and looking inward, while Mama is looking off into the distance as though she has seen something there. All three of them are serious, although the shadow of a sad smile shows at the corners of Tyja's lips. Those were three separate photographs I found at my aunt's in Ohio. When Ed was stationed in Munich, I went to a special photographer's and he put them together into a family picture, but each of them remains withdrawn and alone.

The Germans walked around with Ukrainians and a long list of names. When my father saw that they were approaching our house, he ran out the back door into the garden, but the Ukrainians noticed the opened door and ran after him. He ran out without his jacket and without saying goodbye to us. And he wasn't there any more. They also took Tova's father, Ita and Lula's father, the three Flam brothers who had a shoe and clothing store, the two Feldmeister brothers who owned a tannery, and both Flekmans who were assistants at the University. They took two hundred people. Mama didn't react when they came for Father's books. Three Germans in uniform, very polite, placed the books carefully into crates and took them out to the truck. They worked half the day without help from any Ukrainian. The truck was grated, like those in which they took away people.

Mama and Tyja had to go to dig ditches and pave roads. Mama came back bloodied and bruised because one of the Ukrainians didn't like her work. And they kept on wanting something from us. First, gold and silver. Then nickel, copper and brass. Then furs, carpets and feather pillows. They announced it through bullhorns in German and in Ukrainian.

In the ghetto, we lived in one room with three other families, just women and children. There was only one kitchen for the whole house, and one toilet in the courtyard. We slept on bunks. Mama still went to dig ditches, but Tyja managed to get into a workshop where they made sweaters, socks and scarves for the army—they got soup and black coffee for that. The children who were too young to work didn't get anything, so we dug out two holes under the fence and went over to the other side.

We went one by one. We left our outer garments with the yellow star in a hide-hole beneath the fence, but everyone knew where we were from. We stood by the shop out of which women came with their purchases, we knocked at doors. They drove us off, set dogs on us, swore, but sometimes they gave a carrot, a cucumber, a potato—or else they sold them. They asked whether we had money and gold. I took Mama's small ruby ring. Two women were coming out of the shop, nicely dressed, made up. One of them was carrying a string bag in which a loaf of bread glowed golden. "Please give me a piece of bread," I asked. They looked surprised and didn't reply. "I'll pay." "Show me," the woman said. I took out the ring. "Is it really gold?" "Really." She tried to squeeze it over her finger, but it wouldn't go on. "I can give you an egg." "Is that all? Maybe just a piece of bread?" "Two eggs and that's it."

I came up to the hole when I heard from behind me, "*Kudy ty idesh?*" "Back to the ghetto," I answered. "Do you have a pass?" "No." "Where's your patch?" I didn't reply. "What have you got there?" he pointed to my bulging pockets. He smashed the eggs on the pavement, pressed my head to the ground and rubbed my face in the mess. My face was scraped and bleeding, but I was proud that I hadn't revealed the hole.

Two days later, they caught Tova with a loaf of bread. She lay in the square which everyone had to cross on the way to and from work. She was looking straight up at the sky. Her lips were open as though she was speaking to someone up above. The sun was stroking her angelically golden braids. She lay like that for several days, as though she was resting. Instead of the yellow star on her bodice, a crimson stain.

In that same place, they set up a gallows later and summoned us all into the square. They brought in three Jews who had tried to escape. We weren't allowed to turn our heads away, because guards stood all around, ordering us to look. We were not allowed to close our eyes. The square was small and we all stood close to each other, but we didn't hear any complaints beneath the gallows, only the prayers and sobs of those who had to watch, and the laughter of the guards who were smoking cigarettes and joking. Mama drew me and Tyja close to her when the hanged tried to climb through the air to the sky. One of them had holes in the soles of his shoes. They, too, remained in the square many days.

In the winter, women could be seen by the wall, most often with small children. They sat dead in the frost. It wasn't much warmer inside the houses. When Tyja fell ill, I went to work in her place in order to have something warm to eat. I went out of the ghetto in her group. People weren't surprised. They showed me where to sit. I knew how to knit, but not as fast as the big girls. A German stopped behind me and started to shout. I tried to work faster, but I kept getting the stitches wrong. The German snatched the needle out of my hand, and shoved it underneath my nail. I fainted and fell off the bench. There was no iodine, nor any other medicine. Mama exchanged her wedding ring for some vodka to wash my finger with, but that part of it fell off.

I sat in the house with Sheyndele who couldn't get up any more. Her mother and older sister went to work. I gave her water. "Do you want a drink, Sheyndele?" "No, I don't want anything any more." "Are you cold?" "No," she replied. When she began to rattle, I wrapped her up in my sack. She grew quiet and turned ashen grey. Her older sister just didn't wake up. The mother had to go to work, so she covered her with a potato sack. People came and took her away. The mother didn't come back at night. They found her sitting by the wall.

In spring, when there were only a few of us left, they moved the ghetto down to the river. It was surrounded with a fence and barbed wire in the same way, but only on three sides, because on the fourth side was the river. People knew that the ghetto wouldn't survive. They built hiding places in houses, covered the entrances with wardrobes. They thought, the Germans and the Ukrainians will come, they'll see that there's no one here, so they'll leave. Grown-ups sometimes think like children. Mama looked for a hiding place outside the ghetto. One evening she came home from work with good news. She had managed to arrange two places for us.

Tyja put on two layers of clothing, we embraced and she left for work as usual. In the evening, Mama came home happy that Tyja had managed to vanish. And then we, also, put on two blouses and skirts and our winter shoes, even though it was the beginning of summer, and crept out in the dark with our small bundles, not waking those who lived with us.

We had a place arranged at Kalinets' in Skobelka on the other side of the river. We used to buy milk, butter and eggs there before, they were cheaper and fresher than in the shops. We got into the water between bulrushes, and Mama kept repeating, "Remember, we are going over to the other side, then left, and then right." "Mama, I know very well how to go to Kalinets, I've been there lots of times." Suddenly, shots rang out. We went back into the bulrushes. When the shooting died down, we set off again, but again the shooting started and we had to stay in the rushes. In the morning, the shooting grew even worse, and fires flared up in the ghetto. We heard screaming and saw people hiding in the bulrushes like us. The bank of the river was high there, and protected us, but over and over we heard the shout, "Get out, Jew, I can see you!" People stood up to their necks in water and fell into it with a splash, on all sides moans rose from the rushes. When night came, Mama took bread out of the damp bundle. It had gone soft in the water. I didn't want to eat and the bread tasted dreadfully of mud, but I ate because Mama made me. I held her by the hand and kept dropping off to sleep, and when I woke, I grabbed her hand even more tightly.

Mama reassured me that we would definitely manage to cross to the other side tonight, and kept on reminding me how to get to Kalinets' cottage. But again day came, and we were still sitting in the water. Towards the end of the day, the shots fell less frequently and it seemed that no one was left in the rushes, apart from us. Mama stuck the rest of the bread and mud into my mouth. Then I closed my eyes, it seemed just for a moment, but when I opened them, Mama wasn't there. I called—just once, because my voice got stuck in my throat. She vanished without a trace, and a terrifying silence reigned in the rushes.

I sat motionless and waited for her to come back. Then I thought that she probably hadn't been able to wake me, and had gone to Kalinets alone. I felt ashamed for letting her down so badly and decided to get there no matter what. As soon as it grew dark, I set off for the other side. No one was shooting, and the river must have been shallow just there, or else I swam without knowing it. I turned left, and then right onto the main road of Skobelka. Kalinets' dogs knew me, and just growled reluctantly.

Kalinets stood in the middle of the room with his wife behind him, and they looked at me with amazement. "Is my mama here," I asked. "No." "Then I'll wait for her." "What do you mean 'wait'?" Kalinets asked impatiently. "Well, you agreed to hide us, Mama and me." Kalinets and his wife looked at each other. "Yes, but I changed my mind." He was wearing a dirty *kosovorotka* tied with string. From the pocket of his homespun pants, hung the heavy, braided, gold watch-chain which belonged to my father. "You won't even let me wait for Mama?" "If you don't take yourself off, we'll report you to the police," said Kalinets. Kalinets' wife gave me a piece of bread and an apple for the road.

I walked into wheat taller than I was. I walked, and walked, and I couldn't get out of it so I stayed in the wheat. The following evening, I found my way to a cottage where a family sat at the table and steam rose off bowls. "What are you doing here?" the bearded landlord asked. "I'm hungry." "You have no right to be here! We have to take you to the police." The dog in the barnyard started to growl. "But I haven't done anything to you, I just want some food." "And what will you give us for it?" asked the landlord. I ripped a piece of gold out of a seam. They were eating soup and potatoes with bacon fat, but they only gave me a piece of bread. I never went into cottages after that. I stole into barnyards by night, snatched what I could, and left.

I was convinced that I had disappointed my mother, and that it was my responsibility to find her. If she wasn't at the Kalinets', then she must have hidden in the forest. In the morning I noticed a group of people sitting at the edge of the forest, and I overheard some words in Yiddish. They were six of them: a young woman with a baby strapped to her chest with a shawl, a disheveled woman in her early thirties, two well dressed young men, each with a leather briefcase stuffed to capacity, and a middle-aged man with a short beard. The woman with the baby motioned for me to join them. I took out a carrot and handed it to her. She promptly stuck it in the baby's mouth. They all came from nearby towns. I asked whether they had seen my mother, and they asked me about their families. I was glad that I was no longer alone. Suddenly, a bunch of children ran up, "Jews! Jews!" they shouted and ran off. The forest had no underbrush and it was difficult to hide in, so we burrowed into a haystack as deeply as we could. Soon we heard people coming with happy shouts and exclamations, from the grown-ups and the children. It wasn't difficult for them to notice which haystack had been disturbed and they stabbed it with their pitchforks. I heard people being dragged out. I didn't hear any pleading, just laughter and eager shouts. And how they counted them: "*Odin, dva, tri, chetyre, pyat, shist.*" And how they checked, "Did we get them all?" I remained deep down in the haystack, the dust was choking me, but I did not cough. It was a quiet, calm night when I came out. They lay in a row in torn and bloodied clothing. The moon shone bright, but I couldn't recognize their pitted and cut faces.

"What did they have on their feet?"

"On their feet? Nothing . . ."

"And what did they have before?"

"Well, they had good winter boots. Because everyone escaped with the best they had."

"Boots were very important. And expensive. Not all farmhands owned boots. Not even all farmers . . . "

My shoes started to fall apart because I was constantly walking from forest to forest. A forest when you look at it seems close by, but when you start to walk towards it, recedes. I couldn't stop, because I had to get from forest to forest by night, before it grew light. If I couldn't manage it, I had to hide in a barn or a stable. Sometimes, I managed to milk a cow straight into my mouth. That was my only warm food. Once, in the dark, I saw something on the floor of the forest. I walked up, a man and a woman, dead. Out of her jacket, like a breast, poked a loaf of bread. I picked up that bread soaked in blood. I have never admitted that to anyone until now. I cut the wet part off with my penknife and ate the rest. I wanted to bury them, but there wasn't much I could do with my bare hands, so I covered them with leaves and grass.

The gamekeepers rode on horseback, I could hear them in the distance, and I climbed into a tree. Once a gamekeeper left his horse behind and surprised me. "*Skilki tebe rokiv?*" he asked with a nasty smile. His breath reeked of vodka. "Ten," I replied. I was twelve at the time, but I sensed that it was better to lie. "*Hody na policyu,*" he said in anger. I ripped a gold coin out of my sweater. He waved his hand and let me go.

I always searched for heavy undergrowth and covered myself carefully with leaves, but one day again a pair of high boots stood before me. "What are you doing in the forest by yourself?" "I'm looking for my mother." "Jewish? . . . Come with me." He led me deep into the forest. A bonfire was burning there, wagons stood all around, tents, horses grazed. They gave me a bowl of hot potatoes and a piece of roasted hare. I've never eaten anything as good as that. I had been afraid to start a fire, but they cooked and weren't afraid of anything. "Can I stay with you?" I asked. "Do you have a weapon?" asked the man who had brought me here. "No, but I've got this." I handed him my last gold coin. He took it, but he threw his hands up. "You see, we've got a rule that says we don't take anyone who doesn't have weapons." But they let me stay by the fire overnight. When they'd all fallen asleep in the tents, I went up to one of the wagons and found a woolen shawl, boots, raw potatoes and a loaf of bread. The boots—mismatched, but a left one and a right one—saved my life that winter.

I walked through the forests for weeks without meeting anyone. Once, I wanted to spend a day in a barn to hear human voices. At dawn, someone started to climb onto the straw. It was a boy not much older than me.

"What are you doing here? Get out!"

"Let me stay here until dark."

"*Ne! Nehayno!*" he called.

I ran with all my might because it was growing light and I was in the middle of the village with nowhere to hide. All I could do was throw myself into the well. I jumped into the bucket and lowered the chain. I sat in the well until nightfall. I didn't feel cold and somehow no one needed water out of that well that day.

I didn't know where I was going. I walked straight ahead. Sometimes after walking all night, sometimes after several nights, I would end up where I had started from. I was afraid of people, but I felt terrible being alone. In the ghetto, I had been with my mother and sister and everyone who was suffering, and here I was by myself amid persecutors and people who were quite well off.

By day, I dug myself graves in the soft ground of the forest and covered myself with leaves and grass, but in the winter I left traces behind in the snow. The barns weren't safe, because somebody would always come in and, on top of that, the mean country dogs growled from afar. So, I hid in potato mounds. They weren't as warm as the barns, but better than the forest, and I had more than enough potatoes. Raw potatoes are very good when you are very hungry. What's more important, they have lots of water, and I needed water more than I needed food. I ate whatever I could find in the fields: carrots; cabbage; beets, but I was always thirsty. In the winter, I ate snow, in summer I drank out of puddles like a dog. My stomach always ached. I ate ants, caterpillars and worms whose names I didn't know. I came upon snakes and vipers. I wasn't afraid of them. I wasn't doing anything to them, so they left me alone. Not like people. I washed myself in the rain or in streams. Lice bothered me a lot and woke me up at night. I tried to shake them out of my clothes, but I didn't have anything to get them out of my hair with. Once, I got into a pine forest which had no undergrowth. I looked and looked, but couldn't find a place to hide in and I didn't have the strength to go to another forest. I fell asleep a little, but awoke with fright, so I climbed into a tree. A good thing I did, because very shortly afterwards Germans on motorcycles and Ukrainians on bicycles drove up. They lit bonfires, spread themselves out, ate and drank and pissed underneath my tree. The pine needles under my collar itched, but I had to sit there motionless and watch them throughout that whole damned day.

One evening, I didn't have the strength to get up and I stayed in the grave to rest. But my strength didn't return and I stayed another night. And then another. And then I lost count. It was spring and I didn't feel cold. I didn't want to eat. Even the lice weren't bothering me as much so I was able to sleep. Only thirst woke me. I thought that I heard human voices, but I couldn't run, I couldn't move my hand or my leg, like in a dream, so I thought I was dreaming. When I saw a pair of short, soft boots, I tried to get up, but to no avail. I was stuck to the ground. And I suddenly thought to myself, it's good that I can't get up, that it's all over and that I don't have to go anywhere any more, and I wondered why I had struggled for so long. I'd wake up in the back of a truck shaking over cobblestones. "They're taking me to Father," I thought. Someone was shouting in my ear, *"Dyevushka, dyevushka, Hitler kaput!"*

Everyone in the hospital was nice to me. I was surprised by that because I had thought that the days were gone forever when people were nice to me. They gave me big new boots, a tunic to my knees, canned food and chocolate tied up in a bundle. They even offered me a packet of cigarettes and were very surprised that I didn't want it. They asked where I planned to go. I said, to look for my mother.

I was walking with my bundle along the main street of Luck when a woman from Horochów saw me—Sonia who remembered me from the ghetto. She took me to her house. There were a dozen or so Jews in Luck, and they all lived on Pańska Street side by side in a few houses, like in the ghetto. One woman had survived with six children of whom the youngest girl was my age. They had had a good hideout with a good peasant for a great deal of money. An old man and his two grandchildren had also survived at a peasant's. He had a long white beard and every few minutes he went up to the bowl of water to wash it. Some farmer in Markowicze had hidden Sonia.

Together with others, we went in a rented army truck to Tor-czyn, Łokacze and Horochów. Not a trace of the ghetto remained in Horochów. It was levelled, ploughed over. But our house on Mick-iewicz Street was standing as though nothing had happened. I stared at it in disbelief, I didn't have the courage to go in. People came up. "What luck, that you survived, that you are alive!" the Ukrainian women called out in amazement. They told me about Tyja, that she had been led naked down Mickiewicz Street. They didn't know what happened to her after that. They didn't know what had happened to my mother. They said that some of the men arrested along with my father had been shot in the hornbeam grove, and that others had been deported. Apparently to Dachau. That's what they heard. Only the women talked, the men were silent. The hornbeam grove was a park—one went that way to the gymnasium and to the houses where the richest people lived. In the middle of the park stood a mansion which housed the county council. I wanted to go there, but the truck couldn't wait. It was growing late and everyone was in a hurry, no one wanted to stay there until night.

We decided that we should go to Germany, because if there was nobody here, perhaps they were there. After all, not everyone could

have been killed. The Germans had taken people so we should go
after them. We got from Luck to Lwów, and from Lwów to Kraków
in army trucks. The Jewish Committee in Kraków was giving out
American food and money for an illegal night train to Bratislava. In
Vienna, everyone was asked where they wanted to go. I said—to
Dachau.

I waited for a year in Foehrenwald near Dachau. I went to all the
other camps, I questioned all the DP's. I stayed in Bensheim near
Heidelberg. Heidelberg was another world. Beautiful little stucco
houses, carved, painted, like out of a fairy-tale, they had been standing for three-hundred years. And people were living in them as
though nothing had happened. Carefully dressed and combed.
Time had stood still here. Or else it had passed them by. There were
no murderers here. And no one knew anything at all about what
had happened outside of Heidelberg. Centuries-old Heidelberg, the
source, the seat, the breeding place of knowledge—and no one
knew anything. Along these charming streets a thin, dark-haired
student had walked who had been taught that knowledge is the
greatest treasure. He would pause by the picturesque landscape on
the high banks of the river in which the untouched walls looked at
themselves. He admired the wisdom of the builders and the endurance of their work. He ate, slept and laughed in these timeless
houses. He peed in their tidy toilets. And read, and read, and read.
The imprints of his fingers remained on the gilded and silvered
books, on thousands of pages and on all the catalogues. It would
have been completely natural if the most beautiful and the most
valuable of the books, which he would collect for the rest of his life,
had arrived in barred trucks precisely here. But no one knew about
that.

I had five aunts in America, so I went from consulate to consulate, but they said a quota was a quota and I would have to wait
three years—there was no exception for anyone. So I applied to the
university. Without a word, they accepted me—with three years of

elementary education. And they gave me, for free, tutors in philosophy, mathematics and German. I managed quite well, because I received American packages from CARE, and each box contained two cartons of cigarettes which were quite literally worth their weight in gold. And peanut butter, also extremely expensive. The journey from Bensheim to Heidelberg was considerably quicker than from Horochów to Lwów.

I went to Horochów with Ed and Steve—through Moscow, Kiev and Lwów—as a tourist. In Lwów they gave us a car and two drivers. And they announced that we could stop in Horochów for only two hours. "Look, look is that hay?" Ed and Steve asked when we passed huge haystacks in the fields. They had thought until then that I had been talking about sheaves and they hadn't dared question how so many people had hidden there together.

I didn't recognize Mickiewicz Street that time. Not a single tree was growing there. There weren't any sidewalks either. And it wasn't called Mickiewicz. We went in the direction of the hornbeam grove, we looked, but the grove wasn't there either. Not a single tree had survived in Horochów. I took Ed and Steve to show them the river. We looked, but there was no river. Nor any bulrushes. Not a trace. And nobody knew anything. Just as in Heidelberg.

In front of the house—no trace of a garden—a crowd had gathered, so Steve went around the corner to take photographs from there. A van suddenly pulled up. Two men in uniforms grabbed him by the arms and dragged him inside. He started to shout for help. I was so engrossed, I didn't hear, but our drivers had keener ears. Ed and I ran after them and we saw our drivers struggling with those men and waving their papers. And what if they hadn't heard? The photos which Steve had taken don't exist, the roll vanished from the suitcase. And they only gave us two hours because this was their Horochów, not mine. If I had only known when to light the candle . . .

Kamionka Strumiłowa, Sokal, Torczyn, Ostróg can all be found in the Jewish encyclopedia. In Kamionka Strumiłowa on July 2, 1941, that is a few days after the arrival of the Germans, the Ukrainians killed several hundred Jews. Six hundred others were killed on September 21, 1942, in Zabuże, where Jews from Busk, Chołojów and Radziechów were murdered as well, the rest were sent to Bełżec on September 15 and October 28, 1942. In Sokal, the Ukrainian police murdered two hundred Jews by the brickwork on June 30, 1941. The Sokal ghetto contained more than five thousand Jews from Łopatyń, Mosty Wielkie, Radziechów, Stenlatyń, Tartaków and Witków. The ghetto was murdered on May 27, 1942. One thousand six hundred Jews lived in Torczyn. Most of them were shot to death in August 1942 in the Jewish cemetery. On October 6, 1941, seventy of the intelligentsia from Zbaraż were murdered in the Lubieniec forest. Hundreds of other Zbaraż Jews were massacred outside town on April 7, 1943. In the forest by Nowe Miasto on August 4, 1941, three thousand were shot. On September 1, two and a half thousand, and another three thousand Jews from Ostróg on October 15, 1942. Eight hundred Jews managed to run into the forest, but they were murdered or given away by Ukrainian peasants and Bandera's men. Thirty survived in hideouts and thirty with the partisans.

But about Horochów not a word. Not a trace.

A Brother in Volhynia

FOR SUE

My grandfather was taken into the army when he was a little boy. He served for twenty-five years and then bought land in Wełnianka and got married. In those days, only a Jew who had served in the army had the right to buy land. Grandfather said that money loses value, but it's just the opposite with land, and that it was easy to take money away from someone, but it wasn't so easy to take land. But my mother's brothers didn't want that land, and one after another left for America. When Grandfather died, my grandmother left, too, with Mama's younger sister. Mama stayed because she had got married.

My grandfather on my father's side owned a water mill in Kowel. When they wanted to take Father into the army, Grandfather pricked his right eye with a needle. Father wasn't able to shoot, but he could still read quite well. He went to university instead of into the army and became a lawyer. Mama didn't want to marry him. She danced beautifully, she won a ballroom dancing competition, fell in love with a professional dancer. "You're not going to marry a Gypsy! You're going to marry someone who'll give you a comfortable life," Grandmother shouted at her, sparing no blows. After the wedding, Mama was embarrassed to take her clothes off because she had so many bruises on her skin.

She had six miscarriages in a row, and it began to look as though none of us would be born. She went to Kowel, to Łuck, nothing helped. Finally in Warsaw, a doctor recommended that she avoid all contact with our father for three months. Mama moved in with Grandma for three months, and it worked. She did the same thing each time, and, in this fashion, my brothers, sisters and I came into the world.

Father bought the land and the house in Wełnianka from Grandma. The house stood right by the bridge connecting Wełnianka and Rożyszcze. We had rye, wheat, potatoes, apples, pears and sour cherries, about fifty cows, all the same—black and white—and eight horses. A land steward supervised the workers who lived in a four-family farmhouse, and Father ran a lawyer's office in Rożyszcze in partnership with a Polish gentile. Everybody who wanted to go to America came to them. Father was arrested once for helping a communist leave. I was five years old at the time and I remember how I cried when the police were taking him away. "And what is it I did?" Father defended himself in court. "I didn't bring any communist into Poland, the reverse. And for this you prosecute? This should be rewarded." That argument completely convinced the judge.

Grandma insisted that we should leave Poland. "Don't you read the newspapers? Don't you see what's going on?" she wrote. But Father didn't want to. "Who would I be in America? A lawyer without a language? What security could I provide for you there? Here, I have everything. What would I have there?" Mama gave him an ultimatum, "Stay if you want to. I'm taking the children and going." So Father went to America to look around. By the time he looked around, it was too late.

The Russians took our land and our cows, leaving only the house. Mama was afraid that they'd deport us to Siberia. She began to bake bread. "I'm a working woman," she said. Then, she opened a bar in our house. Just wine, beer and kvass. She didn't have a license to sell vodka. Somebody informed on her. A Russian came and found a liter bottle under the counter. "Aha! You're selling vodka!" he screamed. Mama smashed the bottle and ground it into the floor. "Prove it!"

As before, we went to school. I to Wełnianka, Misza and Żenia to Rożyszcze, but we were learning Russian. Żenia's teacher made overtures to her. She looked like Mama. Her hair was so thick and so long that she could cover herself with it when she let it down. She got furious when I looked through her books, because she was reading things like *Cleopatra*. Harry was studying in Kowel. He was going to be a doctor. When the Russians were retreating, Harry and Misza fled with them, and then came back. "Why did you come back? Why didn't you keep running?" Mama sobbed. It would have been better if they had taken us to Siberia.

"How nice it is here!" the Germans marvelled at our house. Mama hadn't taken anything down, hadn't hidden anything. "A decent woman," Germans praised her. Other people hid the porcelain, the crystal. Mama did the opposite, she set the table with her best things. "They're going to take it anyway, sooner or later," she said. We didn't have much to eat, but the table had to be beautifully set. She wanted us to know all that. "If I don't show them, how are they going to know how to live?" she explained to the neighbors. We changed for dinner. Misza read us his poems. He wanted to be a writer. He wanted to describe our life in Volhynia. Mama was very proud of him. She used to come out to the bridge with us, we looked at ourselves in the Styr. The bridge was wooden but high, because the Styr rose and overflowed its banks. Sometimes we sailed across the fields in canoes.

"How beautiful all this is," the Gestapo marvelled as they listed down the furniture in our house. And they also appraised Mama with their eyes. They searched for Żenia, but Mama had hidden her in the attic. They pushed Mama into the bedroom. You could hear her crying. When they left, she locked herself up, and didn't want to let us in. Before we went to the ghetto, she threw our place settings and dishes into the well. She gave the jewelry and the furs to our neighbors for safe-keeping. She sewed gold coins into our clothes.

They herded us across the frozen river. We wore several layers of clothing because they wouldn't let us take a large amount of luggage, so it was hard to walk across the ice, and they kept driving us on. Everything they did to us, they did in hurriedly. I couldn't keep up, my legs kept slipping out from under me, as in a dream. A German ran up and hit me on the head with something. I fell onto the ice, blood filled my eye. Mama picked me up in her arms. I had a huge scar on my temple from that.

We slept with four other families in a single room. By day, we stood in line in front of a shop where all they sold were pickled tomatoes. Harry, Żenia and Misza went to the factory. Enia and I stole through a hole in the wall and brought back bread from a landlady we knew. Mama taught us to make the sign of the cross and say prayers like Christian children. They only shot at us once. We managed to hide in a ditch full of water, but all our bread was ruined.

Terrible news reached us. It was said that they'd murdered Dubno. After that, Równe. Then, Kowel. Then, Łuck. People didn't believe it. Maybe they'd murdered some Jews—that always happened. Maybe a lot, even, but not all! When the news came that they'd murdered Kiwerce, our Rabbi told us to put on our best Shabbat clothes and to devote ourselves to prayer, because our turn had come.

Mama dressed me and Enia in our best and sent us to the landlady from whom we got bread. The landlady said the bread wasn't baked just yet, and told us to go into the field with the cows. We came back with the cows in the evening, but the bread still wasn't baked, and the landlady took Enia over to other people. Meanwhile it began to grow dark, and it was time to go back to the ghetto. I ran out to fetch Enia, but Alamor, the shaggy, black, sheep-dog, blocked my path. "Alamor! What are you doing? Why won't you let me get by?" But he started growling and barking even more loudly. The landlady ran up. "Where are you trying to go?" she asked. "To the ghetto." "To the ghetto? How lucky that Alamor wouldn't let you get past!"

In the evening, Marek Dobrowicz drove over in a wagon, and took me with him. He said that he was my brother, and told me to forget about my other family. I also had three other sisters of marriageable age, whose names I don't remember. My other brother, Jerzyk, was the same age as Misza. He played the harmonica, danced the hopak, everyone in the family liked him a lot. They were all very nice to each other. They sat down at table together, said a prayer before eating, I felt good with them. The Dobrowiczes' farm was a long way from the village. The Dołgopoluks, a married couple with a grown-up daughter, also came there. They looked very Jewish. Their son had been killed in the war. The Dobrowiczes hid them in a covered-up potato pit.

Misza immediately gave his gold coins to the landlord to whom Mama had sent him, and when that man didn't want to keep him any longer he came to the Dobrowiczes. Mama had also sent Harry and Żenia off somewhere, but they came back, they didn't want to leave her on her own. Misza and I didn't want to believe that the whole ghetto had been murdered. Perhaps they had taken them away to work, especially the young ones like Harry and Żenia. And Mama wasn't old either. Mama didn't want to run away anywhere, wander around, ask for favors, hide like an animal. It was beyond her strength. She had been told to get married, she got married; had been told to give birth, had given birth; had raised the children as best she could. But she wanted to die on her own terms. She scattered us around as a mother should. She could do nothing more.

The Dobrowiczes hid Misza in the potato pit with the Dołgopoluks, but he couldn't stand it in there, and, because of me, he didn't want the Dobrowiczes to feed him for free. He decided to go to Wełnianka, to the people with whom Mama had left her things. They were Ukrainians who had once worked for us. They had always been decent and friendly, Mama wouldn't have left anything with them otherwise. Their two sons were not much older than Misza. Misza went and asked them to give him something of ours to live off. Those two sons put a cord around his neck and dragged him by that cord into the square. Where they left him. "Bury me," Misza asked, "At least do that for me! I'm not asking for anything more!" He complained that birds were pecking him, that dogs were tearing him. "Look what they've done to me," he said, searching me out with his gaze, which he didn't have because the crows had pecked out his eyes. "Bury me," he pleaded. "Bury me." He came every night, and I heard his voice by day too.

The Dobrowiczes were afraid that Misza might have revealed where I was, and they hid me in the same stale potato pit with the Dołgopoluks. We lay there as in a grave; we came out at night like ghosts. Mrs. Dobrowicz brought food, which was good, but I couldn't eat it. I was afraid of the relentless night, I asked when I would see day again. Mrs. Dobrowicz took pity on me and brought me back to the house. I squinted my eyes in the light, I hid in the shadows. I was helping Mrs. Dobrowicz to wash the dishes when the Gestapo arrived in a britzka. Mrs. Dobrowicz managed to push me into the peonies in time. They passed close by me. I didn't breathe and my heart stopped beating, as though I were dead. One of them came up with a knife, I closed my eyes, he cut the head off a peony. They also looked into the potato pit, but the stale air repelled them.

Marek Dobrowicz led us out into the forest at night, and left us in a camouflaged dug-out. The Dołgopoluks didn't want to stay in the forest, they found themselves another landlord where there wasn't any room for me. I asked them not to go, not to leave me all alone. I lay motionless all day and all night. I was afraid to sleep, because when I shut my eyes, the chewing and the howling of dogs broke out, and the wailing of my brother. Marek came bringing food, and saw that the Dołgopoluks had left me, so he took me back to the pit. In a short time, the Dołgopoluks returned there as well.

In the meantime, Hitler told the Ukrainians, "If you want the Ukraine, murder the Poles." And war broke out between the Ukrainians and the Poles. They murdered people and cows; led horses away; set fire to stables. They took vengeance, and vengeance for vengeance. Jerzyk and Marek would go out with the partisans. Anytime they didn't return, Mrs. Dobrowicz would kneel in front of the crucifix which hung above the door. One night Jerzyk went by himself and the Ukrainians caught him. Mrs. Dobrowicz knelt in front of the crucifix day and night, but Jerzyk didn't come back. The Ukrainians had crucified him. Nailed him to a board. We couldn't revive Mrs. Dobrowicz. Every time she opened her eyes and looked at the crucifix, she would faint again. She wouldn't allow herself to be lifted up off the floor. She lay on the floor with her arms spread out, everyone knelt beside her. It was as though she were the one who had been crucified.

The Dobrowiczes had to flee. Marek drove me back to the landlady who had once baked bread for us. Umek came there to fetch me. His father was my mother's cousin, they owned a blanket factory in Rożyszcze. Umek had been in the same class as my brother Misza. He had stayed in Rożyszcze until the end and had seen everything. They were driven into the forest. When they were told to undress, Żenia let down her braids to cover her nakedness. They lay face down in a huge pit. Then came the shots, and they were covered with earth. Then the next ones were told to lie down. When the next layer lay down, the first was still moving. It seemed as though the earth itself were moving. Umek lay there with them. At night, he came out from beneath the earth which was still moving. Even when he had already gone quite a distance, the earth gave way beneath his feet. A peasant was driving by, a Ukrainian. When he saw Umek, he crossed himself three times, covered him with a horse-blanket and took him onto the wagon.

We walked through the forest nearly the whole night. It was too cold to rest, so when the forest ended, we walked around in circles. In the morning, we saw a lone farm. Umek told me to go there and say that I was an orphan whose family had been murdered by the Ukrainians, and that in exchange for food and a place to sleep I would tend cows and do any kind of work around the farm. He waited near the forest in case they didn't take me.

I carried buckets of water and food for the pigs; washed floors; milked cows. I tried to be working and needed all the time, so that they would be pleased with me, so that I wouldn't have to go anywhere again. I was afraid each moment I wasn't working. I was small, and I seemed even smaller under the weight of the buckets. Once, when I was walking back from the well, a Russian officer on horseback appeared. "How can you carry such heavy buckets, child?" he said. "Oh, I can," I said with conviction. "I can carry water, and milk cows, and feed pigs and wash floors." The officer climbed off his horse, took the buckets out of my hands, and carried them into the cottage.

"How can you make a child work as hard as this?" he asked. "She's eager to work even when no one is telling her to," the farmer's wife said in self-defense. She treated me well. I ate with them, slept in the same bed as her granddaughter, the officer had intervened quite unnecessarily. "I'll be back to fetch you," he said, "And you're not going to work so hard any more."

The officer kept his word. He galloped in ahead of the other Russians, lifted me onto his saddle, and took me to Rożyszcze. He was a Jew, he knew I was a Jewish child, and we rode up to a house where Jews were living. Among them, the Dołgopoluks. Previously in Rożyszcze, most of the houses had been occupied by Jews, now they lived only in one. The officer very much wanted to do something for us, but he didn't know what. We didn't know either. We looked at him as helplessly as he looked at us. He left me with the Dołgopoluks. He said that after the war he would take care of me. He was going to return the following day to bring us army rations, but Hitler discovered that Jews were rising from the dead in Rożyszcze, and he directed his army back there again.

We fled along dirt roads. Someone threw a long heavy coat on me. I kept falling over, and falling back. I threw off my boots, and then that coat. Behind us, guns barked, above us, airplanes growled. I hid in shrubs and ditches. We reached Kiwerce just as twilight fell. Everyone had disappeared somewhere and I stood alone amid darkened houses. Some woman heard me crying and asked in Russian what I was doing there. I said that my parents had died in the bombing. She took me into her house and bathed me in warm water. She was a teacher, her husband was a teacher as well, they didn't have any children. I dreamt about our house, about fields of waving grain, and meadows of luxuriant grass. The grass was swaying, then the meadows started to sway, to give way beneath my feet . . . Suddenly, everything came back to me and I woke up with a cry. The teacher was rocking me in her arms.

The Germans knew where we had fled, and came to Kiwerce after us. Airplanes in front as usual. We ran up to a train. They were freight wagons, an iron stove stood in each. I wanted to warm up, but the train swayed and I fell onto the red-hot metal. The teacher kept pouring cold water on my hand and cuddling me. The burn hurt terribly, but I didn't complain. It felt good to be in her arms. We reached Kiev. The teacher and her husband found a cellar in a bombed-out house. We had nothing to eat, but I felt good in that cellar and I wanted to stay there forever. In Kiev, everyone had to register. I told them my name, and what had really happened to my family. They took me away from the teacher, I didn't have the right to stay in the cellar.

No children lived in the Children's Home, only young war veterans. They fought over food, over places to sleep, over everything—like grown-ups. And they immediately recognized anyone who didn't know how to steal, to swear, to fight. "You want to be somebody better!" they said, narrowing their eyes. That was an insult. I ran away again to the teacher, I found my way back like a dog. The teacher cried, but she was afraid of the authorities and she took me back there again. She moved to a cellar closer by, but then they transferred me to Butchna to a home for girls, in other words for female veterans. They swore, stole and fought with one another just like the boys, but in the girls' home they had less opportunity for prostitution.

We got powdered milk, always scorched, sometimes stinking scrambled eggs, also powdered. The main meal was watery soup, our stomachs were so bloated from it that nobody knew which of the veterans was pregnant. We got points for learning, and for those points a mug of real milk on Sundays. Only I and Teresa, a Jewish girl from near Lwów, got points, because the veterans didn't learn. They fed themselves out of the warehouses and gardens belonging to the neighboring *kolkhoz*. I set out there once with Teresa. We mounted over a tall fence and climbed up an apple tree. When the guard caught us, I dropped the apples from under my blouse— Prove it!

"You too?" shouted the director, deeply disappointed. "Why?" "Because we were hungry." "That's no excuse, a lot of people are even more hungry. Do you know what would happen if everybody who was hungry started to steal? What would become of the world?" We didn't know, we thought about it seriously, what more could possibly happen? We lost all our points for milk.

When a lady doctor arrived who wanted to look after some child, the director pointed to me. We were arranged in a semi-circle, but the dark-haired, dark-eyed doctor came up to me right away. She wasn't young; her husband and son had perished in the war, and the rest of her family lay in a ravine which didn't exist any more because it was filled in with those who had been killed. She was more of an orphan than I was because I could still have a husband and son. And she was far more lonely, because Kiev was a hundred times bigger than Rożyszcze and a hundred times more Jews had been murdered there. We went to concerts of classical music and children's films. The music brought me peace and great solace, but I couldn't understand the fairy-tales for children. Once again, I ate off a white tablecloth with a knife and a fork, and the doctor read poems at the table. Sad poems by Russian women poets.

I would go to Kiev by train. When it grew cold, one of the teachers lent me her coat. It reached down to my ankles, but it was all the warmer for that. I went to the toilet in the unheated train, and turned the flaps up. It was probably then that the teacher's party identification card fell out of the coat. The NKVD came and locked me in a room for questioning. "What did you do with that party card?" "What party card?" "To whom did you sell it?" "I didn't sell anything." "Who did you lend it to?" "I've never laid eyes on it." "Confess and we'll forgive you." "What will you forgive me for?" They came every week. Each time, a different one came, but with the same questions. In the end, they ran out of personnel, so they stopped.

When the doctor wanted to adopt me, the director remembered that I had a father in America. "You can't do that to your own father," she said. "So why did you keep sending me to the doctor's?" I asked. "So that you would know that there is still civilization, even here." The doctor cried quietly into her handkerchief. I didn't cry any more.

On the envelope I wrote, "To the Dołgopoluks in the town Rożyszcze." And a reply came. They also sent a certificate saying they were my guardians. I came to Rożyszcze in July. Nobody waited for me at the station, nobody knew the day nor the hour of the train's arrival. A man in glasses came up to me and asked whether I was the lawyer's daughter . . . It was my father's pre-war partner, who had found himself at the station quite by accident. He had a brother in New York who used to write to my father in Omaha.

The bridge across the Styr wasn't there. One crossed on pontoons which lay somewhere else. Low, flat, they gave way under your feet. The square had broken benches and overgrown bushes which nobody pruned. Above them, shady trees. The unmown grass had gone to seed like rye. I walked in the grass for a long time, but I didn't find anything. As though nothing had happened, as though my brother had never existed. The Dołgopoluks had made inquiries about Enia, but all traces of her had vanished as well. I didn't go to our house. I didn't even think of going there.

Again, we had to run away from Rożyszcze. This time, west, to Gliwice. Everybody was taking cows with them, so Mr. Dołgopoluk also took a pair. When we arrived, he sold them right away, of course. Umek found us in Gliwice. I didn't recognize him in a Russian uniform. After he had left me at the farmstead, he found his way to the Russian partisans. He was happy to be a soldier. He planned to go to Palestine. All the young people were going. They said it was the only place for us. I would have gone, as well, if I hadn't had a father.

Father wasn't a lawyer in Omaha, but he had a lawyer's mind, and acquired a few inexpensive houses. By contrast with other landlords, he liked children and when a child was born to a tenant, he let him off a month's rent. When it was a Jewish child, he let off two-months' rent. The people in America didn't believe it when the terrible news started to reach them. Just as we in Rożyszcze hadn't believed it. They didn't want to believe it. "Try to forget," Father asked, "I'll reward you for those years, I'll do everything so you'll forget." He sent me to a specialist, who made the scar on my temple smaller. He didn't want to talk about it. When it was talked about, he left the room. He took sleeping pills, but I would always find him by my bed, when I woke up screaming. He married only when I married. To a widow whose family he had once helped leave Volhynia.

In his safe, we found a photograph which he had never showed anyone. Navy-blue blouses with white trimmings. Navy-blue bows in braids. Me and Enia with bouquets of flowers. My bouquet bigger, because I was a head taller and it was probably my birthday. At our sides, two cousins, little like Enia. They didn't have flowers, just little handbags. At the very front, the smallest cousin, a very cross-eyed boy in a jacket with a round collar buttoned at the neck, like a uniform. One of the little girls was also cross-eyed, but not as badly, and the other one not at all, but with the same expression of insecurity and embarrassment—you could tell they were siblings. "To our cousin, a token of our remembrance. Best wishes, Tsalel and Bashya," it said on the back of the photograph. And in the middle, a stamp: Phot. I. Gurfinkel—Rożyszcze. I didn't remember Tsalel and Bashya. I didn't know how those two little girls and their funnily cross-eyed little brother were related to us. I didn't know their names. Only their childish faces had emigrated from Volhynia. Otherwise, I wouldn't have known they existed.

My brother's voice kept waking me at night. My husband explained to me that it was me wanting to punish myself. For something which wasn't my fault. That I shouldn't, because my brother had perished through no fault of mine. That I couldn't have kept him at the Dobrowiczes, or asked them to do more for him. That I couldn't have gone with him, because then I would have perished along with him. That I have a right to live, even though he had been killed. That I had offended no one, by living. My husband was a good doctor, and sessions with him helped me a lot, but my brother didn't stop calling to me. He stopped only when our son, Michael, was born.

Nobody knew where to look for Enia. She was taken under an assumed name, and she didn't remember her real one. Once, a photograph of a young woman appeared in the paper. She had won a beauty competition in Israel, and had been brought to Hollywood. She didn't know where she came from, she remembered only a house by a bridge, and bringing bread through a hole under a wall. My cousin brought me that paper. "Look! Her story is like yours, and she looks like you." I sent a letter to Hedda Hopper of the *Los Angeles Times,* and that photograph with Enia when we were small. I received a reply from my sister, saying that there was no certainty that we were sisters, and even if we were, it didn't change much because I didn't need her when she was nobody—only now, when she was a film star. She came here once to Baltimore to promote her television series. I went to the studio, but they wouldn't let me in. I phoned. They said she was no longer there. Shortly afterwards, she stopped performing, she got married. She became a rich widow in California. That was how I lost my sister, Enia.

I saw Umek in Tel Aviv. He found me in a hotel by the sea. I didn't recognize him after all those years. He said he recognized me right away, but you just say that. I don't recognize myself any more—only the scar on my temple's the same. He came in a light holiday suit, without a tie. His shirt collar out over his jacket, the way the boys in Rożyszcze used to wear it. He showed photographs of his sons and grandchildren. One of his hands was paralyzed as a result of a wound from 1948. His wife looked like a nice woman, but Umek didn't smile once. His smile had not survived.

Michael became a psychologist in Baltimore County. He treated drivers who had had accidents under the influence of narcotics or alcohol. He wore side-locks, a beard and tassels at his waist. That happened when he was still in college. The followers of the Lubavicher Rebbe used to come to campus, to convert—the

Jews, of course. Everybody else wanted to convert the Jews, so why shouldn't the Jews do it? They demonstrated how to put on the tefilin. They asked, "Who wants to try?" He tried—that did it. I thought he'd get over it, but he didn't get over it. He converted his girlfriend and went to Jerusalem to study. She went, too. Her parents didn't want to give her the money, so some other Jew paid. Even their four-year-old son wore side-locks and tassels. They would come every Sunday with their little ones—two, four and six years old. Others were on their way. Against Hitler. The Lubavicher taught that monuments made of stone are brittle, that the strongest monuments are children. That Jews are needed against Hitler—out of blood and bones, not stone. Not stone, but living souls. "Against what Hitler?" people wondered. "There is no Hitler any more . . . " "It only seems that way," the Rebbe replied.

They would come only on Sundays, because on Saturdays they couldn't travel. And they wouldn't eat anything, because it wasn't kosher. "It's your food that divides us, not ours," said Michael quoting the Lubavicher. "Everybody can eat ours." Three times a day, he pressed his tefilin to his forehead and to the artery of his left arm. He said that this was the best therapy. In our family, nobody had done that for a long time. In our parts, there were no Hassids.

Perhaps the flood washed my brother's bones into the Styr and the Styr had buried them. Where? In Volhynia. Across the whole of Volhynia.

Elgena

FOR SONYA, BLUMA AND KALMAN

My grandfather fled to America, so as not to be sent to war. He was supposed to come back, but didn't. Mother was born after he'd left. There was nothing to eat in Vilna during the war, so Grandmother moved to Święciany. She had no education, but knew about herbs and healed people with them. Mama went to the Jewish secondary school in Święciany, and then to teachers' college in Vilna. She ran from one end of town to the other, tutoring to keep herself in school. Ran because the trolley cost too much. She met gifted young people who couldn't afford school. They said that in Soviet Russia there was equality, justice, internationalism and free education for everyone. She distributed illegal newspapers, was arrested twice for putting up First of May leaflets. She fell in love with Szymon who was hiding from the police. When he fled to the Soviet side, she followed him. All the way to Magnitogorsk. She worked feverishly in the library and received a diploma of recognition from comrade Krupskaya who came in person when she heard how well run the library in Magnitogorsk was.

And then came 1937—*strashnoye vremya!* People went to sleep not knowing what awaited them next day. We are surrounded by enemies, be on your guard, trust no one! In the papers, on the radio from first thing in the morning, at work, at mass meetings, gatherings—this one an enemy, that one an enemy. Every night someone you knew disappeared and every morning someone wasn't at work. How was this possible? We knew them. The secretary of *Raykom,* the secretary of *Gorkom,* the secretary of *Obkom!* New ones came in

their place and disappeared just as quickly. Children denounced
their parents, wives their husbands. All right, so we didn't know
who they were, but it doesn't affect us, because, after all, we know
who we are . . . One night Szymon asked: "What will you do if they
arrest me as well?" "You? That's impossible, for what?" They took
him that very night. Lusia was fourteen months old at the time.

Mama was left by herself with the child, in a strange town,
where nobody wanted to know her. They turned away, quickly
crossed to the other side of the street. It was worse than in the
camps because in the camps you had friends. She stood entire
nights outside the prison to hand in warm clothing and every free
day in line to see the investigator. After two weeks, she got in. "Why
are you holding him? He hasn't done anything." "How do you
know?" "How could I not know, he's my husband." "Good, we'll
check, write down where you live." That same night, they came. A
woman in a leather jacket said: "Your husband isn't needed here any
more, we're sending him out of Magnitogorsk, get dressed, he wants
you to go with him." Mama got dressed while that woman held
Mama's dresses up to see whether they'd fit her. When they were
leaving, she snatched the child away. Mama says, "I'll take her myself." "No, we'll take her." The child started to cry. They shoved her
into the "crow" as they called the black vans in which people were
taken away. Inside were ten other women. They drove them around
the whole night until the "crow" was full and the whole night, she
could hear her child's cry.

"Sign that he's an enemy of the people."

"How can I sign something like that, he's an honest communist."

If you don't, it's standing at the wall. The women stood by the
wall, while they hurled "Spies, traitors, bloodsuckers, whores!" at
them. The interrogators changed every hour, drank *chai* at the table,
and the women stood for a whole day and night. They didn't give
them anything to eat or drink, or let them sleep, or let them sit
down even for a moment. "You're going to stand, until you sign!"
First the walls started to move, then the ceiling, then the floor.

When she fell, they poured icy water on her, so she tried not to fall. They were young, graduates of the Saratov Academy, their diploma assignment was getting everyone to sign. After three days, they said, "You're going to your cell, think about it, you'll realize that you have no way out." The cell was packed—crying, moaning, lamentation: "I want to see my mother," "I want to be with my child!" That was the worst: what will happen to her child, and what will happen to her mother who had nobody but her? She wrote to her from Magnitogorsk every week so that she'd always have a letter on Saturday. What will she do if she doesn't get a letter this Friday or next? If I didn't have a mother, it would be easier for me, if I didn't have a child, it would be easier for me, that's how she thought. For fifteen years, she didn't know what was happening to her child. And her mother never received a letter from her again.

Men sat on the upper story and let down letters on strings: "Women, your stubbornness is not going to be of any use, nothing will help us anyway, do what they tell you, don't suffer." Every night they were taken into a different cell so that they wouldn't make friends. Again standing at the wall for another two nights. They led her along corridors in the night—everything happened at night there—a table at every turn, on every corner, in every nook. They didn't have enough rooms, so they had to use the corridors. She saw men at the walls—hardened, experienced men who had gone through prisons, hard labor, trenches, revolution, civil war. They stood with bulging eyes, like specters, ghosts. What could she do? She signed. There was no court, no trial, just a verdict, it was disgusting. Ten years in the *Sevlag* hard-labor camps—Paragraph 58, Section 10, suspicion of espionage. On behalf of Poland. Szymon had been shot on the spot she learned twelve years later.

She went through the prisons at Chelyabinsk, Novosibirsk, Irkutsk. Lice and bedbugs, they'd bite you to death if you slept. In Irkutsk, they kept them where they had once held the Decembrists. But the Decembrists had sat there in fives, while the communists in fifties. The Decembrists slept any way they wanted to, the communists in tight rows—someone gave the command and they turned

onto their other side. The Decembrists had toilets, the communists
a metal barrel. And dysentery. A mug of water for drinking, washing
your face and everything else. First you have a little to drink, then
you wash your face, then your hands and what ever else you can.
The selection point was in Vladivostok, under the open sky, in a
stadium divided with boards. Men on one side; women on the
other; they communicated through the cracks. She saw Bruno
Jasieński there, the well-known Parisian communist. He was sitting
by the fence, not moving, he didn't have the strength, a *dohodiaga*.
Dohodiagi—that's what they called them. She knew his books, *I Am
Burning Paris*, and *Man Changes Skin*. She organized a bread collection for him, the women broke pieces off their chunks, it didn't help.

In the taiga, at a place called Elgen, five-hundred kilometers
from Magadan, there was an enormous camp for women. There,
she met the German faction, the Austrian faction, the Hungarian
faction—the *Comintern*. Intelligent women, educated, from the
Party Institute to which Stalin had invited them. And the same
paragraph: espionage. She met Johanna Wilke; the wife of Béla
Kun; Yagoda's mother. They took everyone, only those like Dimitrov and Wilhelm Pieck were left. Later, she met hundreds of Polish, Ukrainian and Finnish women. Twenty trees to a pair—with
saws and axes. Ten cubic meters a day. "Day?" They went out at
night beneath a starry sky, and came back beneath the stars. "How
many hours?" Who knows, there were no clocks or watches. It was
even worse during the white nights. Ten cubic meters for six hundred grams of bread is a lot. And if you don't fill the quota, only
four hundred. Take down twenty trees, trim them, saw them. Men
collapsed. The women had more endurance and were more re-
sourceful. Out of one slice of bread, they made two, heated them,
steeped them in water, rebaked them—it was more filling. They
worked every day except when the frost reached fifty-seven below.
The overseer would spit—if the saliva froze in the air, it was fifty-
seven below. Already in September it was twenty below. They
couldn't last.

Mama was young and strong. And optimistic. She spoke Polish, Russian, German and Yiddish. She could recite Jasieński and Mickiewicz's "Oh, Lithuania, my homeland . . ."—everybody liked her. She learned how to lay bricks, plaster, tile roofs, floors, hang windows and doors—for the managers. She plastered once for a manager who had just arrived from Moscow. Humane, completely unprepared for what he saw, he promised that he would find Lusia. Even sawing wood for the settlers—fifteen meters to two women— was a blessing because it wasn't in the forest. Washing or cleaning was privileged work. She carted manure in the winter, fifty below. The manure was as hard as cement, she had to break it with a pickaxe, and the hunger was so terrible that she would have been willing to die if she could just eat her fill beforehand. Once, a Finnish woman from the *poselok* called her into her yurt, her husband was a cobbler. She gave her a bowl of borscht and a chunk of bread. She walked out happy because she wasn't hungry for the first time in a very long time. Suddenly, she hears a song which her mother used to sing to her. Here, in the Magadan taiga? Unbelievable! She stops the horse, listens—the song subsides, silence. She moves on— again that same song. A hallucination? No, it was she who was singing, without knowing it, and the echo carried because it was a forest.

My friend, White Sonya, said that we shouldn't blame our mothers for giving birth to us. Pregnancy had been their salvation. For what was in those four hundred grams of bread? Oats, saw-dust and sand. Pregnant women weren't driven out into the frost. She fed and cleaned horses, so she ate oats and carried them out in her boots. After the birth, the mothers got an additional paragraph for prostitution, and the fathers, if discovered, a bullet in the pituitary gland. On our birth-certificates, instead of a father, there was a dash. As prostitutes, the mothers were kept with the criminals where there was drunkenness, licentiousness, homosexuality. The criminals helped the guards to surround and force the women, sold them. Whoever resisted got the knife. The criminals wouldn't let them near the better work, so they got pregnant again. Fortunately, they miscarried more often than they gave birth.

My place of birth: the gold field Elgen, Srediakovsky *rayon*, Magadan *oblast*. Mama gave me the name Elgena. She thought that perhaps at some time I would find myself somewhere in the world, in Vilna or Paris, and someone would shout—Elgena! And somebody who knew the place would hear, and in this way we from Elgen would find each other and wouldn't be so terribly lonely. A week after the birth, they transported her to gold field Tumannoye, eight hundred kilometers from Elgen. They were transported far so that they wouldn't come back to their children. And an ordinary Russian name like everyone else's was hung around my neck. The mothers of my friends came from Germany, Austria, Finland, but we were all Laryssas, Ludmilas and Sonyas. Mama managed to visit me when I was three, but I don't remember it. Then they took me to Strelki, right on the Kolyma River. I remember a wooden barracks with a long dark corridor. We used to get a hundred grams of milk for which we walked two kilometers. We had hoods with holes for our eyes, grey-blue padded jackets and trousers, reindeer *untas* on our feet. We didn't know underwear existed. Our skin was covered with scabs and boils. The first thing I remember is hunger.

When the Kolyma melted, we caught fish. With nets of bast. The fish were big and called *keta*. We'd hide a fish during the day, and dragged it out at night. We ate it in our beds, in the dark, raw, it was easy to tear. But the Kolyma melted only for four months of the year. We gathered cloudberries and cedar nuts. The grown-ups taught us to smoke, because that stifles hunger. We smoked pinecones and cedar needles. Birch bark smoked well, too. In the winter, we took embers out of the stove—for the smoke. We were hungry all the time. Someone kept a small barrel of cloudberries in the dark corridor of the neighboring barracks. I sneaked in there in the evening and filled my pockets. The frozen berries weren't easy to take out. The people in there saw the scattered cloudberries and waited the next evening, a man and a woman. I don't remember how they beat me. I remember only how our custodian Necha Nau-

movna held me on her lap, fed me warm milk and asked what happened, and I couldn't find my voice. Ever since that time, I stuttered
badly, I couldn't say a single word normally.

Necha Naumovna was an excellent specialist, a graduate of the
Jewish Institute in Frankfurt, and knew the cure for everything. She
treated our scurvy with an extract of pine-needles. She treated the
children of the managers and the guards and that's why they kept
her with us instead of in the forest. For tuberculosis, we had Olga
Nikolayevna, a beautiful blonde with whom the manager was in
love. Her daughter, White Sonya, had tuberculosis of the bones. I
was Black Sonya and she White. I was friends with her and I
wanted Olga Nikolayevna to be my mother.

Well-fed women in sables used to come and choose children.
They sat in a semi-circle, and one by one the children walked onto
the podium—one turn left, one turn right. Women from the *poselok*
came too. Everybody wanted to go to the ones in sables, because
those from the *poselok* needed children for housework and for finding gold, and kept bread under lock and key. Children ran away
from them, preferred to starve with us. The ones in sables weren't
very suitable either, because you need to get up early with children,
and they weren't used to it. They sent children back, but at least
during the time with them you had enough to eat. Nobody chose
me because I had a mother. That's why I hit Necha Naumovna in
the face when she made me go up to a working woman in dirty
overalls. I kept breaking away and running off, and Mama ran after
me, pressing a bag of baked potatoes on me which had cost her a
thousand rubles. She had a shapely figure, beautiful eyes and lips,
she had suffered more than a little from guards and overseers.

Segałowicz also came from Vilna. People searched for their own—
from Poland, from Austria, from Lithuania. When he was arrested,
he turned grey and quickly lost his hair, but he looked handsome
bald. After ten years, he got a permit which allowed him to travel
wherever he wanted—except for the "Big Zone." Mama still had a

few years for prostitution, but Segałowicz promised to get her out. He was very hardy. He walked forty kilometers to see her, the whole night without stopping because he would have frozen to death in the taiga had he stopped. The whole night in one direction, and the whole night in the other, to see her for an hour—one hour a month. He could draw animals and landscapes, and he had a knack for cutting and sewing.

Segałowicz felt sorry for me, and very much regretted that we couldn't speak to each other. One night, a rabbi came to him in a dream and said that soon a large piece of material would arrive, which should be laid out in the place where they had beaten me, and that I should be rolled across that material, this way and that. And, indeed, the workshop shortly received ten meters of flowered percale. Segałowicz and Necha Naumovna laid it down in the corridor of that barracks, he holding one end, and she the other, and I rolled this way and that on it, and I fell about laughing—never before had I laughed like that. And I stopped stuttering.

Everybody who lived in the *poselok* had to give the State a *slitok* of gold a week. It didn't matter where you worked, where you took it from, you could look for it wherever and however you liked, as long as you brought it. So everybody needed gold for that ransom. And for bribes. That's why you paid with gold everywhere, at the tailor's too, and Segałowicz had golden hands. He sewed for the managers and the guards, for their wives and lovers—and collected gold. He gave half a kilo for Mama, a hundred grams for himself, a *slitok* for me and another for the reindeer sled which carried us across the golden snow. Sunrise and sunset glowed pure gold not from the sun but from earth soaked with gold. Segałowicz paid somebody the necessary, and a cold postal airplane lifted us out of Magadan above a diamond sea of ice. Salmonlike *keta, gorbusha, kizhucha, chavcha* hid beneath the ice. We flew like birds for many hours, and we froze on our flight across the stern, forbidding land which had given me birth. It wasn't her fault. She didn't want to. She needed nobody. Not me, not anyone. She had done nothing wrong to anyone, she was simply defending herself. In Vladivostok, we got into a train, which hissed and slithered like a snake.

The manager found Lusia in Kasri, not far from Chelyabinsk. She didn't walk, she just crawled. Nobody treated her, nobody looked after her. She was the daughter of "enemies of the people"—let her crawl. Children whose parents had died loyally in the war received treatment. In the North, there had been no such distinctions. Lusia didn't want to live with us, enemies of the people. It seemed to me that the manager had made a mistake, that this wasn't my sister, while she tried to convince me that this wasn't our mother and that we should run away from her and Segałowicz.

In Święciany nobody wanted to give Mama and Segałowicz work, there was no housing for us either. An acquaintance from Vilna days took Mama as a maid, and housed us in the maid's room—three meters by two. We slept on two bunks, Mama and Segałowicz on the bottom, and me on the top. Lusia was usually in the hospital where they operated on her again and again. Our landlord's daughter was dumb and I had to do her homework. When I couldn't do it, the landlady hit me with her fists. She hit for anything, and I couldn't tell Mama or Segałowicz because we would have found ourselves on the street. Segałowicz went into the countryside to sew and mend clothes for bread and pork fat.

When our landlord started to put the make on my mother too insistently, Segałowicz found a spot in an attic. One half of it was caved in, but the other was all right. Segałowicz put couches together out of boards and linen, a trunk served us as a table. On New Year's Eve, Mama fried potato pancakes and covered the trunk with a cloth. All of a sudden, the attic shook, the doors smashed open with a great noise and two men in leather coats broke in. As enemies of the people, we didn't have the right to live even in an attic. Outside thirty degrees below. Houses on both sides of the street, lights in every window. We knocked at the door of a small house in which my mother had lived before the war. They let only me and Lusia in, and only onto the veranda. They threw us their dog's blanket, his name was Pupsik. Pupsik didn't need it, because on cold nights he slept inside. We wrapped ourselves in the blanket and huddled together so as not to freeze, while Mama and Segałowicz walked the streets the entire night.

The following day, Mama went to the hospital where Dr. Z. was the head of a ward, a Pole who before the war had found her attractive. Dr. Z. took her on as an orderly. In the evening, Lusia and I would go to her in the utility room and amid the bed-pans eat a plate of hospital soup apiece. Doctor Z. recommended Mama to blind Mrs. Żelubowa and Mama begged her to take us in exchange for care and cleaning. There wasn't much room there, but we didn't need much. Lusia slept on a bed which folded up during the day, and I on the table.

From my father who had been an Armenian I got dark eyes, a swarthy skin and a large Armenian nose. In school, Lithuanians, Russians and Poles reviled me as a Jew. They hated each other, but this united them. They didn't let me in to any events or parties, wouldn't even let me join the nature club. I practiced boxing and karate and fought with all of them, but I couldn't beat all of them. Without telling Mama, I went to change my *natsonalnost* to Armenian. They looked at my papers, but instead of "father"—a dash.

First they sought out the cosmopolitans who were mainly to be found among the artists and writers—usually with Jewish surnames. And even if they had Russian ones, Jewish names were added in brackets. They were agents of enemy ideology, and if not agents, then carriers. If not of enemy ideology, then of an ideology which was alien to our nation and culture. If it was difficult to accuse them publicly, they were removed on the sly without any explanation. Jewish poets were murdered this way and scarcely anyone noticed. When the trial of Jewish communists began in Prague, there was no longer any doubt, and the last pretexts vanished when they indicted doctors. Doctor-poisoners, murderers in white smocks, in the most noble of professions. Article after article, commentary after commentary, meeting after meeting: "exposure," "unmasking." A doctor from Vilna was among the accused. Directors, professors, engineers were also removed. Managers of cafeterias—potential poisoners. People cracked, especially if they had a slight faith in communism—leaders of industry, people from newspapers. Some, young mainly, took their own lives. That wasn't written about. A young engineer hanged himself in the stadium so that everybody would know. In January, we heard that freight trains were standing ready, people bought suitcases and ropes. Mama and Segałowicz were sure that they would come for us first. We didn't turn the light on, our things were packed, and we listened.

I was very scared. Not of Siberia, but of beatings. Because they beat you right away. Mama took me to Leningrad where her two cousins lived. The husband of one of them, a highly prized engineer who built the *Dneproges,* said that I shouldn't even visit them. They weren't just afraid, they didn't believe Mama had been imprisoned for so many years for nothing. The husband of the other one was a violinist, they lived in one room, but they found a corner for me with a neighbor in the same communal apartment. The neighbor, an old woman, supported herself by cleaning for the other tenants and standing in line for them. She lost her entire family during the blockade and was no longer afraid of anything. I helped her clean, but I was afraid to go to the store, because people in the lines cursed the Jews—that they murdered our innocent leaders, betrayed our confidence, our innocent trustfulness. No longer cosmopolitans and carriers, but openly—poisoners and damned Jews. Our innocent people were beside themselves with rage. "Can't something be done about them?" they asked rhetorically. Because something could. Their clenched fists and hard faces pointed to that, it was frightening to look at them. They read the papers eagerly and listened to reports. Our fate was sealed, only a miracle could save us.

Mama and Segałowicz didn't write, and I wasn't allowed to write to them. I didn't know whether they had been taken or not. I woke up screaming in the night, because I had dreamed about beatings. A miracle happened at the beginning of March. The devil took Haman—literally—on a beautiful March night when there was no longer a single good doctor by his side. Later, the radio and the newspapers announced that there had been no conspiracy, that Doctor Timoshuk and her colleague Rumiantsev had made it all up, that it had been a hoax and nothing more. The Jews were enormously pleased that they weren't poisoners and that, as it turned out, they hadn't put a single saint to death. All the doctors and the Jewish people were rehabilitated, the joy was boundless and the Jews called this miracle Purim.

Mrs. Żelubowa died and we had to move out. Other people were given the right to the apartment, not us. Before the elections, some wrote at the entrance to the *Gorsoviet* that the Segałowiczes were enemies of the people and didn't have the right to vote. Some people let us have a lean-to. We brought in electricity, we repaired the floors and the walls. When the lean-to had turned into a dwelling, the owners ordered us to move out. We lived with a sick workman who needed care. I caught tuberculosis from him. Doctor Z. arranged shots of streptomycin for me, but asthma set in. Mama treated me with herbs. I asked her whether it had been worth returning from the North. Here, there are enemies everywhere, informers, cowards. There, we had friends, and here all our friends had been murdered. Who murdered them? Stalin, of course. His hands went numb, he had murdered so much. And his legs—so many addresses, so many *vyorst*. But he had endurance, the runt, and strength, even though he was a cripple. Twenty million, they say. Easy to say, but would anyone try to destroy so many people oneself? And if someone had at least helped, put a hand to it. Never mind a hand—a finger. An index finger for example . . .

Mama didn't like to speak about my coming into the world. What I know, I know from her friend, Mira, to whom I went for winter vacations. She lived near Moscow, in a dacha she inherited from her husband, an outstanding chemist who didn't return from the Gulag. She took the dacha away from the chemist who had sent him to the Gulag. In her time, Mira had worked with Lenin whom she respected, but she preferred Trotsky. For that preference she got twenty years, a good part of which she spent with Mama. My father worked in the mine. He had been intelligent and nice. He wrote to his family that he had fallen in love with Mama, and his family wrote back that if he married a Jew, he would have nothing to come back for in Armenia. He didn't go back. Mira said that he died in an accident at the mine, but he might easily also have given himself up to be shot.

Segałowicz didn't want to apply for rehabilitation. *They* should apply for rehabilitation, not him. Let them come to him. Mama wrote to the Ural Military Tribunal. She got a posthumous rehabilitation for Szymon and twenty-five hundred rubles, but she didn't take that money. She had Polish citizenship and wanted to go to Poland, but Lusia started to shout, enemies of the people, she wasn't going to leave her country! That's what they taught her there near Chelabinsk. In the North, at least, no one had taught us anything. Mama couldn't leave her behind sick, so she went for rehabilitation to *Gorispolk*. She had the right to return to where she had been taken from, and she had the right to an apartment there, but she wouldn't have gone back to Magnitogorsk for anything in the world. In Święciany at that time they had built several four-story houses with running water, toilets and, for heating, tiled stoves. She was given thirty square meters with a balcony. Doctor Z. advised her to sign up for a Red Cross course in Svencionelai, twelve kilometers from Święciany. She went there for eight months, on foot, to get a badge of a medical nurse, so that no one would mistreat her again. One nice Lithuanian took Segałowicz into a tailoring shop, but he got migraines from the noise of the machines, so he sewed at

home. Women liked his cut and style and brought him private
work. He sewed at night, because inspectors came around during
the day, and, if they saw private work, cut it up.

First, I took the exams in Leningrad. I got three fives and a four, but
there weren't enough places. The following year, I tried in Kovno,
but there, too, no place for me. In the meantime, I was working as
an orderly at the hospital, and the third time I took the exam with
the workers. I had the best grades in that category, and the longest
hospital training, so they couldn't turn me down. I married a friend
from my year. His father had perished in the war, his mother drank
herself to death, he had been raised in an orphanage like me. I said
to him, let's go North, they pay well there, we'll live like human be-
ings. He agreed, but when we got our diplomas, said he wouldn't
move out of his Lithuania. He had the right, but why did he delude
me? My older son was born when I was in my fifth year. I begged
the dean to give me a practicum in Święciany, so he sent me to
Kretinga—you couldn't go further away than that. Mama took the
little one in, otherwise I would have had to interrupt my studies.

After training, we went to Kuršenai because doctors were given
housing there. We got two rooms in a little summer cottage, with
an iron stove, but no coal was provided, only peat. The stove warmed
us as long as we stoked it, but when we slept, the water in the buckets froze. In the morning, we were scared to put a foot out of bed.
We wanted to add electric heat, but the fire-station wouldn't allow it
because the whole house was wooden. My little younger son got
pneumonia, my mother took him in as well.

My duties included going out into the villages. I went to the
sanitary station where I was supposed to examine four hundred
women of the *kolkhoz*. I stayed a day, another, nobody came. I
asked the registrar, why? She blushed and, in confidence, admitted
that my manager had been there before me, and had warned that a
Jew doctor was coming whom it was better not to see because Jews
infect you with cancer. I went back to Kuršenai to protest but the

manager said, "If you don't like it, go to Israel, why are you staying here eating Lithuanian bread?"

The patients in Kuršenai said the same, "I'm not going to a Jew." I came to the hospital and the chief tells me to go to the operating room, "A difficult case, help is needed." I go in and the manager says, "Your Jewish hands aren't needed here!" I walked out, the patient died on the table. The mortality rate was high. A child died in our ward. I'm sitting at home in the evening, my husband is on duty, someone knocks. I open the door—a woman. "Give me my child back," she says. "What child?" "The one you took for matzo." A hard, dull face. There are symptoms like that, an incurable madness.

In Kuršenai, only Lithuanian was spoken. "What do you need a Jew for, you need a Lithuanian girl," his colleagues kept telling my husband over a drink. Before that, he hadn't realized what a stupid thing he'd done, he understood only in Kuršenai. He stopped visiting my mother. Called his own son "little Yid." Braided a whip out of goat skin and hung it on the wall. Came home drunk, woke the boy, "Show me your notebooks!" An exam. The sleepy child didn't understand what was being said to him, so he'd grab the whip. I couldn't allow that, so I got it instead, walked around with cuts and bruises. It wouldn't have come to that in the North, there was no *natsonalnost* there.

I wanted to leave. A Jew from Święciany who found me attractive was leaving the country, but my husband warned that he wouldn't give me permission for the children. I decided to at least move to Vilna. I thought to myself, it's a cultural city and nearer my family, only hundred kilometers from Święciany. I looked for someone to exchange apartments with, but nobody wanted to change Vilna for Kuršenai. In the end, an officer appeared who was leaving for the Military Academy in Moscow and needed money to pay child support. But his apartment had only thirty square meters, and the regulations for exchanges demanded at least ten meters per person. We wrote that it was for three, but we had to show personal documents. An acquaintance who had spent most of his life in prison undertook to remove one child. He managed it with my ID because it was written in ink, but my husband's, it turned out, was in ball point—a new technology, not yet worked out. The acquaintance offered a page out of his wife's ID, because they didn't have children. We wrote my older son in, and glued it into my husband's—of course, the page numbers didn't tally. We stood in front of the commission, my husband white, drops of sweat running down his face. Had they looked at him, they would have moved us to quite a different place.

I thought that everything would be different in Vilna, but little changed. I was delivering a child with a midwife. The midwife's hand slipped causing a large tear. The head doctor's deputy asked for a review of the delivery, the midwife reported. "If the mother had been Jewish, something like this wouldn't have happened," replied the deputy. The midwife, an honest woman, was embarrassed. "It was me who was delivering," she said, "I turned clumsily, it's not the doctor's fault." At home, a fight with a drunken husband. The following day before an operation, I roll my sleeves up and my whole arm is bruised. When I was sewing up, I had trouble with the knot. "A pity the bruises are only on one arm," said the deputy. "You could use them on both." I threw down the instruments and walked out. Tanya, the anesthesiologist, ran after me, "Come back or you'll lose your job." I went back, my hands were shaking, tears flowing, and this over the operating table. Once, a patient had twins and after a difficult birth, one died. Why? Because I'm a Jew—the accused in a trial which never ends.

Near Vilna, in Ponar, a forest arose out of Jewish children. And near Święciany, beds of flowers on the firing range where the Jews had served as targets. My grandmother lies there in a fragrance of herbs which she once picked. And the mother of the acquaintance who had left, and both his twin sisters who were about ten years old. A small obelisk was erected, and no one reviled them as Jews any more. Quite the contrary: IN THIS PLACE ARE BURIED 3726 INHABITANTS OF ŚWIĘCIANY DISTRICT MURDERED BY HITLERIAN OCCUPIERS—the sign announced. Jews had been shot, but the residents of

Święciany District had erected an obelisk to themselves. Both in Ponar and Święciany, Lithuanians had done the shooting—the husbands, fathers, uncles of those who accused me. That is not insanity, it's logic. They had to accuse me in order to clear their consciences.

"Good," I said, "I'll leave, give me the certificate of termination." The head doctor was a Karaim and his politics were on both sides of the fence. The Karaims are also Jewish, but they don't admit it. I'm not surprised. He transferred me to the outpatients clinic. It wasn't a prestigious position but I had my own office and I worked by myself. I took shifts in the hospital so as not to lose my qualifications. One could work in gynecology or in childbirth. I always worked in childbirth and mostly at night. Forty-eight hours were required, but I always took more. Our unit consisted of three outpatient clinics and a birthing ward, five hundred people in all. Three Jewish women worked in gynecology. Sometimes, a patient forgot the name of her doctor, but remembered that the doctor was Jewish. The senior nurse would open my door wide—"Is this the Jewess who saw you?" When they gave out bonuses, I never got one. Others were promoted, not me. And everyone could insult me. I could have gone back to the hospital when the deputy head doctor retired but I didn't want to.

My husband found himself a Lithuanian woman and moved out. Shortly afterwards, a friend of his showed up, also divorced. He had nothing but an old car, he had left his wife everything else, seemed a decent man. I sold my coat and bought him two pairs of shoes. He was building a dacha. "You make the money for now," he said, "and, when the dacha is ready, we'll start to live." For two years everything was fine, but already I noticed something. For example, he'd be repairing the car and something wouldn't be working out, so he'd say to me, "Take the money out of your stocking, we'll buy a new car." As though because I'm a Jew I had to have money in my stockings. It wasn't clear to me what he was building that dacha with. I went once, looked: entire walls of panelling which was terribly expensive, and a black tiled kitchen costing more than my whole apartment. Once during night duty I had the feeling that I should go home. It was summer, my sons were on vacation at Grandma's. I open the door quietly, look in, he is sleeping—with my friend Gala. Her father was manager in a building company, that's where the panelling and the tiles were from. "Get out!"—I shouted. He took off with everything including both pairs of shoes. And my sons were growing up, those shoes would have come in handy. I once saw his employment record, he'd changed jobs eighteen times. I think he was a stooge and tried to get to Jews through me. But I didn't have Jewish friends. Those I'd had left. And my mother's friends lay in the ground—from Lithuania to Kolyma.

Mama received a pension, but she kept on working. She had kept her beautiful teeth and smile for which Segałowicz walked forty kilometers, and her grey hair looked like a crown. She had high blood pressure but it was under control. She paid for my apartment, bought me clothes. Segałowicz drew snowy landscapes, reindeer, horses and birds, never people. The snow in his pictures was always drenched in gold, high carat, like blood. On the balcony he fed pigeons which he knew by name. He had a heart attack and stomach ulcers, stopped sewing and worked as a shipping clerk in a dairy. Both of them helped me. My older son didn't want to study, he went into the army. He wanted to go to Afghanistan but they wouldn't take him. The younger one took exams for medical school in Moscow. He didn't understand certain questions in Russian, asked for explanations. They said if he didn't understand Russian, he shouldn't be taking the exam. He became an orderly in a clinic, so that he could try in Kovno, as I did.

Lusia underwent fourteen operations, spent four years in hospitals but her legs were like those of an eight-year-old child, limped badly and had to support herself on her hands when in a hurry. She became a school pediatrician, married a workman from a poor family who loved her. She gave birth to a daughter but because of her faulty build, had a difficult delivery, with forceps, and her daughter was born with learning disabilities.

White Sonya didn't grow up, the tuberculosis of the bones caused a hunched back. She became a doctor in a laboratory where she didn't have to see people.

A woman of my age, on her own, has nowhere to run. But I had to.

A Hungarian Sketch

FOR JUDITH

My learned grandfather, called *moreynu ha-rav*, was born in Kraków, but studied in Koszyce and stayed there. He died when my father and uncles were in their teens. My grandmother had a fabric shop, but the business didn't go, so she opened a dairy. My oldest uncle, Herman, deserted from the Czechoslovakian army, where he got it for being a Hungarian and for being a Jew, found asylum in Kraków and married there. Father, who studied in Galanta, in a very good Yeshiva, bought himself a bicycle one day and also vanished. He presented himself very well with that bicycle against the backdrop of the Eiffel Tower—in knickerbockers and a pullover, tanned, with black hair and light eyes. After he had taken this photograph, which had pride of place in our family album, Father joined the Foreign Legion. Nobody there asked who one was, nor from whom or what one was running, but when father undressed, a significant part of the answer was revealed. They tried to dissuade him, but Father didn't back off easily, and the Yeshiva had taught him not to hide from anti-Semites. He came back from Morocco with a bad case of asthma and lay in a Jewish hospital in Bratislava where the nurse was our mother.

My brother Hajim and I came into the world in that hospital and went to kindergarten in Bratislava. The bell at the door was too high, so Hajim lifted me and I pressed. Our youngest uncle, Willi, picked us up. He carried me on his back and I held on to his bangs as though he were a horse. He had light, straight hair, like everyone on mother's side. Father and his brothers had black, curly hair.

Mother and her married sisters wore orthodox *sheytels* on their heads, and little gold earrings with pearls, small sapphires or rubies in their ears. These earrings didn't come off. One got them right after birth, forever, together with a name. Five small rubies twinkled in my earrings. I also had a porcelain doll with blue eyes which closed and opened. Uncle Willi gave her to me.

Father called me his princess, bought me the most expensive sweets and promised to show me Paris. One day, when I came back from kindergarten, Father was listening to the radio from which came shouting, and he took not the slightest notice of me. Mother, also listening, paid no attention to me either. Uncle Willi moved up to the radio and froze as though enchanted. I started to look for my doll, but I couldn't find her. I looked under the beds, in cupboards and in dark corners of which I was afraid. I saw her on a tall chest of drawers. I pulled up a chair, pulled her down by her legs and was terrified. Her head was smashed, she didn't have a face. "What happened to my doll?" I cried, running to my father. Then to my mother. Then to Uncle Willi. Nobody took any notice. Nobody was listening to me. Only to the radio, on which someone was shouting and threatening. I often heard shouts and threats on the radio after that, and our later misfortunes came from there also.

I don't quite remember my grandfather from Szeli—called Saliby then. He traded in cows and horses, and was rarely home. Sometimes, he was attacked on the road, and came home with knife wounds. When they healed, he went again. I was at his funeral. I cried, everybody cried. We came to live in Szeli afterwards with Grandmother and Uncle Willi who had started an apprenticeship with a carpenter in Galanta. The house was big, there was room enough for everyone. The stable and barn housed horses and cows belonging to Uncle Kalman who had taken over grandfather's business after his death.

Our chestnut mare, Kicsi, went around in white socks like a Hasid, had a nice expression on her face and a cheerful disposition. She was patient, didn't kick, and, unlike people, was never angry. She just did not appreciate rides on her back. Why, when there's a cart? She didn't protest when I sat on her back, but wouldn't let herself be steered even into a trot. With the cart, however, she would trot right to Galanta. She also had culinary requirements. Fodder didn't suffice her, she came up to the entrance way and put her muzzle into pots and bowls. Uncle Willi used to say that we didn't need to wash the dishes because that was done by Kicsi. She liked our kosher food, a true Jewish horse.

The boys had religion and Hebrew lessons, and we had embroidery and crochet. But we were also taught prayers and Hebrew letters, and my grandmother told me the Torah which she knew by heart. Reading, writing, arithmetic and biology were taught in Slovak, but when I went to second grade, our teachers vanished and new ones appeared. *Csak Magyarul, csak Magyarul!*—they shouted. Our new teacher was called Roth Peroska. Roth was the last name, Peroska her first one. One and the other meant "red." We called her Roth Piroska Červena—meaning red in Slovak. She came from Mako, where Hungarian was spoken as it should be, not as it was by simple Jews and villagers in Saliby—which was now called Szeli. She was proud of her Mako and her *Magyarul,* which impressed me greatly, because, at home, we had always spoken *csak Magyarul,* even in Bratislava. In school, I recited patriotic Hungarian poems, and wrote long essays.

Hajim and I rode our bicycles to the country for hens and geese which we took to the *shohet.* In the evening, Gypsy women plucked them at our house, and Mother and Grandmother gutted and cut them. The following day, Hajim and I took them on our bicycles to Galanta. Whole or in halves or in quarters, with giblets or without. On order, we also took kilogram-sized goose livers. Grandmother always knew which goose had such a liver. Hajim turned all the money over to Mother, didn't spend anything on himself, but if I asked some for a cake or ice-cream, he gave it to me without a word. Sometimes, we went the roundabout way to avoid the police. Sometimes, a tire went flat and we had to go a long way on foot.

In Galanta, we first went to Dori's. Her mother was our mother's first cousin. They had a saloon and a cellar with wine which they bought in barrels and sold in bottles. People from the whole area stocked up there. We left our baskets there, so as not to ride around town with all our goods. We always had for them the best goose or chicken for the *Shabbat*. Dori, a year younger than me, had huge dark eyes, all the bigger for being set in a slight, delicate face; a Jewish, parchment complexion, lightly sprinkled with dots of juvenile freckles which added to her innocent grace, and thick black hair shone on her head like a diadem. There was no doubt that in Galanta, the princess was Dori.

In Szeli, I became friends with a girl my own age, Bluma. Her mother was my mother's sister, and her grandfather on her father's side was my grandmother's brother. We went to school together and spent our vacations together in the fields. They owned a lot of land. We hauled water to the harvesters, danced after the wheat had been gathered, participated in the births of colts and calves, which we chased when they grew up, picked yellow-red emperor pears or *Kaiserbirnen*—often in other people's gardens. And unripe apricots which gave us stomach-ache. These were always Bluma's idea. Her father had married my aunt when he was a widower. His son from his first marriage, Tibi, was five years older than us, and attracted all the girls. Bluma was slight, thin, had average looks, and braids of an indeterminate color, but didn't lack imagination. She tried to attract a non-Jewish boy from the other end of Szeli and dragged him out for walks, taking me along as bait. I, on the other hand, liked her half-brother, Tibi.

Hajim got a violin from father and taught himself to play from a Gypsy. I wanted to also, but they told me it was just for boys. Hajim wasn't interested in the violin. He played because he was told to. He was interested only in the midrash. He was the best student and rode to special lessons to *Dunajska Streda—Dunaszerdahely*—where the Yeshiva was now. He took after grandfather from Koszyce. He often came home from school with bruises and a bloody face. He went the roundabout way, but they waited for him after school. He was quiet, didn't complain, spoke little. Erwinek, who was younger than us, didn't want to learn anything, didn't do his lessons, ran away from school. I sat with him over his notebooks every evening. Hanele, four years younger—black curls, cornflower blue eyes—had a face like a porcelain doll. "You're a princess? Wait until *she* grows up . . ." people who saw us together said. The youngest, Miriamka, never took her finger out of her mouth. We dipped her fingers in paprika but she never dropped the habit.

The *Bürgerschule* in Galanta cost a lot, but Father persuaded Mother that the school was indispensable for a princess. Mother sewed me a navy-blue skirt and a navy-blue blouse with white dots, as well as a red skirt and a red blouse with white dots for a change. The German language took up half of the lesson time, and everyone understood that one had to learn German. When I had difficulty with physics, Mother handed me a huge goose liver in a cloth on a china plate. The liver shook in the bus and I had to take care that it wouldn't jump off the plate, but I brought it safely to the teacher's house where the maid took it from me at the door. No one bothered me, no one took any notice of me, no one was interested in me. I didn't belong in that school. After classes, I went to Dori's, in bad weather I stayed there for the night.

In spring, came Zoltán Kodály who at some time, as a child, had been reared in Galanta. The concert took place on the school's big lawn surrounded by white orchards and Kodály's head swayed like a white pear tree. The music spurted like nectar from his magic hands, oozed like wine, poured out like the Danube. At a lively pace, and rapturously, slowly and abruptly, the imperial orchards and royal fields played, and above them, danced the soul of this earth, eternally young, eternally giving birth to the variety and multitude of plants, animals and people who didn't lack for bread. He played the promises of my childhood which was ending right then, and my youth which never began. I didn't take much away from this school, but that concert stayed with me.

When the Germans entered Vienna, my father wanted us to escape to Paris. He arranged everything that was necessary, but my mother didn't want to go. "So who was right?" she said when the Germans entered Paris. Then father wanted to move us to Budapest, but Mother didn't want to go without Grandmother, and Grandmother didn't want to go without her remaining children and grandchildren. The people who ran away from the Slovakian side to Budapest and Debrecen hid in locked rooms. Mother didn't want to live like that.

Men from eighteen to forty years of age were taken into military work battalions. The younger ones, like Uncle Kalman and Uncle Willi, were sent to the front. Not as soldiers, but as slaves. They dug ditches, cleared snow, crossed mine fields. They didn't receive winter clothes, just yellow arm-bands. Those who were converts got white ones. They weren't given uniforms or arms, but had to wear army hats. So that the Soviet shooters wouldn't have any doubt at whom to shoot. They were kept under guard. Colonel Muray-Metzger in his speech to the guards said: "You won't go on leave until those damned Jews are dead!" Those who didn't fall from shots or mines, died from cold and exhaustion. And those who weren't tortured to death by Hungarians and Germans, were finished off by Russians. For some Russians this was a double pleasure—finish off an enemy and a Jew at the same time.

One Saturday afternoon, Tibi took me for a walk into the forest and started kissing me passionately. I broke away and ran off, but he told everyone that he had kissed me, and maybe not just kissed. I was quite developed for my age, and it was possible to say something like that about me. I burned with shame and wanted to take revenge. But I was definitely too young for revenge. Shortly afterwards, Tibi turned eighteen and he, too, was taken to the front, so that he wouldn't come back. Then, I regretted it, because had I not broken away from him, the shame would have been the same anyway.

The battalions that didn't go to the front were sent somewhere else for labor. They left only the doctor and our father who wasn't suitable anywhere because of asthma. Every week, Father went to Galanta by bus, and from there by train to Budapest. Sometimes he was late for Shabbat. *Mehaleh shabbos, Mehaleh shabbos,* shouted the outraged children of our neighbors when he arrived after the start of Shabbat, breaking the law. Mother and Grandmother deplored that, and I was ashamed in front of the neighbors' children. But Father assured us that *Hashem* would forgive him.

By night, Donac—a tall, thin Slovak—visited Father. He led Jews across the border. Father arranged and prepared everything, and after they had crossed, he placed them in Budapest. The police would call him in. He would return ill, but when he felt better, would go to Budapest again. When they forbade him to leave Szeli, he went to the post office and carried on conversations by telephone. They took him in twice a week. He came back with increasingly worse asthma attacks. Mother sent us out of the house, so that we wouldn't hear. She asked him to stop, but Father wouldn't give in. Finally, they caught Donac. He was walked through Szeli in handcuffs and with a bare head. He was led by people in civilian clothes. "They've got too many policemen, so there aren't enough uniforms for everyone," Father said.

Father was called in for a hearing at which the postal clerk testified. This time, they didn't let him go. Mother went to Budapest, and told me to go the visiting hour. I didn't recognize Father through the bars. He was unshaven, exhausted, passive, not the same. We didn't speak, just looked at each other with tears in our eyes. I didn't have to say anything. Seeing me alone, he knew that Mother was in Budapest, that she would move heaven and earth. They released him after a week, but the decision was made that he would go into hiding.

One Shabbat eve, our windows in which candles were lit, were broken with sticks. Mother and Grandmother sewed us gold stars on all our clothes. All the girls had to go to weed beets in the fields by the sugar refinery. I went there with Bluma. No one guarded us, nor goaded us on, but we had to weed all the fields which stretched into infinity, so we worked without straightening our backs. We tried to weed as fast and as well as we could. We thought that if we did our best, they would leave us in peace.

People stood along both sides of the road, and looked at our wagons loaded with bags, featherbeds, pots. We were escorted by the *nilas* who had crosses on their armbands—two crossed arrows. They had to carry out old, bearded Shmuel Polak because he couldn't move by himself. They sat him high on the wagon in the middle of the column, over which he towered like Moses with his huge, grey beard. All the way from Szeli to Galanta people stood by the road, thirsty for a spectacle. Every fifth house in Szeli was Jewish, so they had something to stare at. Only the doctor didn't go. He was found dead in his own house, together with his wife. They had no children.

In Galanta we were housed in old barracks and warehouses, several families to a spot. Father casually went out in the evening. Deliberately didn't say goodbye to anyone. Only on the following evening did Mother tell us that Father was safe in Budapest. The knowledge that I had a father in Budapest where he was safe went with me everywhere after that.

After several days, they took us from Galanta to Nove Zámki—which was called Ersekuyvár then—and put us in a brickyard which didn't have walls, just a roof. Railroad tracks ran in under the roof. No one worked in the brickyard. We sat and waited. The April nights were chilly, but Grandmother and Mother knew how to wrap us up. There was no shortage of furnaces and stoves, so the mothers were always cooking something. For now and for the road. Mother cooked up many jars of milk condensing it with sugar. We had no appetite. We didn't know what awaited us. For a long time, people had been saying that the Germans were transporting the Jews far away and drowning them in rivers. We were afraid to talk about it.

"Our life lasts only a single day, we live only today, who knows what awaits us, what we will wake to tomorrow," sang the older girls. It was a song off the radio sung by Katalin Karady, an actress with a dark, sultry voice. The girls who sang it had boyfriends, had some kind of today. I had nothing, and that song annoyed me. I felt wronged. I couldn't understand why nobody was doing anything.

Why no one was asking about the tomorrow which was being taken from us.

The freight cars which were pulled into the brickyard had windows barred with barbed wire. The *nilas* let us take only buckets, bedpans, and hand baggage. With us in a corner of the dark car, rode Rochi, Mother's youngest sister and her three little children— one, two, and three years old. Bluma climbed with her mother into a different car and I never saw her again. Probably Aunt Lina and her children rode in that car, too. I don't remember the names of the wives of my uncles Lebi, Moyse, Jozsi and Miks. Nor the names of their children. Forty-three children went including us and the children of Lina, Neli and Rochi. Uncle Willi wasn't married, and Uncle Kalman had no children yet.

We were very thirsty, many women fainted. We were only given water in Koszyce. I looked out of the barbed-wire window. I had never been in my father's town before. But all I saw were German uniforms and hats which I had also never seen before. Grandmother wasn't in Koszyce then. Koszyce had been deported before us. I helped Aunt Rochi put the little ones to sleep and sit them on the bucket. We didn't know where we were being taken and we were scared—the crying didn't cease day or night. The train stopped once, and we saw with horror that it was spanning a tall bridge. Tense, we listened whether the Germans were opening the cars to throw us into the water. We breathed great sighs of relief when the train moved again and crossed the bridge.

When it stopped again, the doors opened immediately and we were ordered to get out quickly. Men in striped clothes pressed us on. "You won't be needing any of your things!" Grandmother didn't have time even to take her shoes and trod painfully across the paving stones, so Mother gave her hers and went barefoot herself. Hajim held his *tallis* and *tefilin* tight under his arm. We walked in fives. At a certain place on the right-hand side stood several Germans who from time to time pointed their fingers at somebody and ordered them to go to the other side. I don't know whether they pointed at me, I only know that Mother said, "Go!" I didn't want to, but Mother pushed me in that direction. I had two dresses and a coat on, I looked more grown-up than I was. I shouted to Mother that I would find her in the evening and maybe bring something to eat. I could still see their backs at the corner. Grandmother was stepping with difficulty in Mother's shoes, which were too tight for her, and Mother was tripping over the stones in her bare feet. And that's how I remember them. I couldn't see Hajim, Erwinek, Hanele and Miriamka, they disappeared behind other backs.

After that I remember shouting, crying and the swishing of whips. We undressed in a great hurry. Men in stripes took the hair off our heads and public areas with a few strokes of shaving clippers, in a few seconds literally. Men in uniforms ripped from our ears earrings which didn't open. I don't know whether I screamed or whether—as in dream—I couldn't make a sound. And I don't remember whether I felt pain. They left short hair on some girls, among them Dori. Changed beyond recognition, we walked out in the disinfected clothing of other girls and women. In things which didn't fit, we walked in fives across the railroad tracks above which drifted a strong stench of burning.

They put one hundred and fifty of us into a barracks called the children's barracks. Five to a bunk. And they kept counting us. From four o'clock in the morning when terrifyingly bright searchlights were switched on, we stood for hours in the cold and they counted and counted us—as though we were made of gold. When the numbers didn't tally, they threw us onto our knees and Grace appeared. That's what everybody called her. In a tight fitting uniform and high boots, slender as a model, her hair coiffed like a Greek goddess and with her cap rakishly over her forehead, she walked with a swaying gait as though in a fashion show and flogged randomly with her whip.

We received hot black water, a tiny black brick of bread and soup which none of us could swallow on the first few days. We did nothing, we sat and starved. The youngest ones started to rebel. "We want our mothers!" they cried. "You want your mothers?" the Kapo said angrily. "There are your mothers!" she pointed to a thick, low chimney above which we saw fire at night, and black smoke during the day. "That's where you want to be?!" We fell quiet and a deathly silence descended. None of us talked that night, and the following day not one of us mentioned it. We had realized we were by ourselves. In a completely different world. As though it were we who had died.

The devil's name was Mengele. He came in with an impatient gait and ordered all those who had blue eyes to step forward. We approached with our hands stretched out and he moved his finger over the tops of our palms, as though he were checking the quality of the skin. If the skin appealed to him, he pointed towards the exit. We went in fives. I don't remember where, nor what happened next. In the evening, I found myself in the Women's Lager—B2—but I don't know what happened until the evening. Afterwards, I went back to Lager C, but the children's block was no longer there. I don't know what happened to those who didn't have blue eyes and the right kind of skin, nor what happened to the other blue-eyed girls. I met only Adi from Szeli, and Marta from Vag Sellye, and later, in Block 16, we found Dori and we stayed together.

He came twice a week with a squad of Kapos who held each other by the hand dividing the barracks. Stripped bare, we approached in turn with arms raised high and he looked at our ribs. We had to do this at a pace, *eins-zwei-drei,* so that he wouldn't waste his valuable time. The ones who looked healthiest went out. The thinnest he grabbed under the chin with his thumb and forefinger—and with those two fingers threw them into a corner behind the cordon of Kapos. He did this impatiently, as though there were too many of us, as though he were wasting his valuable time because of us. Those who went out got disinfected clothing. Those in the corner were taken out naked on a truck. The rest returned behind the Kapos' backs to waste away before the next selection. We pinched our cheeks to gain color, and hurried forward, because he only selected a limited number.

We didn't have access to the kitchen, but we stole clothing. After the disinfection we would put two blouses or two skirts on and take them to the Kapo. If she didn't have bread, she'd say, "Come some other time." We'd come some other time and say, "You remember the blouse I gave you last week?" And we'd get a piece of bread. I got away with it a couple of times when I hadn't given her a blouse at all.

I saw a German once who had a *Kaiserbirne* in his hand. The golden-red Emperor pear. I thought it was an illusion. An Emperor pear here? Brought even here? It too?! The Emperor wouldn't have allowed it. We wouldn't have let it get to all this. He knew how to guard the earth and its orchards, not let devils, bandits and thugs in. *"Kaiserbirne!"* I called out. The middle-aged German in Wehrmacht uniform looked at me, then at the pear, then again at me—and held it out in my direction.

Everyday we recited *Shema* before sleeping and before the morning *Appel*. I added a personal *pasuk* for myself and for my mother. When the Days of Judgment approached, we sat behind the barracks and prayed beneath the open sky, so that God would see us better. We prayed for all those who weren't there and recited blessings. For bread which wasn't there. And for life which wasn't there. We prayed: Supreme Judge, deliver justice! Deliver it, if that is still possible! And even if it's not possible! Show that you are almighty! We ask only for justice!

Dori became even more beautiful, her face even smaller and subtler, her eyes even bigger, her neck even slenderer, even more swanlike, even narrower and her hands suppler. Mengele lifted her into the air with two fingers. She weighed nothing. "Dori, Princess! My last sister, come back! Don't leave me here alone," I prayed when they took her. And Dori came to me that very same evening, pale and translucent as a ghost. Perhaps because of her beauty, perhaps because of her marked head, or perhaps because she was a princess, some German pulled her off the truck, covered her with his own coat and led her to a barracks where she waited until evening. It happened to nobody else, only Dori, the chosen of God. We recited a prayer of thanks, I assured her the best place on the bunk, covered her carefully at night. I believed that even after the next selection she would come back. She didn't come back, but she was the most chosen. Nobody else went that way twice.

After that, I thought only about my father. That he's alive in Budapest and they can't do anything to him. That was my revenge and my strength. And my obligation, because he will be waiting and will need me. Me, apart from whom, he has no one left. I had to survive, return, tell him everything. So when Mengele grabbed me with his forked fingers and pushed me into the black corner, I didn't even stop but went back behind the hedge of Kapos. He could not have anticipated anything like that. It wouldn't even have crossed his mind. And I didn't get dressed like the others to remain until the next selection. I turned back and, with my arms raised to heaven, moved toward him again. He couldn't have recognized me. Naked, we all looked alike, didn't have faces. It couldn't have occurred to him. I walked past him when he was examining someone else, and went the only way out I had. I made my own selection, I selected myself. He turned his head and looked at me, but the next one was approaching from the front at the pace he'd established, *eins-zwei-drei*. He couldn't waste his valuable time.

We rode in a train for people, and it wasn't even too crowded. Maybe because not many of us were left. We stopped in Katowice and I saw people. They were going around in normal clothes. They were buying lemonade. Reading newspapers. I was most surprised when I saw a mother and child. I had thought there were no more mothers and children.

We dug wide, deep ditches on the outskirts of Wrocław. We slept in stables, covered ourselves with hay. The pick-axe was too heavy for me, and when I pulled it out of the earth, it threw me back like a gun after being fired. The guard who saw it told me to take a spade and to scrape away the earth which had already been dug out. He loudly and eagerly praised my handling of the spade. It didn't help much, I fell down under the weight of the spade. "Help me, can't you see I'm dying," I said to the Kapo. She directed me to work in the kitchen. We cooked potatoes, cabbage and turnips, sometimes, horse meat—that's how important our ditches were.

I thought that I had escaped from the devil, but he found me and I saw him again face to face. He had thin, crooked lips and a crooked nose. A bony, squared-off forehead beneath which horns hid, and in place of eyebrows, thick, Neanderthal brow bones. Beneath them eyes looked out, which he didn't have, which I didn't see, because I couldn't look. He had a black uniform, black boots and black gloves which he never took off.

He ordered me to guard the darkness and silence. I was the youngest, the least experienced. He knew that I lacked ruthlessness and strength. That was his diabolical idea. Evening came, but not all the lights had gone out, and human speech, which he couldn't stand, hadn't quite died down. He hit me with the back of his hand and when I got up, with the palm of it. He hit me with his open hand, but knocked me off my feet each time. This repeated every evening. An alcove was adjacent to the kitchen, from which every evening came the screams of the beaten. Twenty-five lashes. I knew I wasn't going to avoid it. When he ordered me to go in, I saw only a lamp, a riding-whip and a wood block. I don't remember anything else. Afterwards, I found myself in the infirmary, where a dentist was pulling the roots of two of my teeth out. Only then I started to scream.

The oldest woman among us looked after me. She held me close to her at night, covered me with hay, took care of me like a mother. On the night of Christmas Eve, all the lights in the stable were turned off, and, in the total silence, we listened to carols resounding from the blacked-out guard tower. *Stille Nacht, heilige Nacht,* sang our murderers in polyphony, with nobility and piety, because every one of them felt *heilig.* Their superior showed up, and the devil conducted the choir.

In January, we left Wrocław. We walked a thousand to a column. We slept in the forest if we managed to reach a forest, and if we were lucky, in stables or sheds. The *bauers* sometimes gave us cabbage or cabbage soup. They didn't have much themselves. The wind caught up with us in the fields, took our breath away, bent us over, knocked us off our feet. And we had to get up quickly, because the devil was coming after us, and shots broke out time after time. I had a reserve of strength from the kitchen, so tried to walk at the front dragging my new mother behind me. I propped her up against the wind, picked her up when she fell, but her legs kept folding beneath her and, in the end, I couldn't pick her up. "Don't waste your energy," she said. "Go!" I didn't turn around when the shot rang, though it pierced my heart. I thought about my father who was waiting for me in Budapest. I had no luck with mothers.

Of the thousand, only two hundred and eighty of us reached Bergen-Belsen. We pulled corpses out of barracks, dragged them into a pile, that was all our work. For that we had walked six weeks across fields where most of us remained. When we had dragged enough corpses, we received soup. We had more than enough work. We got both soup and typhus for it. I fainted from thirst, and awoke with parched lips. I lay by the water tank from which one shouldn't drink because it was poisoned with typhus. Everyone knew that, didn't drink, and died from thirst. The Kapo brought me a boiled, black liquid, and I drank only that. Had it not been for her, I would not have got up again.

One night a storm broke out with thunder and lightning. With the thunder and lightning of shells. In the morning, the SS men stood in two rows. Men in one, women in the other. Most of the women were fat. All of them had white bands on their sleeves—like Jewish converts in the Hungarian army. I didn't see the devil anywhere. Maybe he had changed beyond all recognition. It was they who were ordered to carry the corpses now. Not drag them, but carry them into great pits dug by English machines. They lowered them evenly and delicately into five pits, ten thousand in each. And we stood and watched over them. If any of them dragged or threw a corpse carelessly, we rained curses and stones on them. The SS women grew thinner day by day, hour by hour. The SS men began to look like our "mussulmen."

A shy, nineteen-year-old English soldier brought me a chocolate and a beautiful, shiny toothbrush. One day, he offered me a ciga-rette and said that he had written to his parents and that I could go with him to England and become his wife. I replied that I had to go back to my father who was waiting for me. I liked the taste of that cigarette, and I have smoked ever since.

A military truck carried me as far as Pilsen. There, I boarded a train full of people from the camps. At the stations, Czechs distributed free goulash and dumplings. In Bratislava, I went to a kosher soup kitchen. A list hung on the wall there and everybody signed their name. On that list, I saw Uncle Kalman and Uncle Jozsi. Uncle Jozsi had returned from Mauthausen. From Russia, only Uncle Kalman. From Auschwitz—only I.

I lived with Uncle Kalman in Grandmother's house in Szeli, which was called Saliby again. We did not recover any of our things, nor any memento. The neighbors said the Russians had taken everything. In one house, I saw our tablecloth with the geometric Jewish patterns. They said it wasn't ours. Uncle Kalman went to the country and bought back our Kicsi. At double price. He said it was for me.

Uncle Kalman married again and had a child. I waited for Fa-ther. I went to Bratislava many times and checked the list on the wall. Uncle Kalman didn't tell me anything, he didn't have the courage. His wife became pregnant again. Everybody was getting married, grabbing whomever they found. At an engagement party in Galanta, a cousin who had returned from Theresienstadt, said that my time had come. I replied that I was waiting for my father. It was then that she told me what everybody else had known for a long time.

The Germans lacked trains to take Jews out of Budapest, but the *nilas* still had the Danube. They ran around like mad dogs, and whomever they pounced on, they dragged to the Danube. A woman who sheltered our friends every day ran over to watch. They stood them by the water and shot. Straight into the river. How many thousands, only the blue Danube knows, which lapped up Jewish blood and didn't even turn red. The embassies were giving Jews *Schutzpasse*. Sweden, Switzerland and the Vatican took entire buildings under their care. Father had Aryan papers and eyes as blue as the Danube. He went around town delivering papers to whomever was possible. A *nilas* from Dunajska Streda recognized him. Father's younger brother, Sani, hid from the *nilas* in an attic and, two weeks later, was shot there—by the Russians.

The world had ended, and I was supposed to go on living. I didn't know how. Only Kicsi hadn't changed. She nudged her friendly, loyal head into the entrance way and helped to wash dishes as before, such a very long time ago. She was a member of my family.

I Am from Auschwitz

TO ESTERA

My grandfather on my father's side was a land-steward in Radoszewice, a few kilometers from Osjaków. A lot of land, a huge orchard, a manor house with outbuildings, the landowner came only in summer. Grandfather had a grey beard, and a heavy ring for keys, and was always nicely dressed, because he was the steward. I went with my basket across the meadows to see him, like Little Red Riding Hood. I brought Jewish food to him because he was on his own. Mother was from Działoszyn, near the German border. Her father owned a bakery, and during the previous war, he did good business with the German army. They would give him flour, and he would give them bread. Father served in the Russian army. A photograph hung on the wall: dark uniform, hand at the belt, moustache. He was very patient, never raised his voice, took everything calmly. He would come home tired, sit at the table and look at us. Mother would shout, "Why don't you say something, why don't you take your belt off?" Never. His brother, Mordche-Josef, lived in Częstochowa on Aleja Wolności, I went there on vacations. How was it possible for a Jew to live on Aleja Wolności? He had a huge cellar of butter and cheeses. He took them from dairymen from the whole area and distributed them to shops on his bike. How I liked those cheeses! And there were so many of them, all different tastes. I didn't eat bread, just cheese, cheese and cheese, because whatever got broken went on the table. There aren't cheeses like that any more, flavors like that. She had been a member of the Communist party, but Uncle Mordche-Josef was very handsome and she fell in love. I remember her songs: "*Ring your manacles, your prison chains, let our voice from prison fly to our lovers, mothers, make music with your chains.*" They had two children, beautiful, like out of the movies. They'd leave them with me, and get on their bikes with that butter and those cheeses. When I brought the children into the courtyard, everyone envied me, they were so beautiful. Aunt Golda also lived in Częstochowa. She had five children and they were cramped. Father had two brothers and three sisters, and Mother two sisters and a brother. All of them had children.

We lived in Osjaków, district of Wieluń. The river Warta flowed there, right behind the church. The church rose up tall and could be seen from everywhere, the synagogue was low and hid itself behind shops. The rabbi, a very good, very poor man, had five lovely little children. On Friday, we'd collect money so that they'd have something for Sabbath. We only went to elementary school. The secondary school was in Wieluń and nobody could afford it. Our Wowek went to Łódź where two of Father's sisters lived. He learned to cut clothes there, and took drawing classes in the evening. His friend Fajwł was an excellent student, and the principal, Mr. Nowak, very much wanted him to go to school in Wieluń, but Fajwł's father said he had to help support the family. They sewed men's clothes and took them to markets.

We had seven *morgs* of land and a shop. Flour, kasha, sweets, baked goods. Father worked on the land with hired hands, and Mother and I in the shop. They placed a stool behind the counter for me, because I was too short. We had a large stove in which mother baked challahs. The neighbors bought challas from our stove and not from the bakery because ours were better. In addition to that, mother sewed. As soon as I came back from school, I had to throw my books down and stand on that stool behind the counter, and Mother sat down to sew. She sewed for weddings, for communions, for burials, for everything. A piece of cloth, a piece of chalk, she could do everything. I peeled potatoes, cleaned, washed the dishes, because Mother always had customers, always. Dinner was never on time, because something always got in the way, we buzzed around like bees. Girls would call at the window, "Come on, we're going to play ball, we're going to play hopscotch, we're going to make flower wreaths." And Mother would say, "You can't today, you can see I have a customer, you'll go tomorrow." That tomorrow never came. I cried and worked, cried and worked. Sarenka, two years younger than me, a very clever little girl, would take off, and could never be found. She'd appear for a minute and disappear again, like a ghost. She didn't want to do anything in the house. Mother's sister in Działoszyn died, so we adopted little Gizelka. I nursed her and fed her and she'd follow me everywhere with her eyes. She had plump little hands, rosy cheeks and a little mouth, like a doll. When she started school, the teachers would take her home to play with. They taught her poems, which she recited at the end of the school year. Kozłowska, Czajkowska, Gnauch, they were all single, weren't marrying. Klara Gnauch, of German descent, went to her family in Łódź for the holidays. Knopf was also of German descent and also came from Łódź to teach us.

We were close to the border. At five in the morning, bombs fell on Wieluń. Everyone ran out of the houses. "Ah, those are our soldiers. It's maneuvers." An hour later people from Wieluń and Działoszyn came running in their nightshirts. Poles entrenched themselves in Działoszyn, in the Jewish cemetery, and shot down two *Messerschmidts*. Great joy, Poland had repelled the Germans. An hour later, German squadrons flew over and bombed the whole of Działoszyn! Uncle Szmuel-Zalman's two sons, fifteen and sixteen years old, perished as did Aunt Genendl's daughter with her little child, and Aunt Ester's husband. Those were the manuevers!

As soon as they arrived, the Germans told the Jews to open their shops, and told the Poles: "Take what you want!" People from the whole area came and cleaned out everything down to the wrapping paper. The owner had to leave and not show his face. The president of the *Judenrat* was Posalski, a horse-dealer, who travelled to faraway places to trade in stolen horses. He could neither read nor

write, but he found people for himself who could and had everything he wanted. Wowek came back from Łódź, so Mother packed
his backpack and told him to go to Russia. He went, froze outside
many days and nights because the border was closed, came back
sick. He was tall but slender and delicate. They sent him to the
Poznań area for forced labor, Posalski put his name down on the list.
Wowek got sick and couldn't work, so they beat him. Józek Dawidowicz from Działoszyn was there and saw how they beat him to
death. Dawidowicz was heavy-set, the type that survives. They took
Father for roadwork, ten kilometers out of Osjaków, to break
stones. They wanted to have good roads. And swimming pools. The
Jews dug them. They made a big pool in Wieluń out of headstones
from the Jewish cemetery. When we found out that Father had
come down sick, I went to Posalski and asked him to take me and
let Father return. He said I was too young, but I cried and begged
until he agreed.

There were fourteen of us girls from Osjaków. We levelled the
ground and dug trenches. Then, they sent us near Toruń to dig
dikes because in spring it flooded there. We stood in water, and in
spring the water was cold. The German who guarded us had no fingers, a bandit. They let them out of prison to guard Jews. Jewish
boys from Piotrków Kujawski, Dąbrowica, Radziejów worked there,
and Poles from the vicinity. There were two big pots, one for Poles
and one for Jews. The Poles had bicycles, rode home on Sunday and
brought bread and pork fat back for themselves. In the winter, we
thinned the forests, because the Germans didn't like dense forests.
The Polish *vorarbeiter* told us that they had cleansed Poland of Jews.
That they had transported them out of the ghettos. Where there
was no ghetto, they locked them in churches. In Wieluń, there was
a huge church so they kept the Jews from the whole district there,
without food and water, before transporting them all to Chełmno.

Us, they took first to Hohensalz, that's what Inowrocław was
called, and kept us behind wires in a huge square. They brought
everyone from the camps in the Poznań region there, and Fajwł

found us there. I told him I was cold so he covered me with his jacket. After that, I didn't see him, because they took the men separately.

We only had stripes and wooden clogs, no underwear or stockings. A piece of string to tie around oneself was a treasure, because it was warmer. When they got soaked, we took our stripes off and lay down on them to dry them. A thousand of us lay in the barracks, on bare boards, three tiers, ten on each bunk. The corpses lay in a separate place and rats chewed them. But the rats preferred bread. We hid our bread on our chests so that nobody would steal it during the night, but the rats stole it anyway. If you felt anything on you when you were sleeping, it meant it was a rat. We had to throw them off with force, because they weren't afraid of us. The bread was divided by Czech women who knew German well. They didn't wear stripes, they had real shoes and canes and had the right to hit. *Polské svině* they called us. *Polské svině, ted' zemřete!* They were Jews, but when Jews are by themselves, then this one is Polish, this one Czech, and that other one Hungarian, like at no other time. They wrote down the number, if someone couldn't get up off the bunk. One was a Christian. *Ježiši Kriste!* she shouted. *Ježiši Kriste, ted' zemřete!* One shouldn't say what Jews did to other Jews. Our barrack was near the wires. All night, we could hear the rumbling of trucks, the crashing of platforms, shouts, children crying. During the day, we saw the *Sonderkommando* pushing wheelbarrows of ashes. Dead birds hung on the wires, and every day they switched off the electricity to take someone down. Intelligent, educated women from big cities went to the wire. Not us, we were from the provinces.

Every Friday there was a selection. They turned us out at five in the morning to stand for hours and die of cold until the SS got up, had breakfast and decided who was still able to go to work, and who wasn't. And every day, wherever we were standing, they made a selection, on their own, for the fun of it. And if we didn't get up off the bunk, if we fainted at the *Appel,* if we fell at work, if we didn't manage to cross those kilometers there and back—a selection every hour.

We met men's *kommandos* at work. The SS men couldn't stand in one place, they had to walk. After they had gone by, a Pole put a piece of bread in my hand. Perhaps because I was the youngest, the smallest. He wore a cross on a string around his neck and said that he was from Kraków. Tall, around twenty years old, I can still see him today. We met very many Soviet prisoners-of-war, the Germans picked them up like chickens. I told one of them that my father had served in the Russian army. The next day, he showed me a little pile of stones, "*Dyevushka, dyevushka, vot tam!*" I found a piece of bread there. They were building a *Truppenlazarett* for German soldiers, large brick barracks, a few fruit trees grew near by. Nothing was left on them any more, just one pear remained at the top. When the SS men had moved on, a small, slant-eyed Russian climbed right to the top and threw that pear down at my feet. They saw him from the distance and ran up before he could get down. They didn't shoot him—it would have been better had they shot him—they beat him to death with the butts of their rifles. We in Auschwitz had few tears, but as I ate that pear in the latrine, I washed it down with tears. A *piccolo,* Leo, came up to us once, a fifteen-year-old. He asked if anyone was from Warsaw. They cleaned boots pressed clothes and tidied rooms for the SS and the Kapos. They wore arm-bands with "Piccolo," were washed and cleanly dressed. The Kapos slept with them. He looked at me and asked, "Do you have anyone left?" He didn't have anyone either. He pointed to a nearby bush. "Something will always be there for you." I would find a bowl of soup and run with it to the latrine. It was thick, warm, wonderful, I'll never forget that soup. One day I found a drawing: an open gate, two hearts in the gate, and above it, "Freedom for you and for me." I hid the paper under my stripes, because, of course, they would have beat me to death for that. I always carried it on me, slept with it. When they took us to the showers, I hid it among my rags. Suddenly they started beating, there was confusion, and I didn't find my stripes.

Once, after our SS women had walked away, two girls from Salonica ran into the latrine. Two girls from a neighboring *kommando* ran up asking "Who's from Kraków? Who's from Częstochowa?" Suddenly, the SS women reappeared, so everyone grabbed their spades because when the SS were watching you had to work. Those two came back from the latrine and didn't have anything to dig with. "Why don't you have spades?" They didn't know how to explain it in German. When those German women started to hit them, the canes turned red with blood. And those girls from Greece were fragile. So I said, "*Frau Aufseherin,* it's not their fault . . ." She looked at me and said, "*Kom mit!*" The SS had their booths there, to rest in, warm themselves up, flirt. Why not? The SS women were attractive, and the SS men also looked good in their shiny boots, and their uniforms cut by the best Jewish tailors. She led me into one such booth. I remember a stove, a kettle, a camp-bed. I came back on all fours, covered with blood. None of the girls came up to me, because you were not allowed to help, they just said, "Get up because the dogs will eat you." Everyday, we brought back tarpaulins with torn up human flesh which the SS at the gates counted, because the numbers had to tally. In the barracks, Genia from Sompolno—we called her Angel—handed me a sooty pot of hot water. She very much wanted me to live.

Every few weeks, they took us to the baths, but not always for showers. Sometimes, they told us to go where Mengele was sitting in a white coat and white gloves. We walked up to him naked, one turn to the left, one turn to the right, like models. Show your tongue, they searched. If they found anything, they wrote down your number and it was over to the other side. The SS men watched from a distance, to entertain themselves. Sometimes, they'd call you over, put a gloved hand on your neck and turn you left and right and laugh. Three times, I passed. The fourth time, they noticed that my skin had been bitten by lice—to the other side.

We didn't have to put our clothes back on. We sat naked, on tall steps, like in a theater—so that we could be seen. We sat the whole night. We didn't say anything. We wondered only whether they would give us enough gas, because if not, then it lasted for a long time and sometimes the *Sonderkommando* put people who were not quite dead into the fire. In the morning, the block elders came in and ordered us to get dressed quickly. We were frightened that they were going to take us somewhere and burn us or bury us alive. They never told us, what or where, just herded us. And we returned to the barracks, because that night enormous transports had arrived and they ran out of room in the gas chambers.

They stopped us by the gate once, *Stehen bleiben!* SS men and SS women with dogs, but instead of leading us to the showers, they lead us to a courtyard with high walls. Two of them selected—one tall, one short. They pointed their fingers: this or that side. They didn't say anything because that would have tired them. Most of the women, twice as big as me, healthy looking, went *that* side. The SS women and the block elders held each other by the hand and didn't allow anyone through. I knew I didn't have a chance, and kept moving back to the rear. Did I want to live an hour longer? There were sisters, cousins, friends from the same little towns who didn't want to get separated. If it's the gas, it's the gas, but together. But they didn't ask whether this was your sister or not, they pointed a finger and that was that, the finger decided. The girls rebelled and broke through the cordon. Chaos ensued, the tall one started shooting. The girls standing in front of me moved back and I suddenly found myself in front of the short one, and I no longer had anyone to hide behind. He probably saw that. I saw the finger, this side. *Ježisi Kristi, ta mala se vratila!*—the Christian girl was amazed to see me back. Only Rywcia and I were left from Osjaków.

Rywcia worked in the sorting room. She would go there just in her stripes, and come back in underwear, bringing some for me as well. Then she'd say to me, give those panties to somebody in exchange for bread, I'll bring you others. Once, she brought me a sweater. To have a sweater under your stripes was worth as much as life! Rywcia discovered that Mrs. Nowak, our teacher, the wife of our principal, was sitting in the *wiza*. She told me to take her some underwear and a pair of stockings. The *wiza* was a bit of trodden earth behind the barracks, in German "*Wiese,*" means meadow. The new arrivals, for whom there wasn't any room yet, sat and waited there until we died. I searched among the shaved heads: "Mrs. Nowak, Mrs. Nowak!" She crossed herself when she saw me. "Oh, little girl, I am dying," and she kept making those crosses. Her husband had been taken too, because they had been teaching children in secret. I came to see her twice, and then I couldn't find her any more. She was too old to survive.

The last summer they gave us kielbasa, two slices each—such things you remember. In August, a heat wave, and everyone got sick. Fever enough to make your head burst. The barracks was long, without a lavatory, blood ran down our legs when we ran to the latrine, and there was no place to put our feet. They made us go to the *revier* for pills. They let ten in at a time, and hundreds waited in the heat, so I turned around, I'd rather die in the barracks. They would throw us chunks of clayey bread. I pulled it towards me, but I couldn't eat. In Auschwitz, to refuse bread meant that you had reached the end. Berta from Zawiercie—she's in Israel now—brought me two heads of garlic for that bread. I couldn't eat them, either, so she crushed them and pushed them down my throat with her finger. Most of the sick died. They wanted to show that we were sick, that they were treating us, and that we were dying normally. At the same time Dr. Mengele wrote up his experiments and places freed up which they needed for newcomers.

In the fall, they started to transport people, nobody knew where, because with the Germans everything was a secret. I went crying to Rywcia that they were to transport my *kommando* somewhere. Rywcia gave a pair of warm panties to Tina, an acrobat from Holland who had an in with the block elder. I stayed on Rywcia's bunk and they took me into the SS *Wäscherei*. The manager was a German civilian out of whom they had made a Jew. They discovered that his grandmother or grandfather . . . He himself didn't know anything about it, but they made him manager, because he was, after all, a German. He wore a suit and tie and a white shirt, the girls were attracted to him. I revived a little because I was working inside now, cleanly dressed. My hair had grown a bit, and I painted my cheeks. If you spat on a piece of chicory wrapper, you could make yourself up a little—to look healthier. You gave up your bread for a piece of paper like that. That manager had a room next to the sorting area. He called me in there, patted my cheek, "*Du bist so schön.*" I started to cry, the tears streamed down my cheeks all by themselves, like never before. He turned around and told me to leave, but he moved me into the sorting area because the floors in the laundry were cold. You sometimes found gold in the clothes when sorting. Rywcia handed them to the SS man, discretely, together with the piece of clothing. She only had to glance at the SS man and he knew. She was clever, she knew how to walk through a hurricane.

One night, the Allies flew over and dropped a few bombs, so the SS chose the clean women's *kommandos*—from the laundry, the sorting area, and the ammunition factory—and quartered us among their own blocks. So that the underground would send word and they wouldn't bombard. It was beautiful there: individual bunks with ladders, walls painted with gardens and mountain views. They had artists from the whole of Europe, after all. It isn't true that the Allies couldn't bomb. When they wanted to, they could. It isn't true they were too far away. The Russians stood so close that they could smell the smoke, without the underground and without reconnaissance, they stood there for half a year. Why didn't the Russians bombard? Liberators! No one even asks them.

They took us out by night in a terrible frost. First, the men. Their stiffened hands and feet stuck out in the snow, we tripped over them. Every moment, someone fell and didn't get up anymore. They herded us with dogs. And there were so many of them, both dogs and SS men, more than ever before, all wanted to flee. Beatings, screams, barking. They drove us first in one direction, then in another, they themselves didn't know where. When we had no strength left, and wanted them to kill us, they led us to some station and packed us into open freight cars. We rode like that day and night without water, without bread, without lavatories. When we got out in Ravensbrück, half of us were dead, and the other half envied them because they were no longer suffering.

Ravensbrück was so crowded that there was nowhere to lie down and we sat hunched up like hens in an unfinished barracks, on the mud, without straw. I didn't have Rywcia anymore, I didn't know where she was, not a single familiar face. First, we carried wood, then stones. What happened in Ravensbrück? Men passed by on the road, in threes like us, but not in stripes, I don't know who they were. I was walking at the side, at the end of the *kommando*, and one of them pushed a jam sandwich into my hand. That you remember. How often did you get bread from someone? That was an event.

Again, they put us into open freight cars, but it wasn't as cold now. The camp was near the airport, day and night the airplanes roared. We dug pits, one next to the other, pits, pits, pits until in the end there was nowhere to dig. The Czech women brought yarn and said that anyone who knitted would get more soup, so we sat in the barracks and knitted. Later, that work came to an end as well and there was absolutely nothing to eat, because the Czech women stole all the bread for themselves. No one did anything to us, there was neither gas nor a crematorium, we just sat there and died. Peacefully, because we were very weak, death did it quickly. It moved through the barracks like the wind. In the morning, huge Belgian horses pulled wagons up for the corpses. The Czech women said that even if freedom came, it wouldn't help us any, because the camp was mined and we would fly out into the air. The barracks was locked from the outside and even they didn't have the key. It was very quiet, no one had the strength to talk, we sat and we waited until they blew us up into the air.

One morning, we heard a racket outside the door. We were certain they were coming for us to kill us in some other way. Instead, in come women in stripes saying that the Americans had arrived and we could come out. We didn't have the strength to get up and go out. The Czech women went out because they had stuffed themselves. I dragged myself out on my knees and saw military cars. Americans, handsome, tall, were giving the Czechs cigarettes, chocolate, whatever they had. They even took watches off their wrists to give them. Then they got into the cars and drove away. They said that the Russians were near, that the Russians were to take us. I saw that prisoners were coming out of the warehouse on the other side of the square, each one with a package at her breast. I dragged myself there on all fours, on my knees, in what ever way I could. The packages were in huge boxes with a red cross on them, and there were enough of them, more than enough for us. Loaves of bread lay by the wall in rows, hard as bricks and a thick dust rising from them. I took a package and crawled back on my knees. All the prisoners dragged themselves there and back across the square, most of them on their knees like pilgrims in Częstochowa.

We came back to the barracks, each one to her own place, and again it was quiet, everyone was eating. I opened everything at once, chocolate, sardines, meat, powdered milk. I picked at a little of everything, then I opened my mouth wide and poured in a handful of dried milk. My jaws suddenly stiffened and I couldn't move them, because they hurt terribly. I could neither eat nor say anything, I couldn't even moan because I was glued together with that dried milk. I sat with my mouth open and nobody took any notice of me, they thought I had died, and I would have thought I was dead, too, were it not for the pain. In the night, I heard moans all over the barracks, death—this time painful. My mouth had come unstuck by now and I could move my jaws a little, but I didn't eat much because it still hurt. In the morning, the Russians arrived—unshaved, dirty, drunk—getting to Berlin from Russia was no joke. They saw the distended bellies—*dyevushki, dyevushki, davay*. Dead women here, half-alive ones there, they don't look, they tread on them with muddy boots—*davay*. I was as small as a child, thin as a finger, so they went on. Hanka from Białystok and her sister, Estusia, covered themselves with straw and pretended to be dead. Then Hanka said, "Let's get out of here, because they'll be back." We hid ourselves in a German airforce barracks, barricaded the door with a wardrobe, and sat there for a day and a night. Their father had been a teacher and a lieutenant, the Soviets took him prisoner of war in 1939, and Hanka kept repeating, "Our father's alive, our father's alive," it became sickening.

We walked out into the road, saw a village. Beautiful houses, all identical, in two rows, like soldiers. There was no one in the village. Bowls on the tables, plates of unfinished food. Pantries full of jars, preserves; wardrobes full of dresses. We washed and dressed ourselves, packed dresses into bundles. They had these little carts with handles which they used to pull shopping home, so we packed our bundles on one of those carts. We reached the main road which was filled with army and civilian vehicles. It was barely possible to get across. Night was approaching, and the Soviet army was everywhere. If they hadn't raped us there, they would rape us here. Hanka said, "Just walk straight ahead, don't look at them." An officer came up. "Don't be afraid," he said, "I'm a Jew." He took us to his place, gave us something to eat and army blankets, "No one is going to touch you here." In the morning, he came out onto the road with us, and stopped a wagon pulled by strong horses. Three boys our age were sitting on it, and a woman with a small child, Poles who had worked for a *bauer*. The officer told us to go to Stuttgart because trains were going everywhere from there. We drove all day, we went into a barn for the night. We lay ourselves down on the hay. Suddenly commotion. The barn doors open. Russians with flashlights. Right away, they go to the wagon, through our bundles. And there are dresses in the bundles, so *dyevushki, dyevushki, davay.* We dug ourselves into the hay. They rummaged through it, trod on us, shouting, "Where are the *dyevushki?* There aren't any *dyevushki,* the boys said. The Russians waved the dresses, and what are these? They are for our sisters, our mothers, our fiancées. They shouted, swore and left. They took the dresses—for their mothers, fiancées and sisters. In the morning, we had scarcely driven out onto the road, when Russians came up, unharnessed our horses, and gave us skinny ones, barely alive. We drove and walked in turn, and it was a hell of a long way to Stuttgart.

Hanka and Estusia went to Białystok, and I got out in Łódź. I went up to a woman, "Do you know where the Jews are?" She was surprised, but she knew. In the Jewish Committee on Śródmiejska Street writing covered all the walls. I read and I read, I didn't find anybody. I went through Koluszki and Radomsko to Sienkowice, and from there to Osjaków it was only seven kilometers. A *Volksdeutsch* from the eastern territories was living in our house with his wife and children. He had not done anything to anybody here, so no one touched him. They gave me supper, made a bed, and said that two Jews had been killed in Wieluń. They had owned a paper mill there. I couldn't sleep all night. My grandmother's brother had land in Chorzew near Sienkowice, so I stopped there. The people occupying his house said that his grandson, Józek, had slept there for a couple of nights and then left for Łódź.

Józek lived with a Jewish girl, but kept on travelling to Chorzew to sell land, and Polish girls grabbed him, and there were always scenes at home. I also had land, and was owned a few years' rent, so I travelled as well. I was always sitting in trains, I couldn't settle anywhere. When I was there, I'd take off for Łódź, when I was in Łódź I'd scurry back there. I slept over with girls from school. They'd say, "Take the land back and give it to us." Boys wanted to marry me— Janecki, Pietrzak, Mielczarek—I could have had the handsomest boys for that land. I travelled there and back, I spent all my money on travel. Józek would shout, "Go to school, study." I came back once, and his girlfriend said, "There were some boys here, they're going to Czechoslovakia, to Palestine, they asked for you, didn't want to move away from the door." From Piotrków Kujawski, from Sompolno, anyone who saw my name on the wall came, everybody was looking for their own. One was going to Germany: "Come with me," he said, "my brother is there, he doesn't eat bread, only choco-late." Hanka and Estusia from Białystok got married and were wait-ing in Łódź for papers to France. Their father was dead. A boy came who remembered me from the camps in the Poznań area, but I had to sell my land, I couldn't just leave it. Because of that land, I didn't leave. And when I finally sold it, the communists had changed the money and I had nothing.

From Osjaków, Marian survived, older than me by seven years. From a communist family, they had been in the Polish Under-ground. When those two Jews were killed in Wieluń, he fled to Łódź. He came and talked a lot about my grandfather and my par-ents, we got married in a civil ceremony. I thought that I'd sell the land and we'd leave—for France, Australia, wherever, as long as it wasn't here—but he started to go to meetings, to give speeches. He knew how to give speeches, and they needed people like that, they took him so well in hand that he stopped walking on the ground, he just flitted from one meeting to another. And always with Poles, because with Jews he always quarrelled. The Poles didn't say much, listened, while the Jews knew everything themselves without him. He worked in a Jewish tailoring co-operative, but didn't sew, just solved problems, there wasn't a national or international problem he couldn't solve. A friend of his wrote from France telling him that a tailor like him could make a fortune there, but he had his meetings and his speeches and didn't need anything else. He came home late, sometimes didn't come home at all. He was never there for me or the child, always in that balloon. The higher he flew, the lower I sank, and an ambitious young Polish girl caught him. In those days, a Jew in the family was proof of positive attitudes, internationalism, evidence the prejudices of the past were gone.

I applied for emigration. "Why do you want to leave?" they asked. "Because I am from Auschwitz," I showed my number. "I haven't got anyone here, everyone is in Israel." I had Rywcia in Is-rael. "All right, you can leave, but your son cannot." "Why?" "Why don't you ask him, he'll tell you." "But he's only fourteen years old, what could he have done?" "Why don't you ask him." I went home and asked. "What do you want? I eat, sleep, go to school, nothing else." I went a second time, "What do you want, he's done nothing." "Why don't you sit down with him, and ask him a hundred times." Marian grew concerned, went to militia. It turned out that the boys were meeting after school and thinking how to get to Israel. Someone travelled to Warsaw and brought back brochures from the embassy for them. The police followed them, they had already interrogated somebody. The *machers* from the Jewish club on Śródmiejska Street were so scared that they were ready to send them to the gallows. Marian was also terrified, and leaned on all his acquaintances so that his son could leave with me as soon as possible.

Marian went to Sweden in 1968 when the Polish communists no longer needed Jews. He sewed furs and earned good money, but his ambitious Polish girl fell in love with a Swede and threw him out of the house. He came to Tel Aviv to talk to me about our son, but talked about her the whole time—that she had done him wrong, that she had taken everything. I say to him, "What do you expect? She's a smart woman. I'm stupid, but she's smart. She's got a handsome Swede now, and look at you! A wasted Jew."

Rywcia had a café on Dizengoff Street, so I worked for her. She found someone for me right away. He had a children's shoe factory, a beautiful apartment, a car. "For all you didn't have, for all you suffered," said Rywcia. He had lost his wife and child in Poland. He was delicate, couldn't eat in restaurants, needed someone to look after him. But I didn't want to stay in Israel. People perished everyday there, such young ones, Jewish children, everyday they killed Jews there.

Zeev finished secondary school and went into the army. Saturdays and other holy days, he slept at home. The bell rang, I opened the door, a soldier. Where's Zeev? I said he was sleeping. He went in to him, closed the door behind him, they talked quietly together.

When he came out, Zeev was already dressed. "Mama, give me some underwear, socks and a lot of bread." I said, "Zeev, is it war?" "Of course not, I've just got to go on duty, we'll play cards as usual." I said, "Zev, it's war!" "What war, what war, you're imagining things again." And he left.

They had bunkers in the desert, electricity, everything they needed. They ate, slept, washed there, a thousand of them in those bunkers—against the entire Egyptian army. Practically no one came out of there alive. A doctor and a nurse in a white apron would come to the door. First, they'd give an injection, and only then tell you he was dead. The whole of Neve Sharet near Ramat Gan, long, four-story blocks, from Poland and from Russia, everyone sat and waited. I didn't want to sit at home, I couldn't. Had they come, they wouldn't have found me in. I lost half my weight, I looked like I did in Auschwitz. Somebody pushed a card under the door: "Mama, I'm alive." All his friends were killed. He had their photo, tiny heads. When he returned, he drew circles, the whole photo was covered with circles.

Fred—Fajwł from Osjaków—came from America. For the first time in my life, I received flowers. I left with him. He was a manager for his uncle, women's clothing. When his uncle died, he bought the business. They sewed for a big company which sent them fabric, already cut, for a thousand dresses. One day the company declared bankruptcy, on purpose, the way they do in America, and he lost everything. He fell seriously ill, they had to cut open his throat so that he could breathe. Then he joined a partnership which sewed men's clothing. I said, "If you like, I'll wash floors, whatever you say I'll do, I just don't want to hear anything about business." He got pains in his right side and half a year later was dead.

A cantor from the Moscow Opera sings in the largest synagogue here. When he sings, the walls shake. Because of him, this synagogue is the richest, everyone wants to have the pleasure. In the

other one, a cantor sings whose parents came from Poland. When
he sings, everyone who's from Poland cries. Every Friday there's a
lunch for seniors, a piano, violin, someone sings, kosher food. You
pay two dollars, and the congregation pays the rest. Anyone who
wants to comes—blacks, the slant-eyed, and no matter what religion. And they're not at all poor. An old German woman who lived
nearby used to come, dripping with gold. Tall, upright, in a sailor's
hat. With a short, restless, clever American, a lot younger than she
was. No one sat with her, so I sat down and said, *"Ich bin eine
Deutsche."* She was pleased. "Oh, that's good, perhaps you'd look after me, because he's taking the gold out of my house." I asked her
why she was wearing a hat like that. "My husband served in the
navy." So I said, "You know what, I used to meet attractive German
women like you when I was a young girl . . . *"Waren sie nicht Aufseherin?"* Her eyes sparkled, she looked the hall over, *"Heruntermachen
mit der Scheisse,"* she said in a hard, strong voice. I told a Jewish
woman from Hanover. "Oh, she's just an old crazy, she doesn't
know what she's saying." I told the girl who was running the program. "She pays her two dollars, what can I do?"

A rabbi gave a lecture here at the center. When I hear there's a
lecture, I always go. About thirty people came, there was coffee,
cakes. The rabbi was very nice, he spoke about Christians before Jesus, and about the principles Christians and Jews hold in common.
I liked it all very much. Suddenly, a woman asked, "Rabbi, why the
Holocaust?" I jolted upright, such a clever man, it's interesting,
what he'll say. "Well," he thought a moment—he began every sentence with "well." "They hadn't kept the Shabbat." That's what he
said. When I heard it, I was flabbergasted and couldn't catch my
breath. Someone behind me began to stroke my back, but it didn't
help. I yelled, "You are a Nazi," and walked out.

One Sunday morning, I switched on the television and saw a
rabbi and a pastor. Dressed the same, but one with a candlestick in
front of him and the other a cross. I don't know what it was about,
because I switched into the middle of the program, but I heard the

rabbi say, "The Holocaust was a gift for the world." A gift for the world!

"Maybe the pastor said it?"

"If it had been the pastor, it wouldn't have cut me to the quick."

"What did the pastor say?"

"I don't know, I didn't listen any more, I had to grab my keys and leave, because when I hear something like that I can't breathe."

There are films in the National Gallery on Saturdays and Sundays. About painters from all over the world who starved in garrets, under bridges, lost their eyesight. About writers who perished, fled, emigrated. About popes and bishops who erected beautiful cathedrals and ordered people burned. I saw films about Jews there— *Samson, Korczak, Holy Week, Promised Land.* And about real Jews—like *Tevye, Fishke, Moti-Peysah, Yidl mitn Fiedl*—entire Jewish villages, looking like they were alive. Come Saturday, Sunday, I have to go, you can't stop me. Like others go to church or synagogue.

In winter, there are free concerts in Constitution Hall. Huge balconies, room for everyone. The Air Force orchestra, the Singing Sergeants, men and women in tight uniforms. "Don't sit under the apple tree . . ." Cowboys in wide hats, operatic soloists, Blacks from New Orleans, one of them ninety-two years old, they had to carry him on. The old music of bygone years. That's my medicine.

Around here, for a long time, they didn't know that I'm from Auschwitz. When they'd see my number in the shop or on the bus, they'd ask, "Excuse me, madam, can you tell me what this means?" Children would ask their mothers, "Is she a criminal?" They'd turn away from me in the synagogue. They didn't like me, didn't want to talk about it. Everyone's got their problems, they'd say. So I didn't open my mouth.

Now, there are books, films, monuments. Now, we don't grate on them, now, we don't bother them, because we're not here anymore. Like those painters—when they're alive, no one wants to know them, and when they're dead they make money off them. They still think they're better, that it couldn't happen to them, and they still don't really want to know.

My son finished university here and got married. He hasn't once asked me how it is that I am alive. He's like a stone. She won't let it be spoken about, particularly in front of the children. He doesn't ask, she doesn't allow it, I don't say anything.

A Mass for Us All

IN MEMORY OF JANINA

Father came from a well-to-do farming family near Lublin, but didn't want to stay on the land. He graduated from the Higher School of Business in Warsaw and worked for the Wedel chocolate company as a sales manager. When he inherited the land, he sold it and established a bank in Puławy. He made us learn French and the piano, if we didn't study we got the strap. My older sister Elka studied, but I didn't want to, ran off and got the strap. Elka got straight A's in school, while I got F's except in gymnastics and religion. I was ashamed that my father was the bank director. When people asked what my father did, I'd say he was the janitor there.

Mama belonged to the School Mothers and taught children for free. When father went to the club to play cards, everyone gathered in our dining room, and Mama walked around the table with a ruler. The greengrocer's son peed on the floor from fright at the first lesson. Mama was friends with the mayor's wife who taught music. On Sunday, the mayor's wife and the director's wife took baskets of food and went barefoot into the forest with children for the whole day to pick blueberries, blackberries, mushrooms. Everyone came back dirty, scratched, happy, but Father was very displeased. When I grew older, I also took snotty-nosed, dirty kids to the Vistula and into the forest, showed them herbs and birds. Kostek Bociarski, a washerwoman's son, asked, "Miss, do fishes and frogs shit and piss?"

We lived in Honigsfeld's apartment house with a large court-yard and garden beyond which the fields started. His son Benio, a doctor, lived on our floor. Old Honigsfeld was cunning and nasty, but Benio tended the poor for free and even gave them money for medications. He was our frequent guest. "What's for dinner today?" "Partridges in cream sauce." "I'll be there." He ate with us on every holiday. He was short-sighted, leaned over his plate, the sauce splashed on his glasses. Our little Romanek came down with a high fever at night and started to choke. "Benio, save the child!" shouted Mama. Benio came over and made an incision in his throat—ever a skillful doctor. After dinner, he'd lie down for a nap and call Romanek to scratch his heels. His sister, Regina, an excellent dentist, married Dr. Dawidson, a communist. Benio married a Jewish deportee from Berlin. She was very proud of being from Berlin. Nothing appealed to her about Puławy, everything was better "in Beh-leen . . ." She died in the ghetto in Opole Lubelskie, even before everyone was deported to Sobibór.

Mechl Borenstein, a tailor, lived in the apartment house. He was married to the daughter of a *shammos* but smoked cigarettes on Saturday, something his father-in-law didn't know about. He'd sit cross-legged on the table and sew—horribly. Mama gave him work out of pity. She ordered a coat, the collar stuck out behind, looking dreadful. So she said, "Mechl, but the collar . . ." "Madam, that's room for a scarf." "So be it," Mama agreed. What else could she do?—four small children, the oldest, Surka, had TB. The youngest, Monius, came running once, "Mrs. Koprucka, I saw a white rat." "Where did you see it, Monius?" "I saw it in our pantry." On Sabbath, they ate little fish. Mrs. Borenstein just cut off the heads and tails, and chopped the rest fine. That was their best food.

Helenka, our maid, brought warm onion flat cakes from the Jewish bakery every morning. The butter melted when you spread it, Father liked them with coffee. But the baker's ragged, snotty-nosed children walked barefoot in the frost. Once when I was little, I took them a gold watch, a diamond ring and a cameo—"Buy yourselves something for winter." Mama asked, "Helenka, my jewellery was on the dressing-table. Where is it?" "I don't know, madam." Mama looked at me, "What did you do?" Helenka went with me, they gave it all back. Mama didn't even get cross.

I took food out as well. Later, when we didn't have enough for ourselves, I gave my own away, saying I wasn't hungry. The sight of that poverty made me lose my appetite. Hadaska Goldstein in my class was always hungry. They owned a tinsmith's shop by the bridge, you went up iron stairs from the workshop to their apartment, always dark and damp. The mother had died, the father remarried, lots of children. I'd say, "Come down to the courtyard," and I'd bring out a cutlet, a slice of apple cake, she'd eat it all on the spot. She was small, but had a pretty Semitic face and went to the photographer every year. On those occasions, I'd lend her a coat with an opossum-fur collar which Aunt Kada had sent us from Warsaw. She looked exquisite in it. The newspaper man, an old Jew, always got something to eat in our kitchen as well. In exchange, he'd leave us magazines, "I'll be back in an hour, look through them." Elka and I would look at the illustrations and the marriage ads. Elka said once, "Let's write: Young, wealthy, back from Africa . . ." We got scores of offers in response, photos in ball gowns and swimsuits, each bragging about how cultured, how well brought up she was. We told Hadaska that the handsome young man from Africa had asked about her. We fitted her out in that everlasting coat with the opossum collar. Elka put on trousers, a jacket and Romanek's cap, drew a moustache on with charcoal. They strolled along a shady, secluded pathway the whole evening, engaged in intimate conversation and Hadaska was happy for the first time in her life. The poor thing asked us about that handsome young man from Africa for a long time after that.

Matla, I don't recall her surname—red-haired, freckled, severely cross-eyed—was a mathematical genius. Her father went door to door collecting electricity money, they, too, were poor. Lonia Eisenszmit, from out of town, lived at an old Jewish woman's on Błotna Street, they had no electricity and in the winter the water in the buckets froze. She studied by candlelight, smelled because how could she wash, but was an excellent student as well. The teachers favored these Jewish girls because they wanted to learn. Why wasn't I born Jewish? Why didn't I go with them, my Puławy poor?

Only Hanka Edelman didn't study. Her parents and their cousins co-owned ships on the Vistula: Kazimierz-Puławy-Warsaw, and Hanka had an instinct for travel. Once she came and said, "We can sail to Warsaw." At night we snuck below deck where chickens were transported, squatted the whole night in the stifling stench, and in the morning disembarked in Warsaw covered with shit. Hanka sailed away to Costa Rica just in time, she had the instinct, and of course the money.

Grey-bearded Moses used to appear in Puławy, kneel on the road and recite the Our Father. "Moyshe, Moyshe," we'd call out to him, but he never reacted, as though he neither saw nor heard us. We didn't know who he was or where he was from, but he looked like Moses. He knelt and prayed like a Christian, but he looked like a Jew. Sometimes a graceful, swarthy, curly-haired young Jew would ride by on horseback, the girls would ogle him. We didn't know where he was from either.

At evening parties at our house, Elka played piano, someone would bring a violin, and Józek Żytkowski of the Warsaw Conservatory would sing. "Spring, spring has come, to the country, and to the town," he'd sing whenever he saw me. I was a lusty wench with blonde braids. We'd recite Franciszek Karpiński, the playboy who later pulled himself together and wrote hymns in praise of God. Mama and Aunt Kada came from nobility and Karpiński was one of our ancestors. Elka graduated from school with honors and wanted to go to the Sorbonne. Father was very proud of her. By then, he already had a lot of problems at the bank, and Benio insisted that he go to Truskawiec for a break. Mama went with him. On the way, they stopped at Aunt Kada's who was appearing in Lwów. In the evening, Father felt ill and an ambulance took him to the hospital, by morning he was dead. We didn't cry, we barely knew him. He came home, ate dinner, lay down, and we had to be quiet. Evenings, he spent at the club.

Instead of going to Paris, Elka became a governess and went into the country. Then she moved to Warsaw where someone found her a job as a cashier in a hospital supply warehouse. Aunt Kada would send us her stage costumes which Mechl Borenstein altered for us. That gabardine coat with the opossum collar was worn first by Mama, then by Elka and then by me.

I said I didn't want any more schooling, or a career like Elka's, and signed up for a course at the Red Cross in Warsaw. Józek Żytkowski found me a cot behind a screen at shoe-maker Kwieciński's on Warecka Street. Professor Bródkowski slept on the other side of the screen. He had a degree from Oxford, an apiary in Radość, was writing a book on bee-keeping, and spied on me when I washed. Some unwashed charwomen, a pretentious old governess and an out-of-work jockey slept on straw pallets. It smelled of feet and bedbugs. Mrs. Kwieciński had a stall on Tamka Street, and in the afternoons I went there to wet down the vegetables in exchange for a plate of soup. Once Professor Bródkowski said that his nephew, a diplomat, had an apartment which needed cleaning on Tamka Street. I took the key and went. I was starting to scrub the bathroom when Bródkowski crept in, arms out like a somnambulist, trying to rape me. I smashed his hands with the scrubbing brush and rushed out to the elevator. Every month, I got ten *zloty* through the mail anonymously. From Józek Żytkowski.

At the end of the course, I was sent to Ujazdów. Huge military hospital with a medical corps school, its own power-station, repair shops. General Horodyński, an aristocrat, was the head of the surgical department. I observed every operation, learned to administer anesthesia, put on plaster casts. I came at six in the morning and was the last to leave. I liked to work. The head nurse in the department would give me the dinner of a patient who was to be operated on, and the senior nurse when she was on night-duty would say, "Go into my room." So I had a chance to bathe and to sleep on clean linen.

Bródkowski immediately wrote to Mama that I was misbehaving, staying out at night, and Mrs. Kwieciński didn't like me washing every day and evicted me. I come to the hospital in the morning swollen from crying, and my supervisor informs me that I have received a grant of one-hundred and fifty zloty a month from the

Rockefeller school. The nurses fitted me out, because I needed a grey dress with white collar and cuffs, a hospital apron, black stockings, two pairs of black shoes.

The school, located in a six-story building on Koszykowa Street, had well-equipped laboratories; a lecture hall for a hundred; a sitting-room with armchairs, palms, asparagus ferns and piano; a recreation hall for gym, religious services, balls; and a terrace on the sixth floor with a view over the whole of Warsaw. All that for Rockefeller's ten thousand dollars. We lived in sunny single and double-rooms. Flower-pots on the window sills, flower vases, washrooms with showers and baths. Waitresses in little white aprons served us quickly and efficiently because we had to hurry to lectures, demonstrations in the operating room, practicums in the outpatients ward and clinic, hospital duty. We were taught by instructors trained overseas on Rockefeller's money. Professors from the university and Warsaw hospitals lectured us in anatomy, physiology, pharmacology, psychology—we were all in love with Lecturer Stefanowski. The military gave us instruction in life-saving and anti-gas defense. Ethics was taught by the chaplain, Fr. Jachimowski, who later perished in the Uprising.

In the clinics and the hospital we were taught to fight to the end for life, but also to face death calmly, respect it. The dying were not to be abandoned. A hand which was growing cold had to be held until the end, so that no one would die alone. Respect was also due the body of the dead, the bed had to be wheeled gently from the ward. And right away one had to smile at the sick in the neighboring bed. To comfort the suffering, assure them that they would have help in the worst moments. We'd return from our shifts exhausted, but with a sense of fulfilling an important, difficult duty, perhaps the most important and the most difficult. Many girls from wealthy families studied there. Each course ended with a ball attended by cadets from the medical corps, officers, society ladies, university students. Those were the most beautiful days of my life.

Our course ended without a ball. Our diplomas were handed out along with our mobilization cards. I was assigned back to

Ujazdów. Ula Turkiewicz arranged to be on the front line with Lecturer Stefanowski, picking up the wounded from the field. I learned from her that Józek Żytkowski had his leg blown off by shrapnel, and bled to death before he could be brought to the hospital. The hospital was enlarged by the one hundred and fifty beds of cadets who had gone to the front, but it wasn't enough. Wounded were brought in day and night; day and night operations were performed. There were not enough surgeons, so veterinarians operated. A box of arms and legs stood in the corridor.

And constant air raids, and we had to turn the lights off constantly because there were no black-out curtains. They bombarded us, even though huge red crosses were painted on our roofs. Fires broke out continually, and the sick who couldn't move perished or received fresh wounds. A sergeant with a bullet in his stomach asked, "Sister, if I die during the operation tell my wife I was thinking of her." An air raid interrupted the operation, and when it was over the sergeant was dead. Lieutenant Doliński, a very handsome cavalry officer, had his lower jaw blown off, food had to be poured through a funnel into a tube and carefully mixed so it wouldn't bubble. When I was going off duty he asked, "Sister, come feed me, I don't want someone else doing it each time." Sometimes, he'd ask, "Kiss me." He had almond-shaped eyes with thick, long lashes, so I'd kiss him on those lashes. "And now I'll kiss you," he'd say, and flutter his lashes against my cheek. He was operated on many times. Dr. Krotowski of Poznań, a miracle-worker, reconstructed the lower part of Lieutenant Doliński's face from his thigh, but he still drooled, mumbled, and couldn't eat normally.

After the capitulation, still more wounded and sick, and nothing to treat them with, post-operative wounds grew infected. And the Germans would burst in at night and drag people out of beds. They'd pull up in a "Green Berta," and take all those who could move, leaving only the paralyzed and the amputees. The wounded would flee across the fences. General Horodyński ordered plaster casts put on to prolong sicknesses as "internal bleedings," "complicated x-rays."

Grandpa also ensconced himself there this way. He'd drink cit-ric acid, feign indigestion, stomach pains, but was always in a good mood and always after me—"Perhaps I can help you, Sister?" Per-haps this, perhaps that—always following me around. He was over forty, bald, no front teeth, so I called him Grandpa. A long, crooked nose too. He came from Kraków, from a mountaineer family— that's where the nose came from. He graduated from a business school in Vienna, spoke excellent German, knew Berlin, Paris, had even been to Stockholm. He said he had a high position on the rail-road, and, if I married him, we'd travel all over Europe.

A heavily wounded Lieutenant Kobielski, an artist, dean of the Fine Arts Academy, lay on the officer's ward. His abdomen had been torn, was operated on again and again, but the shit kept seeping through his intestines. And this Kobielski had to fall in love with me, too. He was well-to-do, so he had layer cakes brought in for me. But Grandpa had dollars as well, so whenever he saw the woman with the cakes, he'd buy the whole tray. When I came down with the flu, Kobielski ordered dinner for me from a restaurant. And Grandpa asked, "Daughter, do you have warm winter panties?" There wasn't anything between us, but he bought me warm panties and felt boots mountaineer-style. An elegant woman from Kraków lay on the women's ward suffering from rheumatism. "Ah, Sister," she'd say, "I see Mr. Węgrowicz adores you, I'm sure he's in love with you, you make such a good couple . . ." And Kobielski was green with envy.

On night duty, I did the rounds of the sick, checked their con-dition, who'd been operated on, who needed something. I walk onto the officers' ward, and there's Grandpa's face across half the wall: long hooked nose, huge protruding ears, glaring devilish eyes—like one of those caricatures the Germans pasted on walls, and a drunken Kobielski shouts out at me, "Jewish whore!" I started to shake, the medications fell off the tray, I turned back into the corridor, and he kept on shouting, "Jewish whore, I'll call the Gestapo, Horodyński's hiding Jews in the hospital"—he could be heard the length of the corridor. Suddenly, I see Jędrek Korczak from the Home Army on the stairs. "Jędrek, did you hear what he was shouting? Calling me a Jewish whore. Is it true that Grandpa is a Jew?" "Of course not, it's rubbish. I know his entire family, landowners from the south-east, our estates were adjacent." That calmed me down a little. After some time, Grandpa comes up, "Daughter, I want to tell you something." We went to the end of the corridor, sat in a niche, and he says, "I'm a Jew."

They'd had themselves baptized before the war. His wife, a devout Jew, prayed as ardently in church as she had before in synagogue. When their daughter was denounced, the wife lay prostrate on the church floor and prayed to the Mother of God asking Her to save her child. He was also denounced by someone, on the street. He showed a medical certificate that he had phemoza and had had to be circumcised. They bashed his teeth in, broke his ribs, poured cold water over him when he fainted, "Admit you're a Jew!" "I'm not!" In the end, they came to the conclusion that a Jew couldn't have withstood such a beating, and let him go. After that, Grandpa disguised himself as a railroad worker and came to Warsaw, but already at the station a school mate recognized him, "What's that Jew doing here?" The certificate was useless, and they took him and his wife to Treblinka. They were ordered to throw all their valuables, jewelery, dollars onto a sheet—death if you didn't. Everyone did, but Grandpa thought to himself, they'll kill me anyway, but what if I survive? So he bent down as though he were throwing, and picked things up again and again. Then, they selected several stronger men, put them back in the train, and Grandpa was one of the chosen. As they rode at night, they managed to push out the bars of the window. The German shot, but missed him. Cut and bruised, he dragged himself to a settlement where he saw a church. The priest gave him clothes and money for the train, because he couldn't pay in dollars. When he got back to Warsaw, his friends said: "We'll introduce you to Jędrek Korczak of the HA who is hiding in the Ujazdów hospital." In this way, Grandpa became one of General Horodyński's charges.

So I say, "You've got to run away." "No, I'm staying," Grandpa says, and tells me that the colonel on the officer's ward is a Jew, a pharmacist who'd studied along with Horodyński. And the major is also a Jew, a music teacher. And the quiet, devout soldier with the bamboo walking-stick who wears a crucifix on top of his pajamas. And that rheumatic lady who claims that we're suited to each other, Grandpa knew her well in Kraków. Even poor Lieutenant Doliński had a Jewish mother.

Grandpa goes off. Suddenly, two masked guys, guns in hand, jump in through the window, and ask for Kobielski. I point to the ward. "You son-of-a-bitch! Hurt one hair on the General's head, and you won't get out of here alive!" Kobielski was shaking like a leaf. Besides, he could see that Grandpa had stayed and that shut his trap. But the colonel-pharmacist fled that same night, and the quiet one on the soldier's ward swallowed poison which he'd carried in his bamboo walking-stick.

And Grandpa says, "Marry me." I say, "Grandpa, if you want to so much, why don't we just live together, why marry?" "No, I love you, I want you to be my wife, not my lover." In the end, I said, "So be it." He had papers, so we went to post banns. The priest looks at me and says, "You are so young, do your parents give their permission?" I chickened out and fled.

The HA men who slept with the rats in the old oil mill and came onto the wards to eat during the day, learned that Governor Frank was coming to Warsaw and they needed money for arms. Grandpa spoke excellent German, so they dressed him up as an inspector and sent him to a rich German's house. Our telephone was in Physiotherapy which closed at four o'clock, the Sister would take the key and go home. Grandpa promised to call by four. Four o'clock approaches, Physiotherapy closes, the phone is silent. "So it's all over with Grandpa, he's lying in pieces somewhere," I say to Jędrek. Then the phone rings. What are we to do? We break the door down. All right, it's Grandpa. The following day, "Who broke the door down?" Me. Report to the supervisor, the colonel, the general. The soldiers on my ward barricaded themselves in and said they wouldn't let anyone in if I didn't come back. "General, it was a matter of life or death," I said. Horodyński closed an eye, "All right, but don't let it happen again."

The attempt on Frank failed. All of them were captured and shot in Aleje Ujazdowskie opposite the hospital, their mouths stuffed with plaster from our hospital. Blood flowed along the pavement, people came, threw flowers, so they were captured as well.

And Grandpa kept going on, "Let's get married, let's get married." Finally, I got tired of it and said, "All right, what will be, will be." We were married on Three Crosses Square. I didn't tell anyone in my family, there were just a few nurses and my supervisor. I wore my uniform, Grandpa a suit made out of an army blanket he bought on Kercelak market.

On our way back to the hospital, the German guard says to Grandpa, "*Du bist Jude!*" "Who, me?" says Grandpa appalled. "I'm on my way back from church where I just married this girl. Do attractive Aryan girls marry Jews these days?" Then he pointed to the Gestapo building on the other side of the avenue, "People in there know me from Vienna, we can go and find out . . ." Flooded with a torrent of fluent Viennese German, the guard gave up and we walked on. I go into the room and my substitute tells me, "Everyone is saying that your husband is a Jew." "What is this rubbish you're concocting? Jędrek of the HA knows the entire family." Grandpa and I went into the park and I started to cry, "What are we going to do? Everyone says you're a Jew?" "All right, daughter," Grandpa says, "I'll be off, tomorrow I'll set out for Hungary, and after the war we'll annul the marriage." I cried even more, "Oh Grandpa, stay, we'll manage somehow."

Aunt Kada had a large apartment on Widok Street which she shared with the theater manager whom she was supporting. She got up at five in the morning and sold rolls at the bakery because she didn't want to appear on stage during the occupation. I called to say that I was married and could we rent a room. Then I went to see Elka who worked for a German building company. Her boss, Major

Priese, a very decent German, found work for our Roman which protected him from being deported to Germany and, through him, Roman arranged an *Ausweis* for Grandpa. Neither the major, nor Roman knew that Grandpa was a Jew, only that he needed cover. And only I knew that Elka and Major Priese were in love. The *Ausweis* from the German company revived Grandpa's self-confidence. He rode in *nur für Deutsche* compartments, bought in German shops, traded.

We went to see Mama in Włostowice because the Germans had driven all the Poles out of Puławy. I introduce my husband, and Mama takes me into the kitchen, "Child, what have you done, he's a Jew." "Of course not, Mama, Jędrek from the HA knows his entire family." "And I'm telling you he's a Jew, old at that, and probably married." It was the period of May Devotions, so Elka says, let's go to church. We come back after the service and Elka says, "He doesn't know what to do in church at all." "Maybe he's not a churchgoer. What do you want from him, and if he's a not a believer, so what?" The attorney from Puławy also says to my mother, "Your daughter's husband is a Jew." "Nothing of the kind, I know his entire family from before the war!" Then Grandpa and Mama started trading together—hard and soft dollars—because Mama had a head for business as well.

I had leave in summer so I say to Grandpa "I'm going to visit Mama for a week." I traveled in uniform, because the Germans had respect for a uniform. The train stops in Dęblin, but there's no search, nobody's pulled off. We look, the airport is on fire, and people tell us that the Germans are fleeing and the train isn't going any further. I got to Włostowice on foot, but had to hide because all the young people were being taken, so we fled to the Parchackie Mountains and huddled in the caves. By night, artillery thundered and flashed like a storm. In the morning, we heard a very long "Hur-r-r-ah" and then silence. We come out, see a burned-out tank and a dead Russian on the ground, his mouth open as though he were still shouting "Hu-rrrah."

They put us up on bundles of straw in peasant huts without

floors. Fleas, lice, bedbugs—you name it. I nursed the sick, Elka—
who, after parting with the major, didn't know what planet she was
on—read fortunes from cards. A general's widow and her son were
quartered in the neighboring enclosure, and he made passes at me.
The winter was severe, so we sat and played cards by candlelight.
One evening, a knock at the door. Mama goes into the entryway
and yells, "Antoś!" The general's son leaps to his feet and out the
window as though heaven knows what was after him. In walks
Grandpa wearing a woman's angora cap, his feet wrapped in newspaper and string, icicles hanging from him. He'd ridden all the way
from Pruszków to Lublin on top of a locomotive. He met that attorney there, the one that had said to Mama, "Your son-in-law is a
Jew," and found out where we were. He looked at the open window,
then at me, "Daughter, aren't you pleased? Come on let's go outside."

A crackling frost, silvery snow, brilliant stars—it looked mar-
velous. "I can see, daughter, you aren't happy, so nothing'll come of
it," said Grandpa. I started to cry and got cramps, but there was no
outhouse anywhere. "Grandpa, what shall I do?" "Go here, no one
will see." I had no paper, so Grandpa pulls out a fistful of money,
"Here, wipe yourself with these." Later in the hut, he throws a wad
of banknotes on the table. Mama asks, "Antoś, where did you get all
this money from." "I sold a typewriter to a Russian." "So typewrit-
ers are that highly rated now?" "I told him it wrote by itself."

Grandpa got a passport, and a car with a chauffeur, and started going to Berlin on official business. Along the way, he found us a
house in Toruń that had belonged to a German. Mama lived with
us, while Roman took Elka all the way to Sopot, to be as far away as
possible. I got pregnant and asked Grandpa, "Do you want a boy or
a girl?" "Oh, a girl, a girl, girls are so graceful and charming!" I gave
birth at home, Mama helped. Grandpa comes home at night and
Mama says, "You wanted a girl, you've got one." Grandpa runs upstairs, unwraps the diaper—a son. He jumps for joy, calls the chauf-

feur. I'm amazed, "You said you wanted a girl." "Was I going to say I wanted a boy? And what if it had been a girl?"

He went back and forth to Berlin and then one time didn't come back. Major Lolek Zagórski, a Jew in Polish uniform, arrived by car. "Your husband said that you should come to Berlin with me." "To Berlin? I'm not going, I don't want to." A month later, Lolek shows up again. "Your husband said that if you don't come with me, he'll come here and be arrested." And in his letter, Grandpa says there'll be a villa and a goat to give Tomczyś milk. "So, do you want your husband to go to jail?" "But I have no papers, besides Mama has to come, I'm not going anywhere without her." "All right, she can come too."

We get into the car and go, with almost nothing, just a few diapers and a bottle of milk for the road. At the border, the Russians approach. Major Zagórski presents us: "The General's wife, the General's son, the General's mother," and we drive across. I say to him, "And what would have happened if they'd asked for papers?" Lolek spread his legs and patted the automatic rifle which he had under his seat.

In Berlin everything was in ruins, rubble. We arrive at the address, the house is half standing, and Grandpa isn't there. We drive through the rubble looking for him. Lolek is furious, "You know what? If I had the gas, I'd drive you straight back to Toruń. What is this? Where is he?" Grandpa finally shows up, "Ah, daughter!" Mama asks "Where's the villa?" "There isn't one at the moment, but there will be." We go to some brothel of a hotel. Pimps going back and forth. Tomczyś, Mama and I in a double-bed, Grandpa on a torn couch. I got scabies from the polluted linen. I say, "Grandpa, I've got a small child, what are we going to do?" "Don't worry, daughter, everything'll be fine." He turned Mama and me into Jewish women and we went to a Jewish camp for food. He looted a baby-carriage for Tomczyś somewhere, we come in with that carriage and tin bowls, and see a Jewish woman from Puławy in the line. "My good lady, what are you doing here?" she asks Mama, and looks at us in surprise.

We got a room in a German old people's home. Mama worked in the kitchen and we started to live more like humans, but I couldn't eat, threw up, lost weight, and looked like a ghost. I say, "Grandpa, maybe I'm pregnant?" He found a doctor somewhere, a German woman. Yes, I am pregnant, but I should have an abortion because I am too weak. I agreed. But I shouldn't have, because women gave birth even in the camps. It should have taken half an hour, but she pierced my uterus and sewed me up for two hours, the blood flowing. When Mama came, I was half-conscious because there was no blood for a transfusion. Mama called in a priest. She said later that Grandpa knelt at my side, crying, "God, don't take her away from me!" The priest said there was an American military hospital somewhere around. Grandpa ran over there and begged and wheedled some blood. After the transfusion, I had a million red cells and should have had four million. My lips were white, and I couldn't close them. The newspapers wrote about that doctor later, she was a morphine addict, had left needles and scissors in people, killed more than one woman.

There was a villa with a garden. It belonged to a general released from jail because no crimes could be proved against him. Grandpa persuaded him that on account of this innocence, he should let us have the ground-floor. Grandpa travelled to Paris now, trading in money and everything else that was forbidden. He had partners: Laksman, Feingold and Fuchs, swindlers who'd saved themselves by cheating, and couldn't shake the habit. They opened a large shop selling postage stamps and seated beautiful hookers at the albums—always full of customers, terrific business, each partner had a car, chauffeur and a hooker. An Australian with a very good passport came, they gave him something to take to Paris. He took it, and said later that there'd been an inspection on the train and he'd thrown it all in the Seine. That's what the crew was like.

I had a hemorrhage again, and the ambulance took me away. Grandpa was in Paris, Mama went with me. They did a biopsy, "Your daughter has cancer, everything has to be removed." Grandpa came back at once, "I don't believe my wife has cancer, it's impossi-

ble!" They tested the tissue again—a mistake, no cancer. But I was
ill all the time, and they had to operate and I couldn't have any
more children. The Lord God punished me. Rightly so, because if
women in the camps gave birth, I could have too. He punished me
severely.

When the blockade started, Grandpa decided that Mama and
Tomczyś would go to Sopot, and he and I to Paris. I say, "How can
I go to Paris, I don't have any papers?" "Don't worry, daughter, I'll
get you a passport." My passport arrives—some ugly, hairy Jewess.
"Grandpa," I say, "I'm nothing like that." "Spitting image, daughter, I've never seen such a likeness!" We board the sleeping-car,
Grandpa hands the conductor the passports with dollars inside, and
says not to wake us. I lay down and slept, and Grandpa walked the
corridor the whole night. We arrive in Paris and I say, "Grandpa,
you look so tired, didn't you get any sleep?" "Ah, daughter, if they'd
come in, turned on the light, and looked at you and at that passport, do you know what would have happened?" "But you said it
was a good likeness." "And what was I to say?"

Grandpa's cousin Charles let us live in a garret above his fur
shop. But I still didn't have papers, so Grandpa says, "You'll go to
the Prefecture and say that you came here across 'the green frontier'
to be with your husband. If they ask which way, across what
frontier, you'll say through a forest, across a little bridge, a little
stream . . ." I went and they immediately arrested me, and packed
me into a big room with hookers and thieves from all over the
world. The following day I was taken into an office, told to strip,
measured and weighed like a criminal. They wrote down particulars
and sent me back to the hookers. On the third day, a hearing. I remembered French from school, so I said that an officer had escorted
me. "Which way?" "Through a forest, across a little bridge, a little
stream," I recited like an idiot. What Grandpa didn't tell me was
that if they discovered my husband had no means of support, they
would pack me off to Poland. "What does your husband do?" "He
works," I said. "Where?" "For his cousin." "How much does he

earn?" I didn't know their money at all, so I said something like fifty marks. The policeman lost his patience, and told me to clear out of his sight, but I got a *titre de voyage* and went to Poland to get Tomczyś.

In Paris, Grandpa made a Jew out of me again, and signed us up for Aguda where the men and women were always kept separate. He went around in a yarmulke, and kept reminding me not to un-cover Tomczyś because he wasn't circumcised. One day, he said, "Daughter, you deserve a rest, wouldn't you like to go to Milan?" Poldek Fuchs was in Milan. Grandpa bought me a luxurious cos-metics case with silver-backed brushes. I said, "Grandpa, it's so ex-pensive." "Nothing's too expensive for my daughter." I arrive in Milan, Poldek throws himself on the case, "Where's the silver brush?" He pries open its handle, it's full of dollars. Later, I say, "Grandpa, how could you, what if they'd found that on me?" "Daughter, had they found it, you would have sworn that you knew nothing about it, and they would have taken one look at your hon-est face and known you were telling the truth." He did with me whatever he wanted.

Laksman, Feingold and Fuchs moved to Frankfurt, and per-suaded Grandpa to move as well. There were no vacant apartments, so we moved in with a German family. He was an engineer. He drank, brawled, broke windows, and she had a lover, an American sergeant. She sat in the garden all day playing a mandolin, and their sons went around dirty and hungry. They stared when I cooked, so I would give them something to eat, on the sly, because she'd throw fits, how dare I feed her children. Finally, the engineer committed embezzlement and went to jail, and she let us have the rest of the apartment for quite a sum of money. The house was damaged, burned out, needed new windows and floors.

Feingold, the genius, fell on the notion of setting up a Jewish bank. They opened the bank on the Zeil, appointed a very re-spectable German as manager, but who was to be the director? Everyone wanted Grandpa. I said, "Grandpa, I beg you, don't be director." So Laksman's and Feingold's wives go after me saying a wife should promote her husband's career, not hinder it. But I dug in, and, thank God, Fuchs became director.

Józio came from Africa—handsome, elegant, exotic Mediterranean features, thick black hair—all the German women were attracted to him. His parents had owned a bar by the station in Kraków before the war. His father had lost a leg in the previous war, his mother worked like a slave. Józio never took any money from them, tutored and made sandwiches in the bar. In a photograph, the father wears Austrian dress uniform buttoned to the throat, white gloves, hand tucked in at his waist, a curled mustache; the mother, in a long black dress with a raffle and pearls, thick hair pinned up high, holds her husband by the arm against a backdrop of delicate moldings and fringed, brocade draperies.

Józio used to don that black dress like a toga, climb onto a chair, and deliver legal speeches which were so moving that his beloved niece Marylka and the girl who worked for them wept as they listened. Józio got to Russia, from Russia to Persia, from Persia to India, from India to Africa. His father had a decoration from the first war, so the Germans didn't take him to the gas, but shot him in Słomniki near Kraków. His mother asked them to allow her to stay with her husband and she supported him at the pit where seventy people were buried. A cross stood there when Józio returned, so he had them exhumed and buried in the Jewish cemetery. He also had wedding photographs of both his brothers in black dinner jackets and white bow ties, the brides in white with veils and bouquets, against the same brocade backdrop. His older brother, sister-in-law and little Marylka were sent to the gas. The younger brother didn't have children, so he and his wife hid, each one separately, but because someone said she had a lover, he went to her and both got caught.

Józio hooked up with an American lawyer and was waiting for papers to Canada. He often ate with us, brought pralines and flowers, courted me. When we had guests, he helped me prepare appetizers. He could make a hundred canapés in an hour, each one like a flower. Fuchs's wife would say to me, "Why aren't you nice to Józio, he loves you? Don't you know Grandpa has a lover?" Her husband did, too, but she didn't know it. When she and her girlfriends saw that I had not gone to bed with Józio, they couldn't forgive me. And later when they saw that he truly loved me, said to him, "What do you want with that *shiksa*? Leave her alone."

One day, it came out that the bank had no money and they all fled to Argentina, Australia, Canada, only Grandpa stayed. I carried pots to the jail, and the Germans laughed. Our house administrator said, "Look, how she's carrying lunches to jail for the Jew." And all of them said, Jew, Jews. The papers were full of it, I was ashamed to go out into the street. If a German went to jail, that was fine, but God forbid if a Jew did. Who can understand them? Józio and the American lawyer took steps, a rabbi intervened, and Grandpa was let out. Then he said, "Daughter, good you didn't want me to be director."

He went to Berlin on business and phoned, "Daughter, I left my wallet and papers in the closet, take them to Grossman, I miss you, kisses." I go to the closet, take out the wallet, inside it photos of hookers at a nightclub, Grandpa embracing them, loving inscriptions. I came down with a high fever. Grandpa calls, "You don't believe that, daughter, do you?" "But there are photos, Grandpa, you're hugging those whores." "I'll be right there, daughter." He left everything and was there in three hours. "I'll explain everything, daughter. Look, this whore and that one, I had nothing to do with. They were Szeps's. His wife's a harridan, so he says, 'Nelek, hide it, you know what a harridan Irka is.' I don't know those whores at all!" "So why are you hugging this one so tenderly?" "Look, daughter, I met her by chance and she looked a lot like a girlfriend of mine from before the war, so I said, let's take a photo, that's all! They're not worth a hair of your head, daughter, let them croak of scabies in a Jewish hospital. Come, let's burn them. Let them croak!"

It was always like that. Józio finally had enough, came over and said, "Nelek is at the hotel with a whore again." I said "I don't believe it." "Come and you'll see." We went. Our Chrysler was standing in front of the hotel. Grandpa came home, kissed my feet: "My holy one, my all, my God!"—as was usual when he came back from those escapades—some kind of split personality, I don't understand it. I said "Grandpa, I can't live like this, I want us to part." "All right, daughter, we'll divorce. You'll be a rich divorcée, you'll marry Józio, I'll go to Vienna." He packed a trunk and left. He thought I'd call him back, but I locked myself in the bathroom and bit my lips bloody so as not to call to him. Józio came, saw me crying, so he said, "I'll phone him and tell him to come back." "No, it's over, don't phone." "He'll be back, you'll see." Józio came every day wanting to phone Grandpa, but I'd say I didn't want him to. One day, I'm sitting having breakfast, the bell rings. I open the door, Grandpa with a suitcase. "Daughter, I can't live without you, you'll have to put up with me until I die."

He summoned Józio to a café and said, "Józio, I'm going to die soon. Swear you won't leave Janka and Tomczyś. She's so trusting, she won't be able to manage." Józio says, "Nelek, what are you talking about?" But Grandpa wrote down who owed him what, here and in France, and Józio took those notes. The following day, December 31st, New Year's Eve, Szeps calls from Argentina with good wishes, so Grandpa says, "I want an ocelot fur for Janka, the Argentinian ones are the best, find the most beautiful." Then said he had an appointment with somebody in Zeil, and left. Józio and I waited at home because the three of us were supposed to go to the Opera that evening. It was already dark when the phone rang. "Daughter, I don't feel well, bring me my heart medicine." I went with Józio. A hotel, a brothel, Grandpa on the bed, white as a sheet. We call a doctor, he examines him, something's wrong with his stomach and gall bladder, he's to have dry rusks. I ran to the shop because it was New Year's Eve and things were closing. I come back with those rusks, and Grandpa says, "Daughter, I want to go home." There was no elevator, and he was so heavy when we were taking him down the stairs, and strange. We get into the car, Grandpa at the wheel, I next to him, Józio at the back, and we go. Suddenly, Grandpa says, "Oh, I feel so . . ." he didn't finish, his head fell onto the steering wheel. "Grandpa!" I screamed, "Grandpa!" He didn't reply, the car kept moving. I hid behind his back, put both arms around him, and closed my eyes. Józio jumped out of the moving car and called for help. He bruised himself, his kidney cracked, but I didn't know it. I was just riding with Grandpa and wondering, "Grandpa, where are we going?" because it took forever. The car crashed into a tree, and nothing happened to me, because I was riding behind Grandpa's back.

The house in Berlin, bought in partnership with Fuchs and Laksman, turned out to be so heavily mortgaged that practically nothing was left. Everything else was mortgaged, too, nothing to live on. So, I said to Józio, "Let's collect on our debts." Lopek owed us, and Szeps and Charles. Szeps says, "I took nothing." Józio replies, "I was there when Nelek said over the phone that he'd transferred it to you." "That was a story, he transferred nothing to me." We went to Paris. Charles says he has nothing, Nelek took everything. Lopek says the same. Nobody gave a penny back. So, I said to Józio, "You've got some money, I've got a bit, we'll open a sausage stall, and live off that." Fuchs's wife says to Józio, "She's so unworldly, absolutely no sense of money, go and save the house in Berlin." And because of that she-devil, Józio went to save the house in Berlin. He had to make new debts to pay off Laksman and Fuchs. When he couldn't get any more because of the interest, Fuchs's wife came and made a scene, "Where's the money?" I opened the door and told her to leave, so she slapped my face. Both of them apologized, but things were still bad and there was never enough. I used to borrow from a Jewish woman upstairs because sometimes I didn't have enough for dinner. Józio looked dreadful, was losing his health. Why did he marry me? I didn't want to. I had said to him, "You're young, you'll marry someone, have children, we'll be friends." "No. I love you, I've never loved anyone else." He was supposed to go to Canada, instead got stuck here with me.

Tomczyś was christened and attended religion classes with

everyone else. He wore a holy medallion and always reminded me when he left the house, "Mama, mark a cross on my forehead so God will look after me." Grandpa said, "I'm not religious, raise him as you want to, I have faith in you." One day Tomczyś came home in tears. "Why do they call me *Jude?* I'm not a Jew." I said "You're half Jewish because your father was a Jew." So they started calling him *halb-Jude.* When he found out what his father had been through, and what had happened to Józio's family, and to my Puławy Jews, he wrote to Senator Ribicoff that he couldn't live in Germany. Ribicoff wrote back that he should sign up for the exam to the American school near Wiesbaden. He'd get up at six in the morning, take a streetcar to the train station, a train to Wiesbaden, and then a bus. He was one of the best students, got a prize for an essay on the United Nations. Józio was proud of him, there wasn't a thing Józio wouldn't give him. He still wore the medallion I'd given him but said, "Mama, don't get upset, but I feel Jewish."

I visited him when he was studying in Massachusetts. "How did you bring me up, Mama?" he complained. "Here, they steal from the school bookstore, and laugh at me, 'Take it, you fool, no one's looking.'" He came back on vacation and one morning says, "My throat's very sore." I take his temperature, thirty-nine centigrade. We called in the doctor—strep throat, she gave him antibiotics. But the antibiotics didn't help, he threw up and got worse and worse. We called again, the doctor did an EKG and said he had to go to the hospital immediately. In the hospital, he had a forty-degree fever. Józio brought in the best hematologists in Germany—no hope, severe leukemia. Tomczyś says to the doctor, "I have to go back to Massachusetts, I've got important classes." He had more and more difficulty breathing and was choking. *"Atem, atem!"* he begged. I couldn't watch, I fled. Józio stayed, and I, the mother, fled. Then the nurse comes and says, "It's all right now, everything's all right." I was amazed, "Who's all right?" "He is," she said, "Nothing bothers him now."

Józio broke down. Nothing interested him any more. He cancelled the weeklies, "I can't, it tires me." He was told to stop smoking, but it was too late. His blood vessels broke, he went blind in one eye. He wanted to go to Israel once more, got a new suit, shirt, tie, consulted me on the color, looked beautiful. The doctor warned me to be prepared for any hour, so when I went for groceries I phoned from town and breathed more easily when he answered. I rang the doorbell, because I was afraid to open the door myself.

That day, we went to town together. Suddenly, Józio says, "I've got to go back, I've got something to do at home." "I'll come back right away, too," I said. I quickly finished shopping and turned into our street, an ambulance was standing there. So it's standing, I didn't think anything of it. I come up to the house, the blind in the study is lowered. That's nothing, I say to myself, he probably lay down to sleep. I ring the bell, a policeman opens the door. "What's this? What are you doing here?" I ask. The policeman says nothing, just leads me into the study. In the study, another policeman, a doctor, a nurse, and Józio sitting at the desk. He had phoned, prepared the passport, everything . . .

I washed his feet, dressed him in that new suit, he looked more beautiful than he did alive. The urn stands in the Hauptfriedhof, next to Tomczyś's and Grandpa's, mine will stand there as well. Everyone can be there, regardless of religion. In Israel, in Tel Hashomer, three hospital wards bear their names. I also sent money to the Pallotinian Fathers for a perpetual mass—for us all.

Blue-Eyed Maria

FOR LODKA GROSMAN

Mother's first husband dealt in furs in Moscow. Jews weren't allowed to live in Moscow, but he was an outstanding furrier and Russian aristocrats, including Mr. and Mrs. W., couldn't get by without him. When he was killed by the Bolsheviks, Mother took her two children and fled with Mr. and Mrs. W. to Warsaw. There she married my father, a widower with three children. I was the only child they had together, which I didn't know right up until the war.

My name was Leah but at home I was called Lodka. We all had extra names: Mordechai-Max, Isaac-Ignaz, Moses-Little Max, Pesa-Pola, Ita-Justyna. We also considered Rafałek a member of our family. He escaped from Russia alone, had no one and ate with us. Mother matched him up later with a well-placed widow from building next door. She was already grey, but looked quite beautiful with that grey hair. They came over every Saturday, and our parents visited them.

Father was a bookkeeper at the Goldbergs' clothing company and worked hard to send us to schools. He brought papers from the office and pored over long columns of figures in the evenings. He shaved and dressed normally, but attended synagogue on Saturday and Mother lit candles on Friday. We lived in Feinbaum's building, 38 Nowolipie Street. Marble staircase, private bathroom—it was one of the best apartment houses. Only Jews lived on Nowolipie and the neighboring streets, and only Yiddish could be heard. At school, we were taught Polish, but only Jewish children went there and all the teachers were Jewish. For a long time, I thought that all people were Jews. At home, my parents, brothers and sisters used Yiddish, Russian and German, but I spoke only Polish. My classroom teacher, Maria Zagraniczna, was an excellent Polish instructor and taught me a love of books. Mother complained to her that I was constantly reading. Through Mother, Maria Zagraniczna became friendly with Mrs. W. and when Mr. Zagraniczny departed for America leaving her with three daughters, she became Mr. W's mistress, of which Mrs. W. was well aware.

When I turned eleven, I was selected for ballet school of Tatiana Wysocka. There was only one place for our entire school and I was by no means the most talented, but I was a blonde with blue eyes. Because I didn't look Jewish, I was sent as school representative to the Castle for President Mościcki's name-day. And I was also hired at the theater where I opened and closed a play entitled "The Massoubre Family." In the stills, I wore a white fur and sat between the famous actors, Elżbieta Barszczewska and Junosza Stempowski who held me on his lap. The "family" was supposed to be French, but they picked me—they must have found me somehow different from Polish girls. My parents, sisters and brothers went up to the theater and proudly showed the stills to friends, but never came to the play. I don't know why. At the Landau-Goldman gymnasium, also attended by Jewish youth only, I took part in "Search for Happiness"—a play by Szelburg-Zarembina. The director was a ward of Janusz Korczak. We performed at the Summer Theater in the Saski Garden. The entire family, neighbors and friends came to that performance, and Big Max brought me a box of chocolates in the shape of a book.

Big Max was a pharmacist and owned a drug store at the corner of Wronia and Pańska, because Jews were no longer allowed to open full-time pharmacies. He married well and got a steel and concrete building at 9 Tarczyńska Street through his wife's dowry. That steel and concrete survived. Ignaz became a bookkeeper for a German firm, Kaliko and Geyer, 3 Boduen Street, which manufactured synthetics. Shortly before the war, he married Tola, a poor girl with whom he'd been in love since the first grade. Justyna married a handsome tailor—I don't remember his name—also poor, and had time to give birth to two children. Pola worked for the same company as Father and always dressed well. I remember her large beribboned hats and high heels. She had black hair, a porcelain complexion, blue-green eyes and everyone said she was beautiful, but she didn't make it to marriage. Little Max who was the most gifted of us got into the university—which was very difficult for a Jew at that time—but a year later went to war and that was the end of his career. Friends who returned said the Germans had taken him prisoner near Łowicz and shot him as they did other Jews.

When bombs started falling on Warsaw, everybody ran down to the front entrance considered the most firm part of the building, but I hid in the cupboard and read. The brother of my courtyard friend, Ewa Dalman, had lent me *Mein Kampf* and that's what I read. It was clear from the book that if the Germans came, they'd murder all Jews. I was terrified and told Mother about it, but she just yelled at me: "You with your books! You're not normal!"

First they robbed Jewish shops and homes. Poles also broke in and stole whatever they wanted because the Germans let them. Then they made us wear arm-bands. I didn't want to and fought with Mother. Everyone listened to Russian radio and to Stalin—he was the God, only he could redeem us. But they took away radios. When they put up the wall, people said that was good because it would protect us from the Poles, but food prices went up immediately, ten times higher than on the other side. An egg for noodles became sacred. "Careful, an egg is there!" Mother would warn us. I buttered a piece of bread—she took the knife from my hand and scrapped it off. That had never happened before, I was always the most spoiled in the family.

In the beginning, the ghetto wasn't quite sealed and children slipped in and out. Kuba Dembiński, a toll boy, lived by the wall on Elektoralna Street, so I'd climb on his back and jump over to the other side. I'd walk into a grocery shop and stand in line like everybody else. The Germans couldn't tell, only the Poles had that extra sense, even if you didn't have the look, but I always got away with it. There was a shop on Żelazna Street through which you could get to the other side, in both directions—a small oversight from which everybody profited, most of all the police. Three policemen stood at the gate: a German, a Pole and a Jew. You'd put a hundred zloty into your *kennkarte* and give it to the Pole. But you first had to make sure that "the juke-box plays," meaning that the German takes bribes. He usually did.

Max left his drug store and beautifully furnished four-room apartment on Pańska Street to a couple of friends, fellow pharmacists who promised to transmit his dividends to the ghetto, and he moved into one room with a kitchen from which the previous tenants had taken out all lamps, switches and doors. We remained in our apartment on Nowolipie Street, and they didn't even squeeze anybody else into it, while on Karmelicka, the neighboring street, entire families had to squash into a single room. An epidemic broke out, so warnings were posted on the other side of the wall that Jews meant typhus. Mother's sister, her husband and both sons died, only Reginka was left and Mother took her in with us. She was my age and looked very much like me. Father's little toe started to rot. We put him in the hospital on Leszno Street. They first cut off the toe, then the foot, then the shinbone, but the gangrene, caused by a clot, moved further up and there was no medications to be had for any amount of money. Towards the end, he lost his speech and was dying in silence. We were devastated. We didn't know then how good it was to die in one's own bed and be buried like a human being.

The Germans would burst into the ghetto time and again and snatch people for hard labor from which they returned half-dead, or not at all. And you had to get off the sidewalk, doff your cap and bow, or they'd beat you unconscious. The streets filled up with beggars, even well-dressed people stood with their hands stretched out. Mother cooked meals at home and our wealthier friends came to eat, among them the Goldbergs for whom Father used to work. When she had sold seven or eight meals, then we could eat, too, and Ignaz and Tola as well. Max was helping Justyna out, who, with two small children, was the worst off.

I met with my friends and we studied. We read *The Forsyte Saga, The Whiteoak Family, The Połaniecki Family,* a seven-volume *Thibault Family,* Balzac, Zola, Zweig, Feuchtwanger, Gorky, because there was no shortage of books in the ghetto. I borrowed from two libraries—the best one was on Leszno, corner of Żelazna—and read two books a day. We read some chapters out loud and wrote down our impressions. We were short of notebooks, so we shared cutting them in half and wrote in tiny letters. We liked to learn on our own.

Suddenly, Jews with foreign passports showed up: Romanian, Hungarian, American—America was still neutral—and they were treated differently. One of the boys, Oliwer, from a wealthy family—he was very tall and we called him Gulliver—bought himself an elegant Lithuanian passport with gold-embossed letters. The two Pięknowski brothers from Orla Street forged the Lithuanian seal at a printer's, Adek Kuźmiński wrote an official order for such and such forms on such and such paper, with such and such content. They affixed photographs to the forms and stamped them, but the signature of Hahn, the chief of the German police, wouldn't come out right. I picked up a pencil, wrote it in a notebook and it came out right at first try. They said, "Write it for us." "All right," I said, "but I want a document like that, too." They didn't much want to give it to me, but had no choice. I wrote in the name "Kuźmińska," for Adek with whom I was secretly in love, and added three years to my age, so I could get a job more easily.

Mother didn't want to hear about my leaving the ghetto. "Where is she to go?" But my brothers told her she didn't have the right to stop me. I went to those people with whom Max had left everything—108 Pańska Street, third floor—and said, "Max is asking for his money." "We don't owe anybody anything," they said. Max couldn't believe it, and looked strangely at me.

I got on an early train, arrived in Lublin and the same day registered with *Arbeitsamt.* I got a room with a family, ration cards, and a job at Julius Meinl's, a store on the main street for the Germans. They had everything there: cheeses, sardines, chocolates, wines from all over Europe, because they had the whole of Europe then. I was poorly paid, but I had my ration cards for food and took additional from men who were leaving for the front. "You won't need them anymore," I'd say and they'd leave them to me. I knew German partly from school, partly from home, and partly from Yiddish which sounded very similar. The Poles spoke German with difficulty, somehow it didn't come out from their mouths right. But to me it came quite naturally and everyone was amazed. They also wondered why I had come alone to Lublin where I had no family. And my landlady wondered why such a pretty girl was all alone and didn't even get letters.

One morning, I am on my way to work, and the newspaper boys shout that there is war with Russia. And notices were immediately posted for all foreigners to report to the Gestapo. I didn't sleep all night. Ordinary officials couldn't really tell the difference, but how am I going to show my forged documents to the Gestapo? I had no choice and went. They were young, flirtatious, said they had never seen a Lithuanian girl before. So I said, "That's just it, nobody here knows these formalities, and I constantly encounter problems. Would you be so kind as to give your stamp, so I don't have to keep explaining myself?" "Why not?" they said and stamped in a black bird with a swastika in its tail. This was a big win for me because if a Polish policeman saw something like that, he wouldn't touch me. And I was most afraid of the Poles, because a German wouldn't recognize me. I ate in a restaurant for Germans, went to the cinema. The Poles deemed it indecent, but I felt safe there. They screened the Newsreel before the feature, and I saw the Pope bless the armies marching out to Russia.

I felt lonely, so on Fridays after work, I went to the ghetto. The Lublin ghetto was open. People were taken to hard labor and beaten, but they weren't starving like in Warsaw. I chose a family and I'd bring them live carp which I got on ration cards at the Meinl's store. I sold it to them cheap and they marvelled that I was

such a decent *shiksa*: "*Azah voyleh shiksa!*" They invited me to the
Shabbat dinner, the mother lit candles, and I felt at home. And I
heard them saying at the table, "*Dee shiksa hot a Yiddishn hein*"—
this *shiksa* has a Jewish charm.

I once went to a Jewish restaurant because a saxophonist from
Warsaw was playing there. His name was Kazik, he used to play at a
dance-hall on Ogrodowa Street where young people used to hang
out. I walked up to him because I hadn't seen a familiar face for a
long time, and he says, "Watch out, Globocnik is sitting over there
by the wall, he's half-Croat and understands Polish." Globocnik, the
chief of SS and the terror of Lublin was a stout man, a gourmand
who liked Jewish food. I heard the name more than once later on.
He was sitting with another German and the owner of the restaurant was amusing them with conversation.

Suddenly, unknown yellowish uniforms appeared in Lublin. I
asked people, "Who are they?" "Lithuanians." I felt sick. That very
same evening someone knocks at the door: an orderly with a bouquet and a letter. I couldn't understand either the letter or what he
was saying, but I didn't let on and just deluged him with my German. The following evening, he came with a letter in German: the
Lithuanian officers stationed in Lublin would very much like to
make acquaintance of their countrywoman. I felt hot and cold, but
had no choice. I told them I was born in Lida, but orphaned early
in childhood and raised by my aunt in Warsaw, so all I could remember in Lithuanian was *labas* and *labas diena*. They turned out
to be very forbearing.

They were senior officers who seemed outright old to me—I
wasn't quite eighteen then—and they acted fatherly. They had the
same orderly bring me a radio, which I was afraid even to plug in.
One of them went on official business to Vilna and brought me
back a statue of Our Lady of Ostra Brama. I became more familiar
with them and asked, "Why do you have such a bad reputation?
People say you perform the dirtiest work, and as a Lithuanian, I feel
ashamed." "Oh, that's not us, but the criminals they let out of jail
and put into police battalions. We are professional officers who had

served in the regular army—Russian, Polish, Soviet—and now in Lithuanian uniforms."

Periodically, I took a few days off and traveled to Warsaw with a small suitcase stuffed with cheese and meat which I precooked so it wouldn't go bad on the way. I didn't tell anyone in the ghetto, not even my closest friends, where I had been. I've left and that's all. Once I hand the Polish policeman my *kennkarte* with the one-hundred bill inside, and he says, "The juke-box isn't playing"—the German is not taking. I waited in a café for the changing of the guard and went up again—the juke-box was still not playing. Dusk was nearing and, with it, the curfew in the ghetto, so I approached the wall from Chłodna Street where it was closer to home and not so high. I threw the suitcase over and climbed up, but my dress caught on the barbed wire. "Young lady, take your dress off, it'll be quicker!" somebody shouted behind me. I turned around: two Polish policemen were standing in the window across the street and laughing. I must have looked to them like a regular gentile smuggler.

Shortly before Passover, people in Lublin began talking about Jews disappearing from the ghetto and shots being heard from the forest. On Friday, I put a carp in a briefcase and went to see my adopted family, but all the doors and windows were wide open and nobody was there. They'd vanished. Everybody, thirty thousand people. Where? How?

I took the rest of the days owing to me and went to Warsaw. I begged them, "Escape, they are going to kill you!" Mother yelled at me that I was spreading panic, put her hands over my mouth so the neighbors wouldn't hear, and told me to swear that I won't speak of it again. "But Mother, they've killed everybody there, so they are going to do the same here! Can't you understand? Why don't you run away?" "And where are we to go?" she asked.

The day after I got back to Lublin, I'm coming out of work—a Gestapo-man stops me. I knew him, he shopped at Meinl's. "Kuźmińska?" "Yes." "Leokadia?" "Yes." "Lithuanian?" "Yes." But we've been told you're a Jew." "What?! How dare you!" "We won't argue in the street, let's go!" he says. We went, not far, just to the left of the University. A dark office, huge black desk and a man in black like death himself. Again I say, "How dare you? I'm Lithuanian, our soldiers fight alongside yours, I want to call our Lithuanian commander!" He looked me in the eye. "All right, you're to come tomorrow with your birth certificate, baptismal certificate and all other papers." "As you wish," I said, deeply offended, and went straight to the station. I jumped into the first moving train and returned to Warsaw. To the ghetto, because where was I to go? "Didn't I tell you, there was nowhere to run?" Mother said.

All night one could hear the wailing of starving children. There were no more funerals. The dead were carried out by night and left on the sidewalk with no identity papers. Families didn't report their dead in order to keep their ration cards. They also kept their clothing. A large Jewish newspaper was published, so they covered the bodies with it, and in the morning rickshaws picked them up and took them to common graves.

I couldn't stand it there, but Mother wouldn't let me leave the ghetto again. We had just heard that Adek Kuźmiński and Oliwer were recognized on the street. Lithuanian passports didn't help them, on the contrary, they were taken, as spies, to Daniłowiczowska Street. Oliwer's family tried to buy him out, but in vain because Daniłowiczowska wasn't just a Polish police station, it was Gestapo. They beat them to force a confession, but the boys had nothing to confess, so they beat them to death. How I hated the Germans after that! I prayed that they be all wiped off the face the earth, and lived by belief it would come to pass.

I was afraid to go out of the ghetto, but I was even more afraid to stay among the dead on the street, and I was terrified by the never-ending wailing of children. Max took out five thousand zloty and said, "Go." "Where is she going to go?" cried Mother, but gave me a letter to Mrs. W. "First say you've come from Lublin with greetings from her friend, Renia. You need to sense out what they're like, because yesterday's friends can, today, send you to your death."

Mrs. W. lived at 15 Konopacka Street, on the other side of Vistula called Praga. Her husband was dead, which we hadn't known. He died a natural death, a heart attack. When I walked in, Mrs. W. and her son, Igor, were having dinner—potato soup—a normal life, a different world. They asked me to sit down with them, but I declined even though I was hungry, because I thought, "What will happen when they learn who I am?" I tendered the "greetings from Renia" and Mrs. W. asked, "How is Renia's friend, Maria Zagraniczna? Is she still alive, because such terrible things are happening now . . ." I saw tears in her eyes, so I said, "I'm very sorry, I lied, I'm Lodka Grosman," and I gave her my mother's letter. Mrs. W. burst into tears and said, "As of today, you're my child."

She was slight, dainty, with grey hair carefully swept up, wore elegant hats with a veil. I brought her lice from the ghetto. She threw all my clothes into a boiler and then ironed them heavily. One didn't see people like that in those days. She cooked and cleaned for herself, but refused to sell her jewelry, of which she had a lot. Igor accused her of avarice and there were severe altercations on the subject. Igor, who had studied at technical school before the war, was working now for a German construction firm. Mrs. W.'s daughter, Ludmiła, married a Russian Orthodox priest who served as a secretary to the metropolitan. They lived at the church on Podwale Street. Her husband wasn't to know anything about me.

Mrs. W. introduced me to Mr. Pawełek, administrator of the building, who traded in identity cards on the side. He offered me a forged birth certificate for five hundred zloty or a genuine one for five thousand. I had five thousand from Max, so I took the genuine one of dead Maria Chojnowska from Lwów. Later, it turned out to be forged, too. "Now you have to go to work," said Mrs. W., "Because if you stay at home, people will suspect that you're hiding." Mr. Pawełek advised me to go to Tłuszcz where his sister-in-law worked in an engine-house. I went, and she said, "You know German, go to inspector Volkmann, they need you at the telephone exchange."

I operated forty numbers, from eight to six with a break for lunch, not hard work. The girls at the depot found me a pleasant room with a very respectable woman whose brother was a priest. They were all nice to me, impressed that I was from Warsaw. A construction engineer, Mr. Marszałł, who built for the Germans, used to come to the depot, because he often needed a line to Warsaw. He brought us chocolates and took us to lunch. We sang, recited poetry. He didn't try to woo us, he was happily married with a four-year-old son to whom he was very devoted.

Sundays, I would go to Warsaw, stay with Mrs. W., and at dawn on Monday, go to Żelazna Street because Ignaz's group passed that way to work outside the ghetto. I picked up packages from him—silver from his wedding presents, suits for which he would have gotten nothing in the ghetto—and sell them to the railroad workers in Tłuszcz. One morning I was waiting, group after group were coming out and friends were calling: "Hi, Lodka!" "How are you, Lodka!" A grey dawn, no one else could be seen on the street, just a kid, maybe ten years old, was loitering around. Suddenly, a Polish policeman comes up to me: "You're a Jew." "How dare you! I'm a foreigner and I don't have to explain myself to you. If you have a problem with that, call a German." Seeing my Lithuanian passport with the black bird and swastika, he gave the brat a kick in the pants and went off.

Two days later, I come home from the depot, my landlady walks in and says, "I've found out you're a Jew, you have to move out immediately." There were no more trains, curfew was approaching, where was I to go? I locked myself in the room and sat there till morning—she didn't give me away.

I took the first train to Warsaw and registered as a volunteer for work in Germany. I didn't want to go, because I still had my mother, sisters and brothers, but I saw no other way out. They wrote my personal data down and I walked out in the street—straight into Mr. Marszałł whose head office was nearby. "What are you doing here?" he asked. "I'm going to Germany for work." "No, you're not going . . ." "Why not?" "Because they'll put you in a brothel there, and not to work. Let's stop at a café and I'll beat the idea out of your head." We went into a café and he kept beating it out of my head so long that I finally admitted I was a Jew. "I know," he said. "You know what?" he added. "I am building in Małkinia now and you know German, you can go and run my office there."

Małkinia was a railway station, church, and a couple dozen cottages along a dirt road called Church Street. The station was a long wooden barracks. Only the church was built of brick, massive like a castle and surrounded with a brick wall. Our draftsmen, directed by two engineers, worked in a rented cottage. Mr. Marszałł told me one of the engineers was a Jew, but wouldn't say which one. For me, he rented a room with a fisherman's family at 7 Church Street. I slept there, typed—with difficulty—on my typewriter, and lived on tiny fish which my landlord, Mr. Kocisz, caught in the Bug. There was forest all around and quiet which I badly needed, I liked it there.

We were erecting houses, about one kilometer from the station, designed for German railway workers who were to settle there. We employed nearly one hundred men, not counting twenty "dead souls," and I alone did all the bookkeeping, disbursements, allotments. We were allotted coal, potatoes and vodka—small amounts of coal and potatoes, but always more than enough vodka. I distributed what was owing the workers, and then Mr. Marszałł would come and sell the dead souls' allotments to the peasants.

I arranged everything because I knew German. I had free railway passes and travelled with papers to Ostrów whose *Arbeitsamt* we came under, and to our head office in Warsaw, so I'd occasionally spend Sunday with my "aunt." Once, when I was on my way back with money for the workers, the tram stopped in the middle of Kierbedź Bridge: a round-up. Gendarmes pushed everybody into trucks. People waved their *ausweises,* explained, wept—nothing helped. I opened my briefcase: "This is money to pay workers of my company that builds for Germans, they'll say I ran off with their money like a thief." The gendarme thought for a moment—"*Ja, ja,*" and let me go.

All of a sudden, long freight trains started arriving in Małkinia. They were packed with Jews who stretched their hands out through little barbed-wired windows. Ukrainians with rifles stood on the buffers between cars. The trains would stop and then shunt to a side-track leading into the forest. I thought they were going to some camp there. But so many trains went that way, every day and every night, and they were so long, so I thought to myself, "God, where will they put all those people?" Summer was hot, and they had been travelling in crowded freight cars for who knows how long, so people ran up offering them mugs and bottles of water—for a watch, a ring, a wedding band.

And for a bottle of vodka, the Ukrainians brought shoes, clothing and underwear to the surrounding hamlets. The land was poor, sandy with no industry, but people started coming to church in woolen suits and city dresses. What did the priest say? I don't know, because I didn't go to church. I didn't want to, I said I was an atheist.

Everything was at the station: cigarette kiosk, grocery shop, two buffets—one for Germans, one for Poles—and a post-office window. I picked up letters which, after my experience in Lublin, I wrote and mailed to myself from Warsaw, and the German at the window would always call out, "*Ah, Marie mit den blauen Augen!*" Germans had their separate buffet, but the lower ranks liked to come to the Polish one, away from their superiors. I stopped in on hot days for a drink of soda water and heard them complaining about too much work. And I heard how glad they were Globocnik had come and—on the basis of his experience in the district of Lublin—made it all more efficient.

Toward the end of November, Mr. Marszałł sent me with papers to Warsaw and I saw Jews working there on the tram tracks, among them Kuba Erlich whose father had a position with the ghetto police. I was amazed because after seeing all the trains that had passed through Małkinia, I thought all Jews had been taken away. I walked up to him and he said, "You ought to go to the ghetto and see, everyone who's still left has a duty to see it all and know."

I went with them and saw: doors and windows wide open, ripped eiderdowns, empty streets along which we heard the echo of our footsteps. Zamenhof Street, always packed and full of turmoil, was now silent like a graveyard. The silence after the starving children was even more dreadful than their wailing which had terrified me so much before. In our apartment on Nowolipie Street, I found strangers from the Schultz workshops. I knocked at the neighbor's door. She looked at me in amazement: "What are you doing here? Your mother is convinced you're dead." "And where is she?" "On Niska Street, with railway workers."

I went there through cellars and attics because, by then, you were allowed to walk on the street only at designated hours. I came upon Rafałek who was also amazed: "We've had no news from you for so long, your mother thinks you're dead. I have to go and prepare her." His wife was probably no longer there. Only forty thousand people were left in the ghetto, so no one even asked any more. Ignaz reckoned fifty thousand. Let's say fifty thousand. If fifty thousand were left out of a half million, there was no point in asking. Rafałek went and said, "Mrs. Grosman, if you cook me some *pierogi*, I'll give you a good news." What good news can you have for me?" "Lodka's alive!"

Ignaz, who was always very attached to Mother, took her with him to the "railway workers" whose job was to crush stone and throw it on the tracks at East Station. Returning from work, Ignaz always brought something to eat, so they weren't starving. They lived now in a small room with some single man. Ignaz's wife, Tola, was no longer there. Wives were to be protected, but the permits constantly changed—now they were yellow, now blue, now green—and one day when the husbands went to work, they were all taken away. Justyna wasn't there either. She had taken from her own mouth to feed her children and dropped from starvation. Dawidek was four and Rózia three, Mother took them in and, after trying for a long time, managed to place them in Janusz Korczak's orphanage. She thought Korczak would save them, but he left with them in one of the first trains. Pola fell into a deep depression and stopped speaking. Mother put her in a hospital thinking she'd get help there, but the hospitals were the first to go. My cousin Reginka just walked on her own to the *Umschlagplatz*. Max worked at Schultz's knitting factory. He was taken on by Mietek Grynbaum, his friend from bachelor days, who was the manager there because the factory had belonged to his parents. "What a decent man!" I said. "Do you know how much I had paid him?" "But why, he is your friend?" "There are no friends anymore, good he took me on anyway."

People left in the ghetto had special numbers and Mother said that Himmler promised no one would touch them anymore. "Mother, how do you know what Himmler promised?" "Because he was here. He saw how everyone worked and said if we keep on working like this, they wouldn't touch us." I said to Max, "You still have money, run away, it's the last hour." "I can't leave Rega, and she can't run because her looks would give her away." And Mother the same: "Where would we go? They will give us away. It's better to stay here and what happens to everybody will happen to us." And that's how it was. While I was on the other side, I heard all the time: they had found a Jew here, they had found a Jew there. That was the main topic of conversation. Not the war, not the situation on the fronts, but who was hiding Jews. I don't blame people who refused to hide Jews, because unusual courage was needed to do that. I blame only those who denounced and gave them away—it was because of them that so much courage was needed.

I went through cellars, attics, and smashed-through walls to the brush-makers workshops on Świętojerska Street where my friend Ewa Dalman worked. When I arrived, they were having a party. With music: accordion, violin, clarinet. Young people, no elderly or children were around anymore. They ate and drank. They took whatever could be carried out of the apartments left behind by the deported, and sold on the other side, so no one in the ghetto was dying of hunger anymore. Lolek Skosowski was there too. "Only don't tell him you've come from the other side," Ewa warned me. Tall, dark, slicked-down hair, he asked me to tango, but didn't question me about anything. Everybody knew he was an informer.

I had eyes that attracted attention. I couldn't ride a tram without somebody doing a double-take, or some boy saying to another, "Look at those eyes!" Igor, too, as soon as I walked in there, "Oh, what eyes you have!" Not tall but shapely, he had a bony face, aristocratically bent nose, and kept peering into my eyes. I thought he was just being friendly, until one night, without a word, he came into my bed. I didn't know if I had the right to refuse him. Mrs. W. was asleep, should I have screamed that I didn't want to? Mrs. W. pretended not to know, but one day said, "He's not the man for you." I noticed that he often drank, but it was war and almost everybody did. Anyway, he still drank in moderation then, on account of his mother.

At Christmas, I got two weeks off and was spending them on Konopacka Street. I knew when Ignaz's group returned to the ghetto, so I'd go to East Station and join them. "Why go there, why endanger yourself?" Mrs. W. said. "Better forget, forget all about who you are." But I had to. One day Mrs. W. went to her daughter's and didn't return for a long time. Dusk was falling, the curfew was approaching, someone knocked on the door. I thought it was Mrs. W. and opened. A young man in a hat stood in the dim corridor. "Lodka Grosman? I have a letter for you from your mother." I put my hand out—it was a Gestapo badge. "Get dressed!" he said. "Why should I, does it make any difference?" He shined his flashlight in my eyes, and crossed himself. "You believe in God?" I asked in amazement. "All right, what do you have?" he said. "I have nothing here, but can bring you silver tomorrow." "All right then, at noon in the café on Stalowa Street. "Who are you talking to?" called Igor who was doing something in the kitchen. I picked up my coat, ran to East Station and went back to the ghetto with Ignaz.

The following day, the man returned with a Polish policeman and took Mrs. W. to the police station. Igor was sitting in the bathroom just then, and somehow they didn't look for him. Mrs. W. explained that Igor was a womanizer and girls were continually coming over, how was she to know who they were? And if that one was a Jew, why hadn't the agent arrested her? Her son-in-law came running and the Russian metropolitan intervened, and they let her go. Who denounced me as Lodka Grosman? I don't know.

Again, Mother wanted to stop me. "Look, gentiles are hiding in the ghetto from deportation to Germany, and you're afraid to stay?" She took her coat out of the wardrobe because the one I was wearing seemed to her too thin. To this day, I don't know how I could accept that coat from her. I joined Kuba Erlich and his group of thirty people. Usually, nobody paid attention, but that day, they counted at the gate: one too many, so I had to go back. I tried with others, the same thing. I bade my mother goodbye four times, and returned. The fifth time, I said, "I'm not saying goodbye because I'll be back anyway." I go, somebody calls, "Lodka, Lodka!" It was Salek from preschool. In those days, when you met someone like that, it was as if you'd already been in the next world. Salek's group was one short and thanks to me the number tallied, so I passed. We rode a tram, no one was guarding, and no one tried to run. They had nowhere to run, and they had no longer the strength. They thought maybe they'd be left alone.

I jumped off at Vilna Station, and here I was told there would be no train Małkinia today. "But I have to get back to work." "Tomorrow morning there will be a train from Wołomin." I slept over on Konopacka Street and took the early morning train to Wołomin. There they tell me, "There is a train to Małkinia, but from Tłuszcz." Ten kilometers away. I walk down the track and see that the snow on the embankment is red. Then I see someone lying in the snow— someone here and someone there—and gendarmes coming along the track and shooting at the snow. "*Gut Morgen, Fräulein,*" they called to me and laughed. I walked on and saw even more red snow. At Tłuszcz, a girl with broken legs was lying near the track. And peasants were pointing with their fingers, "Oh there is one, and there!" and were leading the gendarmes towards the woods.

I had arranged with Mother that at four I would call the Jewish Council on Dzika Street that all was well. I call and a voice tells me that my mother was taken away and that Ignaz had said, "If Mother's going, so am I, I've had it." Which meant they went on that track, along that red embarkment along which I followed them like an abandoned dog.

I saw the ghetto burning, I went there especially. I knew it wasn't wise, but I had to. I stood on Krasiński Square like others and looked at flaming Świętojerska Street. I saw people on the upper floors throwing out mattresses and eiderdowns and jumping down. And I heard people next to me saying, "At last, there will be no more Jews."

At that time, only passenger trains stopped at Małkinia—comfortable pullman cars, with anti-aircraft guns on the roof. The passengers were well dressed, elegant women, well-cared-for children. People ran up to them with bottles, but they didn't need water, just asked how far it was to the farms where they were to work. They spoke German, so people called me, "Miss Maria, Miss Maria, come here!" What did I tell them? Nothing. I said, "I don't know." What could I say?

One day in Ostrów, I didn't make the train. The dispatcher said there would be a train with Jews bound for Treblinka which stops at Małkinia. Only two cattle cars came, without roof, packed with men who looked like skeletons, a Ukrainian with a rifle stood between the cars. A German who stood on the locomotive kindly pointed me to a place at his side. "Perhaps you'd like to take a ride all the way to Treblinka?" he suggested. I looked at him terrified. "For a concert . . ." he added. "We have the best orchestra there, *die beste in der Welt.*"

Neither the previous summer, nor winter had we smelled anything. It started in March. Easter was approaching, people wanted to air out their houses, and here comes such a stench that it was better not to open the windows. Everyone listened—"Oh, another train coming!"—and immediately closed the windows and shutters. The trains didn't come as often as before, and weren't as long, but the stench was more and more intense and growing from bad to worse, because they were digging up and burning those whom they had transported last summer, autumn and winter: 400,000 from the district of Warsaw, 300,000 from the district of Radom, 100,000 from the district of Białystok, 35,000 from the district of Lublin, 20,000 from Slovakia, Bohemia, Macedonia and Thrace. They had all fitted into the gas chambers, but had not been digested by earth because that was beyond her capacity, so they were dragged out again, laid in layers on grills made up of scrap railway track, and sent, like burnt-offerings, to heaven. The stench was worse than in Auschwitz because they were burning already rotting bodies—day after day, night after night. Sultry heat came, but one couldn't even open a slat because it was just a few kilometers away by ground, and even closer by air. "When will they finally finish, when will our torment end?" people complained. Because this really was the most odious place on earth.

The Germans in the buffet spoke about how many thousands they'd managed to burn yesterday, and how many today. Today's figure was always higher than yesterday's. They calculated how many months of this hard work was still left, and praised Globocnik for showing them the most efficient way of burning. They smiled at me and tried to start a conversation, and I politely answered their questions. *"Ah, Marie mit den blauen Augen!"* called the one from the post-office window, which reassured me that no one could tell anything from my eyes. What did I think about? How not to reveal anything in my face and in my voice. There were no other feelings then. Each day, each night was a gamble. Middle of the night, I'm awakened by knocking at the door. I get dressed quickly, certain that it's my turn. It's Mrs. Kocisz—by any chance, do I have a thermometer because her child is sick. It's impossible to tell all of this.

There was no more ghetto in Warsaw, but suddenly I hear that hundreds of Jews are staying in a hotel on Chmielna Street, are treated well and are to go abroad. I went there. The place was filled with people. No arm-bands, many were waiting on the stairs. Davvid Guzik of the Joint Committee and two other men were sitting behind a table and registering—a normal, civilized world. I asked Guzik, "Are you going, too?" "Yes, and my family, we've all been registered. And you? Are you Jewish?" "No, but I have friends and would like them to survive." Suddenly, Lolek Skosowski pops up. "I know you, but don't be afraid, get registered. I am sending my wife off, you could be added as a cousin, even without a visa, everyone will go." I didn't quite like it that they were so gracious, it seemed too easy. "Good, I'll come back with my friends," I said. Yes, they all went, but not where they thought they were going. Guzik fled at the last moment, Skosowski was later shot by the underground.

I got out of Małkinia whenever I could. Our German inspector, Tragbar was his name, arranged a pass for me so I could travel the area freely and buy him illegal meats from the peasants which he sent to his family in the Reich. The best raw pork was in Węgrów, the best kielbasa in Kosów. I took it in a suitcase to Warsaw for Mrs. W. Her neighbors knew about the incident with the police, but weren't sure it was about me. One day, Mrs. Kaźmierczak from across the hall called me in and said, "Why do you mingle with them? Don't you know they are sheltering Jews?" The Germans stopped trains and searched luggage, but I'd just say in perfect German: "*Rühren sie das nicht, das ist mein!*" They deported people to Auschwitz for smuggling or could kill you on the spot, just like for sheltering a Jew, but no one was afraid, because no one informed on you for smuggling.

That summer, trains were going in the opposite direction, and they weren't packed with Jews, but with Germans—this one without an arm, that one without a leg, bandaged heads—and they also asked for water. As the front came closer, Mrs. W. moved to her daughter's on the other side of the Vistula. On the first of August, I went with papers to our head office in Warsaw, and was coming

back across the Kierbedź Bridge. Suddenly, shots were heard and
the tram stopped, but there were no Germans in sight, only young
people with red-and-white arm-bands running below the bridge. I
got to the Vilna Station on foot, but there were no more trains, so I
turned back to Konopacka Street and found Igor there.

Afraid that the Uprising would break out on Praga as well, the
Germans ordered, on penalty of death, all men to report at the corner of Wileńska and Targowa Streets for evacuation. Igor picked up
a knapsack and was going. "You're not going anywhere," I said. I
went up to a gendarme on horseback. "We're White Russians, we've
been told to gather there," I said pointing to the Orthodox church
across Targowa Street.

In the church, where in fact several Russian families took shel-
ter, the priests gave us a room and bed, but told us to marry first.
We didn't want to do it without Igor's family, but the priests were
adamant: "You can't sleep in the church without wedding vows."
And I had to change religions, from Roman Catholic to Russian
Orthodox, which, for me, was no problem at all. The wedding was
very elaborate: four priests, crowns, choir. No wedding is as digni-
fied as the Russian Orthodox.

The priests allowed us to sleep and to pray, but didn't provide
food. I walked two hundred meters to the garden plots at the end of
Targowa and brought back carrots, cucumbers, green tomatoes. It
was forbidden to go out onto the streets, but I was hungry. I'm carrying a full bucket, a truck stops. Again I say, "We're White Russians on our own here . . ." When they blew up the Kierbedź
Bridge, we knew it was over, and went back to Konopacka Street.
Two days later, a noise in the street woke me up at dawn. I ran out
to look: a tank with a red star was standing on the corner of Stalowa
Street. I'd never seen anything so beautiful.

That same day they came for Igor. "I'm a Jew," I said, "and he saved
my life." They glanced at each other. "He'll come back today, an officer's word." He didn't come back, neither that day nor the next. I

went from post to post, and from one command to another until I got to a prison camp in Jabłonna. The officer, a Jew, said, "It's not because you're Jewish, and not because he saved you, but we basically have nothing on him." And he let him go.

I had left Małkinia wearing a summer dress and now it was autumn, winter on its way. So as soon as trains started to move again, I went to pick up my things—in a roofless freight car, on snow-covered coal. The bridge over the Bug was blown up, and a hired horse-wagon carried passengers on to a ferry. Riding slowly through a pine forest, we suddenly came across a vast clearing where a crowd of people were clawing the ground. "What is this?" I asked fellow passengers. "Canada," they replied. "What do you mean Canada?" "Don't you know, Miss, Treblinka?" "So what are they doing here?" "Searching for gold and diamonds in the ashes."

People in Małkinia saw I had no clothes, so they offered me various things, and quite cheaply. Mrs. Kocisz held out a sealskin fur to me. I had already reached for it because it wasn't expensive—it had a Dutch name and address on the lining. I still wouldn't tell anyone, either in Małkinia or in Praga, that I was a Jew. Whether it was known or not, you just didn't speak about it. Sometimes I feel it's not myself I'm talking about, but somebody else. Or it's a reincarnation, because one can't live through such things.

In January, the Russians finally crossed the Vistula, so I went with Igor to Podwale Street. The Russian church was no longer there. A bomb hit it during the Uprising and everybody perished, only the maid who had gone to fetch water survived.

Mrs. W. had been right warning me about Igor. I went one day to get the laundry from the attic and found him there with a woman, our next door neighbor. I told him he disgusted me, so he hit me in the face with his fist. I was terrified, didn't know what to do. Nobody had ever hit me before, not even a German. One of the depot girls from Tłuszcz came over, so I went to the store for something to serve her and returned too soon. Once a girl came complaining that he had promised her to divorce me. He came home drunk and had difficulties in bed, so he'd get enraged and beat me as if it were my fault. When I told him I'd leave, he laughed in my face: "Where would you go?" And it was true. He had taken me not as a partner but as his property, a slave he didn't have to reckon with. And nothing changed because I still had nowhere to go.

On the ninth of May, I found out I was pregnant. Marching bands were playing in the streets, victory, crowds of people, but I never felt so lonely and abandoned. I swallowed analgesics, quinine, valerian, everything I had, but I awakened twenty-four hours later and didn't even miscarry. He worked on construction again, but each time he got paid, came home drunk and without a penny. And between pay days, took things out of the house. The baby was given a gold cross by the godparents—because his son had to be christened, of course—he took it off the child's neck and sold it. He was social, invited friends over, neighbors, the janitor, it didn't matter whom, and if I said anything, he hit, kicked, broke glass. After he sobered up, he'd say he didn't remember, took me to church, knelt down and promised it wouldn't happen again. And then would get drunk again, and again rave like a beast.

Walking along Targowa Street, I spotted a Jewish woman in front of me: hair, nose, even footstep, because Jews walked differently, apathetically. I was amazed, I thought I was the only one left. "Are you Jewish?" I asked. She got scared. "Don't be afraid, I am too." She had spent two years in a wardrobe, hidden by a single man thirty years older than her. Everything was fine while she stayed in the wardrobe, but when she came out, everybody could see he had sheltered a Jew. She didn't look the way I did, so nobody could pretend they didn't know. He drank and beat her as well, and she, too, had a child already, six weeks older than mine, but he really had saved her life. She told me there was a Jewish Committee right there, on Targowa Street. There I met Mietek Grynbaum for whom our Max had worked in the ghetto. He told me that in April when the ghetto was already burning, they'd been together on a train for Majdanek, but he'd managed to jump out. I also saw Guzik there. He was a representative of the Joint again.

My father's sister found me through the Jewish Committee. I didn't remember her because she had left for America long before the war. She sent me her photograph in a cardboard frame and asked me in every letter how I liked it, so I finally took the frame apart and found two twenty-dollar bills in it. That was a lot of money at the time. I bought the child clothes—which my husband sold for vodka. Jews who had managed to survive in Russia came back, among them my school friend from Pawia Street, Irka. She saw the bruises on my face and asked, "Are you waiting for him to kill you?" Child in one hand, suitcase in the other, I left without even a note, and stayed with Irka. I told Marlena, the woman from Targowa, to do the same, but she said she couldn't because her husband really saved her life.

The Joint distributed American money and machines for the establishment of Jewish co-operatives. I got a job at a "Solidarity" underwear and haberdashery store in makeshift premises on Marszałkowska Street. The manager got visits from his friend, Marian Szarach from Powiśle, who was fifteen years older than I. He had managed to escape from the ghetto to the Lublin forests and join the partisans of Colonel Korczyński. They didn't want Jews, but Korczyński was also from Powiśle and knew Marian's sister, so they took him. Marian heard that Korczyński had killed a group of Jews from Lublin hiding in the forest. When Korczyński was arrested, Marian was summoned to testify. But he thought to himself: today Korczyński is in jail, and who knows what will be tomorrow, so he said he could give no evidence because he'd just heard about it and not witnessed it. He was awarded the Medal of Victory and the Cross of Grunwald. Later he was supposed to get also the Partisan Cross, but by that time Korczyński was out of jail and they were no longer giving decorations to Jews.

I wanted to keep my Aryan papers like most Jews who survived in that fashion. But when we went to get married, they checked the

Lwów registers and it turned out that Maria Chojnowska had never existed, and that Mr. Pawełek who had sold me her birth certificate was a fraud who unscrupulously put my life in danger. In truth, the fact that I didn't know spared me a lot of fear, but had I known, I would have been more careful.

People searched for relatives, didn't find them and left. But we were too tired, didn't have the energy, even after the pogrom in Kielce. Marian turned out to be a very good father to my son. He worked for the Central Union of Jewish Cooperatives and got from them two rooms with a kitchen in Żoliborz. We went to Thursday Soirees which took place on Królewska Street in a theater improvised from the ruins of the Kronenberg Palace. Tadeusz Borrowski appeared there twice. The first time, he read his poetry, the second time, a story about Maria, his fiancée, with whom he'd been imprisoned in Auschwitz. We were taken aback by his sudden death. A young man who'd survived Auschwitz? Nowhere did it say suicide, just that he had died and that it was a loss of a talent.

In 1964, I visited my aunt in New York. Her whole family chipped in and gave me two thousand dollars which was an enormous sum in Poland. By then, bringing hard currency was not only permitted, but even approved of. Marian bought a used car and became taxi-driver, and still there was money left over for remodelling and wall-papering the apartment. I turned it into a jewel.

March 1968 came. Marian brought a newspaper, I thought it was a reprint of *Mein Kampf.* Even in my worst nightmares, I didn't imagine I'd read something like this again. My son who was studying planning and statistics came home and said, "I don't know about you, but I am not staying here." I met Mr. Marszałł on the bus. "You've got to leave," he said, "I didn't save you for some scoundrels here to torment you again." But Marian was approaching sixty and couldn't make up his mind. Until one day we got a visit from his old friend, Kazik Leszczyński, who had brought him food to the ghetto. "Don't worry," he said, "I've got an estate near

Warsaw, I'll hide you." That convinced my husband. "Nobody is going to hide me anymore," he said.

You filed papers and waited for the permission to come or not. If it came, you had to sell everything and leave within two weeks. Immediately the vultures and hyenas descended, as they had years ago during the relocations to the ghetto. "I'll chop everything up before I'll give it to them," yelled Marian. We had to give up the apartment. The administrator came and said, "The windows are crooked." "That's how they were," I replied. "But I didn't know about it, and besides, the apartment needs to be renovated." "But it's been renovated, don't you see?" "But the new tenants may not like the color . . ." We had to pay eight thousand zloty, three months wages. And thirty-thousand for our son's college education. A ransom for everything. Marian sold the taxi, but you couldn't take cash with you. And only ten grams of gold per person, they could remove a wedding-band from your finger. Everyone was allowed to take out the foreign currency brought into the country legally, but a Jew no more than three hundred dollars. Ida Kamińska, the famous Yiddish actress, stood in front of me at the bank. She had often performed abroad and had brought thousands in, but she, too, was allowed to take only three hundred.

So one bought whatever there was. And there wasn't much, especially because everyone was buying. You paid inflated prices for drapes, curtains and covers which wouldn't go with anything later on. And you had to accurately list all "items for domestic and personal use": each plate and pot, each cup and glass, each pair of socks and stockings, underpants and long-johns. The customs officer carefully read my list, all five pages, and assigned me the date for inspection of the luggage—in two weeks. "But I have to leave in a week." "There is nothing I can do about it, all the days are filled." I put five hundred zloty in an envelope and he found a day. We had to pay with dollars for the luggage. Even porters demanded dollars, or else they wouldn't carry the suitcases. How could we have lived there? How could we have been so blind? This time, however, we had somewhere to go. Israel, Sweden, Denmark, America, Australia had all opened their borders. We chose Australia—the furthest away. Sometimes I think it was just a bad dream, and then I feel better.

And if you are ever in Treblinka, please say a short prayer for me in front of the big stone to the Warsaw Ghetto. I didn't just lose my nearest there, but my whole world. Including Lodka Grosman.

A Family Sketch

My mother's family came from Kutno and from Kalisz, Grandmother was probably from Kutno and Grandfather from Kalisz, but Mother was born in Warsaw. I know because I once retrieved her birth certificate in Poland. Grandmother was Orthodox, from a very unassimilated family. Grandfather had an apartment building in Kalisz. They also had houses in Warsaw which were destroyed during the war, and nothing remained of them, but I know that my aunt—cheating me—retrieved quite a lot of what had survived in Kalisz. Apart from that, Grandfather had a vinegar distillery in Warsaw. I don't remember what they looked like. I probably never saw Grandfather. I remember Mother as through a mist, and I'm not even sure whether I remember, or whether it's an image based on stories I had been told. I have only one photograph, a very blurred one. During the occupation pictures were scrupulously destroyed. That one survived precisely because it wasn't clear. It's a photograph from some party, taken at a table. My mother and grandmother are in it. I had it blown up, because I wanted to see their faces, but it wasn't possible to recapture any of their features, only the silhouettes remained. Mother, as everyone claims, was the living image of Julie Christie, to the point that my father couldn't sit through that film based on Pasternak, what was it called?—*Doctor Zhivago*—and left in the middle. Mother was light blond, natural, not dyed, and had blue eyes. I also had light hair when I was little, but then it grew darker. A certain gentleman who searched me out in New York said, "Your mother was a beautiful woman, you don't look a bit like her . . ." My mother really was very beautiful, so everybody claims.

My father's family, on the other hand, was assimilated and very snobbish. As a result of the slump at the beginning of the thirties they were actually ruined, but they kept up a facade. They were Warsowians. If some of them lived in Łódź, it was as a result of business, because they had an agency and a spinning mill there. They also had business in Gdańsk and trade relations in France. My great-grandfather, who survived and died a natural death in 1945, had made a lot of money in Tsarist Russia. He lived in Petersburg. After the revolution, he returned to Poland, but because he had got divorced from his first wife and married a gentile, he went on to Germany and lived in Berlin. He survived the war in his own villa, the Germans didn't touch him. I don't understand how that happened. Apparently, several Jews who gave a lot of money to philanthropic causes out of Swiss accounts had been left in peace, and my great-grandfather was one of them. It's also very possible that they needed a few such Jews for show—especially right in Berlin—to make an impression on foreign representatives. His wife was much younger than he was. She created a cult out of him, and stayed in the east part of Berlin because his grave was there. She used to write to us, and I know that Great-Grandfather died without knowing what had happened to his closest family. Grandfather—the only industrious one in a family concerned only with spending money— also died a natural death. It was hard for him to survive the things that happened as a result of the economic crash and he died of a heart attack at the age of forty-six.

My parents were married in 1939, in April. They had met some two years earlier in the famous Ziemiańska Café, but father was married and his divorce took a long time. They had a Jewish wedding first, on account of my mother's Orthodox family, but Father forced Mother, and, in any case, if I know him, pressed her to become a Lutheran, and right after, they had an Lutheran wedding on the quiet. Father had converted to Lutheranism in 1938 together with a part of his family. They decided that Lutheranism would be better for them than Catholicism because the Lutherans were also a minority in Poland and accepted Jews more willingly. In any event, quite a few Jews converted to Lutheranism then, and there was a pastor in Warsaw who baptized Jews very readily. Only my father's mother became a Catholic, and his relations with her were always very cool. Actually, he hardly knew her. He saw her for the first time when he was thirteen years old. She walked up to him on the beach in Sopot and asked him his name, after which she introduced herself to him as his mother. When Grandfather divorced her, there was a great scandal in Warsaw, because she had had an affair with the well-known actor, Bodo. She had been a Pilsudski Legionnaire in her time, and apparently kept in touch with counter-intelligence. All in all, she led a very colorful life, just didn't look after her own son. After that meeting on the beach, they didn't maintain any close contact, because Father was sent to school in France. He finished secondary school there and started his studies, but came back to Poland when the family's financial situation was so bad that they could no longer support him in Paris. Father established closer relations with his mother only during the occupation, when, thanks to her various contacts, she arranged Aryan papers for us and other Jews.

I was born in the ghetto, as a Lutheran. When I wasn't quite a year old, I was taken out of the ghetto together with my mother by one of my father's workers and baptized a Catholic, at the insistence of my newly-Catholic grandmother who had become a believer. Father also took his company out of the ghetto. He went to the Germans with his Aryan papers and said that as an Aryan he did not wish to run a company among Jews. He thought to himself, either it will work or it won't. It worked. The gentile industrialist, Adamczewski, helped him—that was a well-known cosmetics firm which produced toilet soap called "Puls." Adamczewski found a place for my father's business on the Aryan side, found him clients, orders, without him it would have been completely impossible. We lived on

Grochowska Street, and the company was located on Burakowska—all of it on the Praga side of the river where one was less likely to meet undesirable old acquaintances from the elegant sections of Warsaw. The whole of Father's family found itself on the Aryan side: his mother, brother, aunt, all his cousins. Not one of them survived. Father—not tall but handsome, slender and dark with cold, light-grey eyes, which could be very deceptive—didn't have any problems as far as his looks went. Like my mother in that regard, but she got upset easily and then she didn't speak Polish well.

On Mother's side, Grandfather, two uncles and the husband of my older aunt, went to Russia, in 1939 or in 1940. They had planned to orient themselves, and then to bring the family over. They all perished, deported far north. I don't know the details, I only know that they were completely helpless and didn't know how to make it over there in Russia.

Grandmother didn't want to leave the ghetto. Keeping it a secret from my father, my mother took me up to the ghetto wall in my pram so that Grandmother could see me from the window on the second floor. Someone, however, told Father and he categorically forbade those walks. Father got my younger aunt out of the ghetto when she was already at the *Umschlagplatz*. A Jewish policeman, who was either in love, or had even had a romance with her, helped him. In any event, he took her from the *Umschlagplatz* and contacted Father. My older aunt and her small child remained with my grandmother, it was hard to take the child to the Aryan side because it was a boy.

I lived on the Aryan side with my mother, father, aunt and nurse, a Ukrainian woman who had been recommended to us because my mother was in bad mental shape and didn't know how to look after me, and my aunt was good for nothing other than romances. She always had some fiancés. She was a pretty girl, had all kinds of friends, and wasn't afraid of anything. Maybe she didn't understand, or perhaps didn't want to believe what was happening.

The nurse brought the first informers down on us, unintentionally. It really wasn't her fault. She turned to Father with a request: could her friend, a Ukrainian woman who was very ill, come to stay with us for a while? Father agreed, the friend came, quickly realized that we were Jews, and as soon as she had recovered, went and snitched. Two Polish policemen came and Father started to pal around with them, paying them every time they came on a visit, and they kept on coming until Father found a different apartment for us. There were also timid informers who literally fainted when they had to blackmail. In any case, it happened that Father heard a knocking, opened the door, and had to revive a middle-aged guy who confessed that he would not have come on his own, but his wife had forced him to. "Don't get yourself upset, things like that happen in a marriage," my father calmed him down forbearingly, and gave him money for his wife, but after that incident we had to change our apartment again.

Aunt got us into it the worst. She went off out of Warsaw, I think to Świder, where her friend was living with her lover. The friend was Jewish. They questioned my aunt about the family and so she told them about my mother, father and me, about my father's mother and brothers, who was where, and how they had got out of the ghetto, she told everything. And at parting, she even gave them our address and telephone number, although our telephone had been connected illegally and only a few people knew about it. The blackmailers came, but Father said he wouldn't give anything. When they left, he sent us all out of the house. I was placed with his friend who had an optical shop in Warsaw. He and his wife liked me a lot and always gladly took me in when things were difficult. Father placed Mother and my aunt separately, and remained behind alone to be arrested. He was taken to the police-station somewhere in Praga. A Pole interrogated him. "So, admit it yourself, are you a Jew, or not?" "It's easy enough for you to check," my father responded apathetically. Then the man re-considered, and a moment later asked, "Where are the two young women and the child that we have in the report?" "I'm not telling." Then the man who was interrogat-

ing him said, "Get out of here, change your address, and if you survive, remember from time to time that there were decent people
here, even among those who worked for the police."

Father once more pulled himself together, changed the apartment and didn't get so depressed again—until Mother was caught.
He also immediately warned his mother to move right away because
the situation was dangerous. Those friends of my aunt's who had
denounced us and knew about the whole family could try their luck
where they might, convinced that if so many members of a good
family were on the Aryan side then they could make money. Aunt
explained that she had trusted them and that it could not have been
they who betrayed us—after all, her friend was Jewish herself. That
was no argument for Father. "And so what if she's Jewish? Doesn't
she need money? She needs it even more, to survive." My father's
shrewd mother, on the other hand, was convinced that the policeman who had interrogated him, and also knew about everything
from the report, hadn't let him go out of a rush of goodwill nor out
of a desire to feel good, but to track us all, and she fell on the crazy
idea of putting Father in prison as soon as possible.

In this way, Father found himself in the Gęsia Street jail, in terrible conditions, and a step away from death. Actually, he was accused only of trading in dollars, which had been found on him, but
his fellow prisoners in the tight overcrowded cell had more than one
opportunity to find out that he was circumcised. Fortunately, a certain burglar of high caliber who was respected in the prison wouldn't
let them talk about it, and, in exchange, demanded that my father
tell him interesting stories out of books, because he was bored in
prison. My father who didn't like novels wore himself out telling
him most of Sienkiewicz's trilogy. He left out *Pan Wołodyjowski* because he hadn't read it, but added *Pan Tadeusz,* stressing the sensa-
tional passages—of course without the rhymes. Apart from that, he
knew very little Polish literature, so he drew on his French resources, particularly *The Hunchback of Notre Dame* and *Les Mis-
érables.* When he ran out of that material, he wove in some of his

own Parisian and Warsaw romances together with bits of Balzac and Dickens. This thousand-and-one nights situation did not last that long, because very few people lived for a thousand nights in a German prison in those days. He was released after several weeks for a large bribe in dollars which he promised a German. Immediately after his release, he phoned his mother to tell her that she would never see him again as long as she lived. He didn't know that it was going to be very easy for him to keep his word, because she was arrested shortly afterwards, not for any economic crime, but because she had been denounced as a Jew.

Everybody in my father's family perished because of informers. Even his aunt, scarcely ten years older than him, a well-known cosmetician, who never left her well-hidden office which she ran the entire time for her most-trusted pre-war clientele. Her eighteen-year-old son tried to escape, but was shot and died on the spot, which was better both for him and for others because he had underground publications on him, so they would have tortured him. Father's half-brother, who had managed to escape from a transport, was recognized on the street by a Polish policeman. He attempted to bribe him, but unfortunately, that policeman wasn't a blackmailer. Both of Father's cousins were denounced. They had tried all kinds of things. There was even a special clinic on Karowa Street in which doctors tried operations to camouflage circumcisions, but the effects of the operation didn't last. Father's cousins also tried a special sticky fluid, which they smeared on before going out onto the streets, but that fluid also didn't work for long and had to be reapplied every hour causing painful abrasions.

After that disaster caused by my aunt, we lived apart. I stayed with my father who claimed I was safer with him, because not only did he have a good appearance, but he could also mix with the Poles more easily. My mother, in fact, didn't have the same freedom, and grew increasingly nervous, especially when she discovered that Father had a girlfriend. At that time we lived in Konstancin, in a luxurious guest-house to which a lot of Germans came. Father thought that was the safest place. In any event, no blackmailer reached us there. The girl who lived with us vanished whenever Mother came to see me for a few hours, but it all came out because Mother started to ask who was dressing me, who was looking after me, and I told her that there was a girl, and when she asked what she looked like, I replied that she was as pretty and well-made-up as she was.

My mother took it very badly. She wanted to have me, but Father wouldn't let her. Once, she came when Father wasn't home, and sneaked me away, but Father brought me back. I don't remember those fights, and I know the details only from various stories. I think I remember Mother crying. It didn't matter to me whether I was with her, because Father was good to me, willingly played with me, devoted nearly every free moment to me, saw to it that I had everything. I doubt if any other child in Warsaw then had more dolls, teddy bears, cats and dogs than I did. And the girl was very good to me, too. She was truly in love with Father. She was a gentile girl evicted from Pomerania, eighteen years old. I suspect that Father had told her that he was already divorced from my mother. She was a truly nice girl, and all Father did was ruin her life.

Shortly after the fight over the girl, Mother moved in with the husband of my father's aunt, the cosmetician who was no longer alive. He was a handsome man. Father definitely opposed their living together, claiming it was unsafe for Mother, but she felt very lonely and didn't want to obey my father any more. She was arrested together with that man at the trolley stop on the corner of Książęca and Nowy Świat, but not because of him. The plainclothes policemen came up only to her, because they had been informed about her. They didn't want anything out of him, didn't even check his papers, but he wouldn't leave her and went with her. She had been denounced by a woman who thought that her husband, an informer, was having an affair with her. Mother removed her bracelet and asked whether for that bracelet they would allow her to call someone to whom she wanted to say goodbye. They agreed, and when she telephoned Father, they waited politely until he came, and they didn't attempt to arrest him, either, nor even to check his papers.

They didn't question him about anything, they weren't at all interested in him, they were just ordinary police. Father offered them all the money he had, but they wouldn't take it, explaining that they had an order and had to take her because she had been watched and that Aleja Szucha had already been informed that they had her so if they didn't deliver her, it would be dicey for them. However, they allowed Father to escort her and they all walked from Książęca to Aleja Szucha very slowly—for nearly an hour—the agents in front, my father and mother behind them, and the man who was living with her, at the back. The agents warned them not to even think of escaping because someone else was there behind them. Father assured Mother that he would do everything to get her out. What else they talked about, I don't know. They parted at a discreet distance from that building on Aleja Szucha and Mother went in there with that man to whom she was closest then. He was an elegant man, and I presume that he was affectionate and good to her. That was already December 1943, and those years must have made her a shadow of herself. Many years later, Father told me that at that time he had wanted to go back to my mother, but I'm not sure whether it was really like that or whether it only seemed like that to him later.

Father truly did all he could to save her. The woman who had first denounced her came to him and said that she had her own contacts, independent of her husband's, a professional informer, and thought that she could get Mother out for ten thousand dollars. That was an enormous sum, and Adamczewski, who never failed to help him, lent Father that money. It later turned out that he employed Jews in his factory and that some of the workers he recommended to my father were also Jews. The attempts to rescue my mother lasted three months, during which time the woman who had denounced her had many opportunities to ascertain that it was my aunt, and not my mother, who had had an affair with her husband. The woman was led astray because my mother had tried to cover it up, as she had covered up many other things her younger sister had done, and she had suffered a great deal knowing that she was having an affair with an informer. Aunt used to meet him in Mother's apartment, and that was undoubtedly the biggest mistake. I learned these details many years later from one of my father's wives whom I contacted when Father was already overseas and, marrying again, he needed the divorce certificate. I discovered then that my aunt had continued her affair with the informer, drinking away with him the money which my father had given him to save Mother.

Three months went by before it became clear that my mother was no longer alive. The woman who had denounced her brought Father back the ten thousand dollars. And when Father expressed amazement, she said, "Why are you so surprised? That I don't need that money? As God is my witness, I don't need it for anything . . ." and she burst out in such weeping that Father found it hard to stop himself from consoling her. He wanted to go to Aleja Szucha immediately, and started to dress me to go with him, but after he had dressed me, he thought how much I looked like my mother and decided that he did not have the right to give me up to the Germans, so he called Adamczewski and asked him to take care of me. Adamczewski realized what was happening and told Father to wait. He quickly arrived with a psychiatrist who immediately gave Father tranquilizers and professional care.

I found out that my mother was dead only after the war when her friend came back from Russia and started to cry when she looked at me. She said that I was very much like my mother and asked whether I understood that I would never see her again. I hid behind the armchair and didn't want to come out. I also hid behind the armchair when she talked about Russia because it seemed to me that she was saying it all on purpose to scare me and I hated her for that. I very often sat behind the armchair later during endless arguments after Father married my aunt.

That's all. It's obviously a skimpy sketch for a story such as this, but it's all that I know. Just like in that photograph. I never allowed any "artistic" enhancement of my mother's and grandmother's faces on the one photograph that remained. I simply belong to those who inherited nothing from their next of kin except sketches. I feel fine in New York. I like to vanish into the crowds on Lexington Avenue and in the subway. I married twice and didn't try after that. I didn't want to have children. I'd rather be by myself.

A Pact with God

FOR HALINA M.

My mother's younger sisters—Rivka, Rachel and Yona—fled to Palestine, one after the other. Grandma went to visit them in 1939 and fortunately didn't make it back in time. Mother's older brother, Henryk, lived in Leipzig where he had a big fur company. In 1937 he escaped with his wife Maria and three sons—Leon, Bernard and Wolf—to Milan and from there to Nice. When they came for them—twelve Frenchmen and one German—Wolf, who had just finished his baccalaureate, was on a skiing holiday in Haute Savoie. Maria slit her veins so they took her to the hospital. Uncle Henryk, Bernard and Leon were taken to Drancy and from there to Auschwitz. Wolf was interned in Vernet along with his mother, but they bought their way out of there with money, crossed over to the Italian side with smugglers and hid in the mountains with the partisans. Father's older brother, Hipolit, had a bacon factory in Gdańsk and other towns. He had himself baptized shortly before the war, talked into it by his lover Rita, a German woman from the Poznań area, who was a divorcée with a daughter, Yola, a few years older than me. Uncle Hipolit soon came to realize that being baptized wouldn't help him much and bought Mexican passports for big money. He took his seventeen-year-old son, Władek, and his widowed sister, Rózia and her sixteen-year-old son, Adam, and they got onto a train on 9 May 1940, as a Mexican couple with children, and went through Italy and Spain to Cuba. His real wife, Regina, also changed her papers and went to live in Piaseczno near Warsaw where a romance with a German supported her alibi. Regina and

Hipolit's daughter Maryla, blonde and blue-eyed resident of the former Free City of Danzig with a Germanic name, had a ticket for a ship to New York—for the World's Fair. "*Sind sie Volksdeutsche?*" "*Natürlich . . .*" She got a visa and sailed to Sweden on 28 September and from there to America. Aunt Rózia's older daughter, Hala, who was studying in Paris, met a Polish aristocrat there and in 1940 left with him for Scotland where she told no one she was Jewish. Uncle Bernard who was a doctor in Warsaw fled from there to Russia with his wife and his son, Jerzyk. Their older daughter Danka and their son-in-law got baptized and stayed in Poland, carefully erasing their Jewish traces. Mother's youngest brother, Jakub, was a dentist living in Radom. He had a wife and three children. They stayed where they were and we never found out what had happened to them.

I was born when my mother was forty-two years old and convinced that she would be childless. We lived on 6th-of-August Street, in a very good neighborhood. Huge black furniture stood in the dining-room, in the bedroom, wardrobes full of my mother's dresses and furs as well as a vanity loaded with cosmetics. I don't remember the kitchen because my mother never cooked. I don't remember my father either, I only recall a dark blue diary with poems which he wrote about me in it. For him, I was like the Messiah had appeared when both of them had given up hope. I had light curls, a round face, a small nose, dimples in my cheeks. "God Lord, it's little Shirley Temple!" people in the street said. But I was most like my Uncle Hipolit and his sister Maryla, twenty years older than me. Father was an engineer with the Majewski company. He had a heart attack on the way to work. I was three years old, but I remember the green benches in the hospital waiting room and Mother shouting "Give me my husband back!"

Aunt Rózia's husband also died of a heart attack. And Father's younger brother, Zygmunt who lived in Vienna. It happened a lot in those days. They were too delicate, too weak, too little hardened. They broke under the burden of insults—they weren't Jewish enough.

I bit my fingernails, which annoyed my mother a great deal. To her, hands were most important. She didn't cook, didn't touch the kitchen, in order not to spoil her hands. She always noticed appearance, manners and diction. People who spoke Yiddish, dressed like Jews, gesticulated like Jews irritated her most of all, and she called them "Yids." Mother and those Jews who had grown away from all this were convinced that the whole misfortune was the fault of "Yids" and their lack of manners.

Opposite our house was a ministry which was bombarded day after day. I can still hear that terrible rumbling in my ears, that howling, and the wailing of the sirens. I am still afraid of sirens, and I can't watch films about the war. Mother's younger brother, Moniek, lived in the Jewish quarter on Leszno Street. Mother took me there—perhaps they'll bomb it less. His wife, Rena, had thick black hair, a long nose and came from a religious family. Uncle Moniek was a fairly prosperous furrier, and Aunt Rena, a dentist, and they had cupboards loaded with food. Their Janka, two years older than me, and I went in gas masks to fetch water and to carry out chamber-pots. The masks were very useful when we were taking out the chamber-pots. One day Aunt Rena said, "Moniek, we don't have anything to eat," so Mother took me out of there. Immediately after that their house was bombed and they brought Janka to us.

I remember that swarms of motorcycles with side-cars moved across the width of the street growling like dogs. We stood on the sidewalk with other people. Mother didn't say anything, didn't explain anything, and I didn't ask about anything, but I saw that something bad was happening and I felt scared. That fear never left me.

Mother bought honey-cakes in a honey shop on the corner of Marszałkowska Street and the Square of the Redeemer, and often talked with Pani Renia who worked there. Her husband, Pan Stefan, was an engineer with the gas-works. One day Mother said to her, "I have a problem. I have to move into the ghetto." "Why?" Pani Renia asked. "Because I am a Jew." "Ah, don't go there." "But I have to." "No, you can't go there." Pani Renia knew a lawyer who was in love with her and who would have done anything for her. His office was near the law courts. Mother was pulling on long gloves as we walked through the court building to the other side. At the same time, she was pushing her Jewish armband into her glove.

Pani Renia also put us in touch with a priest and we went to him at the Church of the Redeemer through the sacristy. He was a prelate who demanded that we know the catechism very well. Late one afternoon when we were returning to the ghetto, green trucks blocked the street in front of us. "A round-up!" people shouted running away. We managed to catch the tram which was going in the opposite direction, but when we reached the courts, the building was locked up and it was almost curfew. Mother squeezed my hand hard when we came up to the guard gate. The guards were busy talking, and the lady in the hat with the girl with blond curls didn't look like Jews who wanted to sneak into the ghetto, and we snuck in behind the guards' backs. Many women and children were shot in the ghetto for illegal crossings.

Our baptism took place in the evening, by candlelight. Long shadows played on the walls, and the echo carried each word high. Pan Stanisław, Rita's first husband and Yola's father, was my godfather. We didn't go back to the Jewish side. Pan Stefan, Pani Renia's husband, went there in the gasworks' van and brought out suitcases with our things to an apartment which Pani Renia had found for us at 7 Miodowa Street. Pani Renia also agreed to take my cousin Janka out of the ghetto to her mother's in Sandomierz, but money was needed for her maintenance, at least half a year in advance, and Janka's parents didn't want to give more than a month's. Afterwards, when they had reached an agreement, it was already too dangerous to go into the ghetto for Janka, and all three of them died there.

Men in black leather coats stopped us on the street by our house and came with us into the apartment. I no longer know whether they ordered me to, or whether I knelt down myself and started to pray out loud. And I don't know which was more effective—my prayer, or the money which they got from Mother. Immediately after that, Pani Renia found me a place with the Sisters of the Resurrection, and Mother moved in with Rita who had married an Austrian and was living in a German quarter on Aleja Szucha. Her husband, Walter, was a lieutenant, who had fortunately become an invalid and was managing a Jewish umbrella factory while Rita was working as a translator for the Gestapo—on Aleja Szucha. She came back from there sick. "Oh, Zosia, how they inform, how they inform!" she would say to my mother. The ones who lay in ambush on the street at least let you go for money. More threatening, and more prevalent by far were the disinterested, often anonymous, informers who gave you no chance. Everybody feared the disinterested and invisible ones most.

The boarding school of the Sisters of Resurrection was at 15 Mokotowska Street. I always remembered the numbers and names of the streets, but nothing other than that interested me. A new name was a new name, I didn't ask about anything. I knew that despite my baptism I was still a Jew, which was very bad. That was enough, I didn't want to know any more. When it became too dangerous on Mokotowska Street, they moved us to Stara Wieś, to a white mansion with a turret and little towers belonging to a prince. Afterwards, I thought that I was touched, that such a place had never existed, but it turned out that it was all true, and that the mansion which stands to this day in Stara Wieś, Węgrów district, belonged to Prince Radziwiłł. German officers occupied part of the mansion. They had a separate entrance on the other side, but they used to come to our chapel. Sister Alma once said to my mother, "Ah, Halusia is so smart, when she sees a German, she immediately runs away."

We carried water from the well and peeled potatoes—two buckets of water and forty potatoes a day. In the summer, we picked mushrooms, strawberries and blueberries in the woods. The nuns made tasty dishes out of them. We prayed in the morning, evening, before and after eating. We confessed every week, and for one day a month we spoke to no one except the cross on the wall. I prayed very sincerely. On these words, which I often did not understand, depended my life not only in heaven, but also here on earth. We went to church for Sunday Mass and Communion, but Confession, Novenas and Vespers were held in the chapel at the mansion. The priest who heard our confessions had escaped from Germany and hidden with the Sisters of the Resurrection because—which we didn't know—he had been born a Jew. Germans also confessed to him because he spoke good German and even had a German last name. How were they to know that a Jew was hearing their confessions?

We went to the village school, but the nuns gave us extra lessons in Latin and German. They also taught us embroidery and to make play things out of paper and straw. They arranged games and theatricals for us. They darned our stockings and repaired our clogs. They cared for us and treated our flu, hepatitis, and scarlet fever. They went into the countryside to ask for milk and potatoes and flour for us. We didn't have enough to eat, but I never felt it. I only felt fear in my stomach. My face grew thin, my nose longer, and fear showed in my eyes, and I looked nothing like Shirley Temple any more.

I went to my mother to Warsaw for holidays. Yola took me to the circus where the antics of the acrobats filled me with dread, and to the cinema where I sat even more anxiously because everything was in German and I only saw Germans around me. Once they sent me to fetch milk from Meinl's, a shop for Germans and *Volksdeutsche*. A moment later, the telephone: "Frau Haslauer, whose is that Jewish child?" Walter immediately took me back to Stara Wieś and I never went there any more. My mother came to me, but I was afraid of her visits. Krysia Janas's grandmother came once and took her back for Easter. They were discovered in the train. The Sisters tried to save Krysia, but one of the Germans told them to desist because it could end up badly for the whole boarding school. I don't remember her face. She was nine years old, the same as me.

We were not taught hatred—only love, above all for the Lord Jesus. But hatred was stronger. Especially when coupled with love. Because how could you love the tormented Jesus, and not hate those who betrayed Him? And how strong must the hatred have been if even little Krysia Janas was betrayed? That's why I made a pact with the Christian God that I would never be a Jew and that, in exchange, no one would hate me. That was Easter 1944.

At the end of July, Walter, Rita and Yola were evacuated to Vienna, and Mother stayed in their apartment. When the Uprising broke out, she fled Warsaw with a German whose name was Kurt. It was still safer for her to pass for a traitor who had taken up with the Germans. Kurt was killed near Kutno, and Mother went on to Łowicz. She didn't say any more and I never asked.

Mother wanted to go far away where no one knew us, and we got as far as Brzeg-on-Oder. It was a small green town with a big Russian base: a regiment of bombers, a regiment of fighters, a regiment of tanks. Our apartment opened onto a garden. I had my own room with a white rug, a white bed, white cupboards. A piano, also for me, stood in the living-room, even though I didn't want to learn to play. The large kitchen, very well appointed, was also not much needed, because my mother didn't like to cook. Crystals and porcelain figurines with flutes and piccolos stood on the cupboards, tables and side-boards.

Mother ran a kiosk with cigarettes—as Mrs. Chmielewska, of course—and I went to church and wore a gold cross which she bought me. We received dresses and beautiful material from our aristocratic cousin in Scotland. The cigarettes were brought by traders from Łódź who bought German tablecloths, tapestries, and crystals in Brzeg. The cigarette kiosk was a terrific business, and the Russians, the main customers, were crazy about Mother. An elegantly dressed Polish *Pani* with well-kept hands—they had never seen such a lady.

A tank officer, Major Lukovsky, paid court to her—a widower, a serious man—but Mother said, "He is a Jew, I don't want to know him." She took a pilot, Grisha Baranov. Grisha had no idea he was twenty years younger than she. He also didn't know that we had once been Jews. He took me to church on Sundays, gave me money for the collection, but didn't go inside. "Halusia, it's all nature . . ." he explained. He taught me to read and write in Russian, took me and Mother to performances of Russian singers and dancers to which Russian women came in German nightgowns and coats made out of German bedspreads. He bought me a bike and a waterproof coat. I had a father, and felt safe for the first time in my life. And I saw a smile on my mother's face—something I had never remembered about her.

Grisha had a brother in a high position, and he went to Moscow to prepare an apartment for us. It's scary to think what would have happened if he had made it. Mrs. Chmielewska? . . . Birth certificate, baptismal certificate . . . And Mr. Chmielewski is buried where? And in which parish were you married? And where is your father buried? And your mother? And your sisters? They were not in a hurry, they had time. There had always been more than enough time in Russia. And what if they had asked *me* a couple of questions? My mother took it into her head to become an officer's wife. In a far-off capital city of a huge country—far away from our past. What was she thinking of? That the NKVD, NKGB or MGB were numbskulls like the Gestapo? An assumed name, concealed ancestry, even the date of birth not real. Marriage to a naive officer of an elite force and off to Moscow? On false papers! And in occupied Warsaw where had she lived? In the German district. With whom? A worker for the Gestapo! And how did she get out of Warsaw? With Germans. And where to after that? To Brzeg-on-Oder, a Soviet base. And a cigarette kiosk because—Soviet airmen smoke. A seasoned old agent who even knew how to disguise her age in order to wipe twenty years off her résumé. And what was she doing during those years? Where was she? . . . People with much simpler life stories weren't able to account for themselves. It really is scary to think what would have happened if the train in which Grisha was traveling hadn't been blown up by the Ukrainian partisans in Volhynia, and if poor Grisha hadn't been killed.

After Grisha's death, Mother didn't want to stay in Brzeg-on-Oder and said, we were going to Palestine. No one in Brzeg could know about it, so we moved to Łódź where our cousin Danka was living. She and her husband had survived as Poles. He had been an officer with the underground Home Army and they still concealed their Jewish origins, even from their own children. Danka's brother, Jerzyk, returned from Russia with the army, as a decorated captain with a Polonized proletarian surname. Uncle Bernard did not come back, he had died there somewhere, they didn't say where, and shortly after, Danka's husband, the decorated Home-Army man, was deported to Siberia.

I didn't want to go to any Palestine. "Go yourself," I yelled at Mother, "I'll stay with Danka, I don't want to go to the Jews." In a letter to Grandma, I put a photograph of myself with the golden cross on my chest and inscribed it: "To my darling Grandma." Grandma thanked me for the photograph and the inscription, only she didn't like my "pendant."

Mother enrolled me at Shomer Hatzair and that helped a bit. I went there in secret from our acquaintances and neighbors to whom we were still the Chmielewskas. I made friends with girls who had returned from Russia, and in summer I went to Lower Silesia with them to a former German farm for *hahshara,* preparation for agricultural work. We sang Russian songs there and danced the *hora.* We also sang in Hebrew, but the melodies always sounded like Russian ones, and the *hora* was a Romanian dance. We sometimes picked potatoes, and the braver boys milked cows, but mostly we danced and sang. Discussions and lectures focused only on what was happening, not on what had happened. They asked, "Where were you during the war?" "In a convent." "Aha." That was all.

We left in one of the last transports on a frosty January morning. We were only allowed to take one suitcase each—as was usual when Jews were leaving. Danka saw us off by herself, so that her sons wouldn't know where we were going. On the other hand, everyone on the platform knew, and stared at us with derision. The conductors looked down at us. The customs men ordered us around loudly. The border guards eyed us sternly and let us through as if they were doing us a favor. High, gloomy mountains blocked our path, and a mad howling pursued us when we slipped away through tunnels. Even the Italian sky clouded over above us, and the bare vines on the hillsides looked like crosses—not vineyards but cemeteries planted with crosses. Incensed at us, the sea tossed us around for three days and nights and didn't let us get to the shore, and we lay on the deck and moaned like the damned.

Mount Carmel was white with snow, but in the port at its feet the sun and mother's three sisters greeted us warmly. Their hair was too black, their eyes too black, and their skin too dark. We didn't see Grandma because she had died before we arrived. She had been fasting for Yom Kippur and wouldn't take a drop of water despite the heat and died, probably because of that. She became very religious there and shared every piaster with the poor. She would wheedle money out of her daughters when she didn't have anything to give. A lot of people came to her funeral, the poor from the whole vicinity.

Everybody lived poorly here. Yona's husband was an upholsterer. My mother once wrote her: "To marry an upholsterer you didn't need to go to Palestine." "And what would I have now, had I married well in Warsaw?" Yona asked. Rachel's husband taught at a secondary school. Rivka and her husband worked on the land in a *moshav*. Rivka placed me in an agricultural school. We didn't dance there and we didn't sing, we had to work. Mother had no husband, nor a profession, so she stayed in the barracks and ate camp soup. One day she was walking along a street in Tel Aviv and hears: "Zosia! What are you doing here?" Who should it be but Pani Renia. Her husband had been killed in the Uprising and she had married a Jew, a doctor who had escaped from the Russian army. They were living in Jaffa, in a spacious, formerly Arab house. "Zosia, you will stay with us," said Pani Renia who always extricated Mother from her problems.

Shortly afterwards, Yola appeared. She had met a handsome Jew from Romania in Vienna and she wanted Mother to take her to a rabbi. Mother went with her to a rabbi and even to the *mikva* to which she herself had not been since time immemorial. Rita, Walter and Erika who had been born in Vienna followed in Yola's footsteps. They didn't want to live in Austria.

I showed no talents at the agricultural school, and Pani Renia recommended that I be put into the army. I was just seventeen years old so they told me to say eighteen. Rivka, a *halutz* and a *Hagana* fighter, had connections in the army and after the course for recruits, I got a job in the Town Council in Tel Aviv. In Jaffa, near Pani Renia's, was a French hospital, and next to it a church—low, small, unnoticeable, like synagogues in Poland. In addition, it was dark inside. I entered it through the sacristy, secretly, as I had done before when I had a secret that only God could know about. Sometimes, I stopped by during Mass on Sunday morning, on my way to the office. I'd stand in a dark niche at the back behind the few people assembled there.

Pani Renia lent us money and Mother bought four by three meters on the roof without a kitchen, without a lavatory. The kitchen, of course, was not necessary for my mother. For the same money, she could have got a proper apartment, but she had to be near the center, near cafés. She worked finishing clothing and was poorly paid, but she never complained. "Your stomach isn't made out of glass, nobody can see whether you've eaten or not." Appearance and style were what counted. She had her two friends from Warsaw and a circle of ladies from Austria and Germany—what more did she need?

Everybody around us was a refugee. And mostly, like Mother and me, they were running from the Jews. Even Rivka, Rachel and Yona, who had escaped in 1929, 1930 and 1931. Jews were not liked here either. People were ashamed of them. Especially of what had happened to them. The subject wasn't spoken about. Heated arguments erupted whenever someone mentioned it. Why didn't they leave? What were they waiting for? Were they worried about their little shops? Why didn't they defend themselves? Why didn't they attack their murderers? Why did they give themselves up? Most criticized were the Jews from Poland. The Galicians said they came from Austria, the Litvaks from Russia—nobody wanted to be from Poland. "Don't be ashamed that you're from Poland," one Romanian boyfriend said to encourage me. There were no Jews in Tel Aviv, Haifa or Jaffa. My grandmother was a rare exception, but she had a particular reason. For whom else had the Jewish God brought four daughters out of the house of death?

After the army, I got a job as a bookkeeper with the taxi drivers' union, and everything was as it should be, but now Mother started to nag me: "Get married!" This was the period when men who had made it in Germany and emigrated to America came to Israel to find wives. The girls needed no persuading, married and left.

Janek was ten years older than me, he came from Mińsk Mazowiecki. After the concentration camp—I don't know which one because we didn't talk about it. He had a men's clothing shop in Connecticut. A good man, but in the concentration camp and also probably in Mińsk Mazowiecki nobody paid attention to how someone ate, sat at the table, or held the knife and fork. He spoke Polish, German and English as though they were all one language and Mother gave him hell, even though he really tried. Three weeks later, the wedding—in the café Bustan, in the garden, in the best section of Tel Aviv. The invitations have been sent, and Mother says, "You are not marrying that Yid." "Mother, the invitations have gone out . . ." "I'll die if you marry him!"

Jack was a few years younger than Janek and had also been in a camp. He was from Kraśnik, so he probably went through Płaszów, then worked on airplane engines—in Mauthausen, perhaps. He came to America with his uncle who had never married but devoted himself completely to him and worked hard in a factory in order to put him through schools. Jack graduated from Yeshiva University, was very intelligent, could have been a rabbi, a professor, a lawyer— didn't want to. He played the horses—legally and illegally—off-track betting. His uncle bought him a supermarket, he lost it. He bought him a partnership in a hotel—the same thing. I went to work. One day I notice my fur coat is missing. "The fur coat? What fur coat?" As though he had never seen my fur. After that, I couldn't find my diamond ring. "You left it somewhere, it'll turn up." He took out loans in my name, he signed checks in my name. Was gentle, never argued and didn't drink, but chain-smoked. He had several heart attacks, but never complained about his health. He died on the operating table.

I worked as a bookkeeper in the bank. In those years in the bank it was also better not to be a Jew. I came from Poland, spoke with a Polish accent, my maiden name was Chmielewska, my religion—Catholic. My husband? Yes, he had been a Jew. Yes, I lived in Israel for a while. With my mother who—only now did I have to lie—married a Jew after the war. My mother came to America under her real, Jewish name, because in Israel they didn't want to issue a passport under the false one. She cursed "those Jews" terribly because of that.

I felt no guilt or shame about lying. Had it not been for lies, I would have long been dead. I was simply still afraid. Besides, I really did not know who I was. To the Americans, I was a foreigner. To the Poles, a hidden Jew. Who was I to the Jews? Considerably more members of my family survived than in other ones, because they all knew how to lie, camouflage themselves, assume protective covering. Like among the animals, among carnivores. It isn't we who should be ashamed.

My daughter joined those who proclaim that one can be both a Jew and Christian. She's an American, and doesn't understand what little religion has to do with it. I tell my hairdresser that I'm going on vacation. She asks where? I say, to Europe. I can't tell her that I'm going to Israel. I can't. On my way back from the office, I step into St. Patrick's. It's peaceful and quiet in there and I can talk to God. In the only way I know how. When I leave the house, I have to cross myself surreptitiously. Norman has caught me at it a couple of times. "What are you afraid of?" He can't understand. But I get angry when Sussie quotes the New Testament to me. I had reasons, does she?

"She does too."

"Because I didn't give her anything."

"You did."

"My fear . . ."

After the war, my uncle Hipolit moved from Havana to Chicago where his daughter, Maryla, was living, and afterwards brought Regina over from Poland and they lived like a model married couple. I didn't know him, he died before I came to America. His son, Władek, worked as laborer in Chicago, changed his Mexican name to a Polish one and married a local Polish girl. He went to church, became a Chicago Pole. Adam married a New York Jewish girl thereby acquiring permanent resident status in the U.S. and a share in his wife's family's business. Their son joined the Baha'is for a while but converted to Hassidism afterwards. Aunt Rózia moved to Hala's in Scotland and died there. Wolf came to New York with his mother who had a wealthy brother here. Wolf's daughter became a fashion coordinator for furs. She appeared on television, went to international conferences. Walter became an electrician and liked Israel a lot. He took part in two wars as a volunteer. His old wound didn't bother him at all in the Sinai. Erika studied psychology and—as a social worker—tried to help people. Yola and her husband settled in a *moshav* and raised chickens, he supplemented their income as a bookkeeper. They didn't tell their daughter who was proud to have been born in Israel as a *sabra* the real family story, because why complicate her life? Pani Renia gave birth to two Israelis: Lior became a doctor, and Gideon traded with Hong Kong. Janek went back to Germany and didn't try to marry again. He died before his time, like Jack. Danka's husband came back after ten years in Siberia. A patriot, an HA man, a national martyr—he got a good position on the railroad. Jerzy, a veteran of the battle of Lenino dec-

orated with all three crosses: Cavalier's, Officer's, and Command-
or's, as well as the *Waryński* party medal, and a valued historian on
the editorial board of the *Biographical Dictionary of the Polish Workers Movement,* died suddenly in January 1990. Of a heart attack. His
own son didn't know what his real name was.

And my mother lies under her real Jewish name in the great
Jewish cemetery on Long Island.

Cousin Benito

FOR BEN, ZOÍLA, MICHAŁ AND BASIA

████████ They came from the Świętokrzyskie Mountains—Chęciny, Przedbórz, in the direction of Pilica. They started moving to Łódź before the first war. A large family, because their father, who had four children when he became a widower, married a second time and begot another two, and when he died, his widow remarried and gave birth to another three, and they all had grown-up or adolescent children, so one brother's son, Beniek, survived, another brother's son, Michał, and one sister's daughter, Regina, who had fled to Russia.

Beniek went to "Yabne," a very good Hebrew school on Cegielniana Street, but he didn't like studying. His twin Józiek was not at all like him, he had a good memory and was a very good student, while Beniek stood on his head, walked on his hands, rode a bicycle—everyone said that nothing would come of him. Their father bought them a violin. Beniek didn't take lessons, but played. Their father sent them to the synagogue but smoked cigarettes himself on the sly on Saturdays. Beniek wasn't interested in God, but he liked Shabbat dinners, candlesticks, a table laid with a white cloth. He went to "Bar Kochba," a sports club, and to the *hahshara* on Kiliński Street, but he wasn't a Zionist. He didn't really know in which world he lived.

Their father made tailor's scraps into yarn and thread for cottagers who wove homespun fabric out of them, and he partly financed their Uncle Sender's lining business. He also lent money to other small manufacturers at one and a half percent a month keeping it secret from the Tax Department. In 1932 he bought a four-story house together with Uncle Sender—at 57 Radwańska Street, near Poniatowski Park—for thirty thousand dollars. He hid for the last years of his life so as not to pay taxes. He died in 1936 of cancer and didn't pay. His older son, Natek, took over the business. Beniek helped, but wasn't very useful, he wasn't suited to it. Józiek became a left-winger, joined the Bund, so they quickly married him off and his father-in-law, who produced high quality fabric, harnessed him into his business. Within three years, Natek doubled his income and in 1939 they had enough money to go to New York for the World's Fair and not come back. Others were doing that, but Natek thought that the war would be brief, because England and France would quickly defeat Hitler. After all, nobody expected what was to happen. Beniek was drafted into the army in February. Józiek not, because he had a secondary school diploma, so they would have had to take him into the military academy—they didn't want Jewish officers. Beniek defended Skierniewice, and afterwards, like others, bought civilian clothes and a loaf of bread from a peasant and went home. He didn't find his mother there, she had fled to Warsaw with the youngest, Mayer, who was eighteen years old at the time. Józiek and his wife left as well. Beniek and Natek stayed to look after the family property in Łódź.

The Germans took everything away from them, herded them into the Bałuty section and penned them behind barbed wire. They had no more news of their mother and brothers in Warsaw. Uncle Sender, who had bricked up his stock papers and gold in a wall of his house on the Aryan side, died of hunger like others, in a dirty bed, alone after his wife and children had been deported. Familial relations existed for perhaps a year in the ghetto and then everything fell apart. You went out to work at dawn, came back in the evening and went to bed hungry. Who could think about family there? Beniek paid money to become a prison guard. People were locked up for robbery, smuggling; for hard currency and valuables. The sentences varied, but nobody ever got out, except by truck or train—for Chełmno or Tuszyn forest. Natek was manager of a warehouse in which flour sacks and oil barrels were kept. A very good position, an enviable one. He was accused of taking scraps from the sacks and barrels. They beat him and then let him go home for a ransom. He brought two diamonds and a gold watch from the safe, so they accused him of hiding valuables. He was sent to the Tuszyn forest.

They dragged Beniek out of the cellar and deported him at the very end, in August 1944. He had a one-hundred dollar bill, a fifty and two twenties in his boots, he threw the singles out. They were allowed to keep their belts and shoes during disinfection. The shoes were lined up in a row and after getting out of the shower everyone handed his pair to the German for inspection. Beniek took the shoes next to his, replaced them after the inspection and put his own on. His cousin Berek took a hundred dollar bill to the *Oberkapo,* a German, so that he would shield them both from work, and then a fifty on top of that for a job in the kitchen, peeling potatoes. In this way, they survived Auschwitz and Czechowice. Towards the very end, on the way from Buchenwald to Halberstadt, the Americans bombed their train. Beniek got a piece of sharpnel in his buttock, Berek's leg was shattered. Beniek could go on, Berek had to remain in the field. Beniek got into the *krankenhaus* thanks to his wound on which he poured salt in order to stay there as long as possible.

When the Americans were turning Halberstadt over to the Russians, he ran away to Eschwege with other DP's. Like the others, he used to go to the PX to trade in American products. He met his beautiful wife there. She had light, gentle eyes, soft, gentle hands, played piano, he hadn't seen a woman like that in years. Like other German women who were starving, she had left her husband and was living with her parents. Ben brought them condensed milk, cocoa and chocolate from Jewish packages, and cigarettes and coffee off the black market. She got pregnant, started crying, so he married her and moved in with them. He had a family again, and a white cloth on the table—after all these years. When a son was born, he took him to the doctor and had him circumcised.

The Germans paid him for forty-eight months of ghetto and camp. At a dollar and a half a day, it didn't cost them much. He opened a stocking and sock shop. When he was sent to Bad Nordheim for treatment, his wife visited him faithfully every Sunday. Six weeks later, he comes back, she's not there—vanished. The shop's closed, no money, no goods, she's only left the child. He waited one week, a second, a third, and then took the little one and moved out. Didn't know what to do with himself. Went to the American Consulate like the others, was told that he couldn't leave without a divorce and wouldn't get one unless he gave the child back.

He sailed to New Orleans with other DP's. They wanted to send him from there to Alabama, but he wouldn't let them. They sent him to California and gave him a job with a Jewish company in Salinas. He went from farm to farm buying up jute chicken-feed sacks which were then washed, repaired and re-sold. When he'd had enough of that, he moved to Los Angeles. He went door-to-door in a white Carnation Company outfit persuading residents in the Mexican quarter to have milk delivered to the door. There on a veranda, he saw an angel in a white Peruvian dress. She had luxuriant, black Jewish hair, dusky Jewish eyes, even his first wife hadn't been that beautiful. He decided to do everything to make her like him, though he had neither position nor money.

Zoíla came from the Yurimaguas area, from Marañón, from the green plains of Loreto flooded by the Marañón on its way to the Amazon. Seventh Day Adventists came there and told marvels about the United States. Finally Zoíla said to her father and mother, "I have to see those United States." The missionaries took her to Florida. When she came down sick with her ovaries, they took her to eastern Los Angeles where everyone spoke Spanish and where their great hospital named for their prophetess Helen White was located. Zoíla knew how to work in the house and on the farm— where she came from, no one had any other work—so after the operation they put her in the salad department. She chopped carrots, radishes, celery—chopped everything. On Saturday, the holy day, she was sitting on the veranda with her landlady, and saw two doctors dressed in white, one carrying small white bottles on a tray. Why have they come? When they said they were taking orders for milk, she ran upstairs to a woman with a baby and to a Colombian who drank milk like water every day, and both of them ordered four gallons a week. With that, one of the milkmen says that his friends who have recently come from Argentina would be delighted to make her acquaintance. The following day, Sunday, Zoíla is still in bed—the telephone rings. Señora Weinstein. "We would be very pleased if you would join us for dinner."

The Weinsteins had escaped to Argentina from Germany and Benito came from Germany. They spoke in their language and all their acquaintances spoke that way, Zoíla was convinced they were Germans. After maybe a year, at a party at the Weinsteins', someone addressed her in that language. "I can't speak German," she replied and everybody laughed.

"Why didn't you tell her? In America?"

"I had neither money nor position, I was afraid that she'd leave me."

"So it was better to be a German?"

"Of course."

"Even after what they had done?"

"Even after that . . ."

Zoíla understood that even less. She knew it had something to do with Jesus. But that was a very long time ago. What was it about now?

Ben had no success distributing milk, so when the Weinsteins decided to open a fur business in New York and offered him work, Ben and Zoíla went with them. Ben sewed on a machine, Zoíla sewed linings by hand. Six months of the year, they would get furs ready for winter and then they would go to Florida. They bought one floor on Coney Island, and later a small house in Queens. Zoíla brought Alejandro in, and then Sofia, then her parents, then Isaac, Fernando and Rafael, only her oldest sister stayed in Peru. Michał, an officer who had been thrown out of the Polish army and of Poland, also came. The Peruvians accepted him as their own brother. They all helped each other. Redecorating, painting, the whole clan came and worked. When someone fell sick, they all looked after him.

Michał came from the airport in the evening, he sits, drinks tea, and suddenly sees that the wall is moving. He thinks to himself that things are moving in front of his eyes because he's tired. He looks— it's not tiredness, but huge, yellow cockroaches marching up and down the walls. He leapt up onto his feet, and Ben says, "It's nothing, they don't bite, or at most each other, they just live here." In pots, bowls, the refrigerator. How did they get into the refrigerator? And in his room. *His* room? It was *their* room, he was just an intruder. But they really didn't do anything to him—tolerant, Americanized, concerned with their own affairs. People came, disinfected, but after a few days new ones moved in, the whole of New York was occupied by them. When the Chinese bought a house like that, they would take it down to the foundations, put in concrete barriers, cover them with tar, and then burn incense in the rooms day and night.

Zoíla's mother cried all the time. She didn't know the language, she felt trapped. She had diabetes, took medications which damaged her kidneys and heart. Nothing could be done. The father who, in Peru, had liked to drink and party, suddenly got a prostate gland attack and had to be operated on. After the operation, he allowed himself to be baptized and even tried to make up for his deficiencies in reading the Scriptures. He didn't complain about pain in his eyes and nobody knew he had glaucoma until his eyes gave out. At first, he used to ask "Where are we?" and after the mother's death, he completely lost track of where he was, thought he was in Peru. He would go to the threshold of his room, lean against the door-frame, and, hand on the back of his neck, talk to invisible people. Zoíla even lit a big lamp on purpose. He'd push his hat onto his forehead as though against the Peruvian sun and question former neighbors about the harvest. He'd address them by name and nod his head in agreement because he could hear them. Then he'd say to Zoíla, "Help me climb up." "Where do you want to climb?" she'd ask. You had to climb to get to their house in Peru.

Ben and Zoíla played in church—he the violin, she the piano. When they practiced, Michał would run out of the house—the cockroaches were nothing! Ben would put on a tie, a carefully pressed shirt, Zoíla would inspect him from all sides. The roof of the wooden church was shaped like a tent, and the curtain in the wall and the podium also resembled a synagogue. Pale, modest stained glass windows, abstract in design. No cross, Jesus had carried it off for them. Nor statues, nor holy pictures—no idols, in accordance with the Commandments. Nor any work on Saturdays except helping the sick. In some countries, they were locked up in prison for refusing to work on Saturday; churches were taken away from them, so they prayed under the trees; forbidden to sing, they sang in their hearts. They didn't observe Christmas or Easter. For others, Jesus was born, died and rose from the dead every year. They knew from the Scriptures that he had been born once, died once, and went to heaven once. And that it was essential that he should come again.

The service was above all a lesson, also like a synagogue. From the Bible, of course. The Bible had once been forbidden by the Church. Inspectors went into houses. A woman was baking bread. Noticing that inspectors were on their way, she stuffed the Bible into a loaf and put it into the oven. The bread was baked, and the Bible saved, food both for body and spirit. The Protestants rescued the Bible, the Baptists popularized it, because there were no Adventists as yet—but nobody studied it more diligently than they did. With them, it was a bit like in synagogue in the old world when you "bought" a piece of *Torah* and such a "bridegroom" gave a reception for everyone. "Bridegroom" because in singing the verses of the *Torah* he was marrying it. You'd pour small glasses of vodka, Mother would serve herring and calf's foot jelly, and the poor would eat as much as they could. Here, as well, you'd bring food from home and place it on a communal table. Not pork, Heaven forbid! Forty-two nationalities used to meet in the small church in Queens. Whites, Blacks, Hindi, Puerto Ricans, Peruvian Indians, certainly not rich, but neatly dressed, prayed earnestly and sang while Ben and Zoíla played. Everyone knew and took an interest in each other, that was important to Ben. God didn't concern him much. For him, it was a place where he could be with Zoíla. He moved into her religion as he had into her house.

She was greatly concerned that Ben had a son somewhere and no one knew what had become of him. She went to the German Consulate and to the International Red Cross. He was discovered in Düsseldorf, living with his stepfather and a younger half-brother. The mother wasn't there because she ran off after the birth of the second one as well. She drank during pregnancy and that second son was not a success. They exchanged letters and photographs, Zoíla had a portrait made from the photograph and showed it off with pride—our son. He came for a visit, handsome, like Ben only a lot taller and fatter. He had a music shop and was doing quite well, but wasn't marrying. Ben asked him whether he would like to take back his real name. No, he answered, because he owed everything to his stepfather who had brought him up alone and who didn't really have anyone but him.

Zoíla couldn't breathe in New York, so they sold the cockroaches to the Chinese and moved to Florida. Ben had a pension from the Germans and Social Security. He made extra as a guard in a supermarket and loaded groceries into cars for old people who spoke to him in "German," while Zoíla did real estate. They bought a small house in St. Petersburg where there was a Spanish-speaking congregation. And then another in North Port where there were hot springs.

St. Petersburg was flat, one-story houses, ten miles by ten. A hundred streets lengthwise, a hundred crosswise, and a church of a little different denomination on each. They borrowed a church from the Baptists on Saturdays for a hundred dollars, but each time

Ben opened it a dreadful alarm sounded, the police and the fire department came, so they gave it up. Fernando took out the wall dividing their living from the dining room, they hung Jesus cut out of a plastic cloth on a nail, put up a podium with a microphone—for what kind of church would it be without a microphone? In front of the house, they placed a large sign *Bienvenidas,* and a small plaque on the door, *Shalom.* The congregation made up of people from Puerto Rico, Santo Domingo, Cuba, Aruba, Ecuador, Bolivia and Peru sat in five rows of seats. Isaac's and Alejandro's daughters dressed in perfect Spanish skirts which concealed and revealed everything as they should, slipped between the rows with Spanish agility and grace handing out Bibles and *Himnario Adventista.* If someone didn't know Spanish, they'd sit down next to them and translate word for word into their ear. When the Messiah comes, there will be only one language, most probably Spanish. *"Cuán dulce en este día de paz,"* Zoíla intoned in a clear child-like voice. *"Hoy el sabado glorioso, santo sabado lo llama es el día del Señor,"* echoed Ben in stentorian tones. Zoíla proclaimed that the Second Coming was near, Ben that the Day of Judgement was at hand. In this way, both the Christian wolf was sated and the Jewish lamb remained whole, but when they knelt, it was sad to see Ben on his knees.

They fenced off the driveway so it wouldn't get stained by the cars' droppings, and put up a table covered with a white plastic cloth. A grey-haired guitarist in jeans and Spanish cowboy boots, a convert, played and sang sentimental tangos—the same as before his conversion, but *amor* now referred to God and rhymed with *dolor* and *Salvador.* And no one danced, just listened pensively, slightly tapping a foot.

The house stood in an undeveloped green area between an old railroad line and a freeway whose roar resembled the sea. In the garden they had oranges, grapefruit, guavas, papayas. They trod on sweet golden *nisperos* which they couldn't keep up with picking. Benito climbed up the roof on a ladder, and from the roof up a tree. He still had dextrous hands and feet. They cut a piece of sugar-cane before breakfast—a heavy stick which they chopped into pieces and sucked its sweet morning cool. They also had sweet lemons which have to be sucked quickly because their sweetness turns bitter a minute after cutting. The mango tree died one night from unexpected frost, so Zoíla cut the dead trunk in March under a full moon and the root sent out two new shoots. They ate Quaker Oats and *kiełbasa* made out of vegetables—a healthy diet is very important if one wants to see the Second Coming. But the refrigerator also contained pickled cucumbers, a jar of herring and rye bread for Benito, because it's easier to change religion than food. The Seventh Day Adventists didn't permit alcohol but on Friday evening an open bottle of sweet Jewish Manischewitz appeared on the table, Zoíla couldn't resist. Zoíla cooked, Ben peeled potatoes—thinly, carefully. And no one said grace before meals—in Spanish or in English—as solemnly as Ben.

Zoíla served her father five kinds of *cabuco,* six kinds of beans, every kind of melon and a long white *navo* radish which can be eaten raw or cooked. She'd put the dish in front of him and direct his hand like a child's. She bathed him, anointed his skin. He looked good and moved around quite well, but, because he couldn't see and that's dangerous at his age, sat in a wicker chair under the fig tree and talked with his friends whom only he could see or napped peacefully, as though he'd never left Peru.

Saturday and Sunday they spent in St. Petersburg, after which they got into a big station-wagon, the kind that hasn't been manufactured for a long time (Fernando picked it out for them at a used car lot), and drove to North Port—with Father, fluffy white female dog, *Oychour* (which means "star" in the Quechua language), white cat *Misho* ("cat" in Quechua—Ben called him Misha), a pair of beige doves and a pair of multicolored chaffinches. The springs in North Port had more minerals than Baden-Baden and Vichy put together, and old people from the entire continent rested there after the hardships of life. Old acquaintances suddenly met in azure baths and on pastures of eternal green after thirty or forty years. "Joe, is that you?" "Is that you, Jane?" Like in the next world. They were people with a various accents and culinary habits, so long self-service counters—both in St. Petersburg, in North Port, and everywhere along the road—offered them boiled, baked, fried salt- and fresh-water fish; grilled, fried and sauteed breasts, thighs and wings of turkeys and chicken; well-done, medium, rare roast beef and steaks; boiled, stewed, raw multicolored bouquets of vegetables; thin and thick sauces and soups for every diet, and columns of tortes, cakes and cobblers out of all manner of fruit to everyone's fancy. And eat as much as you can—for just six-fifty. And for seniors over fifty-five, twenty-five percent off! So they ate, as much as they could and more than they could, and sighed, "God Bless America!"—mutually reassuring themselves in this way that this plenty was still not what their Bible called "green pastures." In the eternally green pastures of Florida, housing cost half what it had in their former life, health care was free for seniors, and there was no income-tax. If you add to that the atrophy of sex, what could be closer to Heaven?

Alejandro brought himself a wife from Peru, but met another woman in New York and had children with both. Because they lived together happily, he was called *cacique*—head of the tribe. Rafael left behind in Peru a woman with whom he had four out-of-wedlock children. He brought two sons up later and they bore his name, but he couldn't become an Adventist. Isaac, married to a Peruvian, had eight children and all were Adventists. Fernando married a woman of German descent who was jealous, irritable and worked hard. She lost her memory totally one day and had to be committed to an asylum. He worked in a shipyard. When orders for seagoing ships ran out, he built spaceships—to the Moon, Jupiter and Mars. It was his work which circled through space, an Indian's from Yurimaguas, tributary of the Amazon where to this day they play on pipes out of human bones. When spaceships stopped being built, he bought himself a fleet of taxis in St. Petersburg, and took up with a dispatcher from Kentucky, thirty years younger than he was, who immediately got pregnant. Fernando had no children in Peru or anywhere else, so no one believed it was his, but he had himself tested and it turned out that he could be the father. The dispatcher doubled in size after the birth and, at two hundred and forty pounds of living flesh, gave birth again—out-of-wedlock, because Fernando still had that wife in the asylum. The dispatcher didn't belong to any faith, said she was allergic to religion. Sofia became a nurse in Los Angeles and married a Korean from Hawaii, a Catholic, who became an Adventist. Their children looked typically Hawaiian. Isaac's daughter married a German who became an Adventist. Alejandro's son, an officer, married a military woman, Catholic, who did not change her religion. At Christmas, both those who recognized the holiday, and those who didn't, met in Florida. Ben and Zoíla played for them. Ben didn't always hit the mark with the bow (that interval in the ghetto and camps had been too long), so he helped himself out with his fingers like on the guitar, and when something didn't work out on the piano, Zoíla would finish the piece on a white Peruvian pipe. Achim also came. Ben sent him a ticket, although Achim could easily have bought it himself. By then, he had several music shops, classical and popular, spoke English and read the *Wall Street Journal*. His stepfather died suddenly of a heart-attack, his brother moved to Berlin, but Achim never went back to his real name. He preferred to be German. The last descendant of a murdered Jewish family. And never married, though his girlfriend bore him a son.

They bought another little house in Pinellas Park, as an investment. The houses had to be looked after, repaired and reinforced, because satanic hurricanes waited at the edge of Heaven. So every few days, they moved from one to another with Father, dog, cat and birds. The station-wagon smelled more and more like Noah's Ark. Ben also began to lose track of where he was. He'd call his cousins, they'd ask "Where are you?" and he'd say, "I don't know where I am." He always went around cleanly dressed and never ate anywhere but at a table set with a cloth, because that was deeply ingrained in him. Otherwise he attached no value to material things and would have taken the shirt off his back and given it away. Whatever he saved, he sent off. Nobody asked him for anything—what was he, a millionaire? He sent money to Regina on the kibbutz, widowed with two small children. The children grew up, did military service, lived in concrete houses in the Sinai and tended cucumbers. Mountains of sand, a few palms, a few camels, suddenly the sands open—cucumbers! After the agreement with Egypt, they had to leave those cucumbers, but with the restitution bought a penthouse in Tel Aviv and a small villa in Hertzliya. Regina married a second time and Benito kept sending. They said to him, "She's got fairly wealthy children who love her dearly, her second husband isn't a loser either, so maybe you don't need to keep sending." "Why are you saying this to me? Whom am I going to help then?" When Michał's daughter was getting married, he sent a letter with a hundred dollars inside.

First, a huge area was cut out for a building-materials warehouse. Then, a heavy truck, light truck and trailer leasing company was built there. Then, Mercedes and Volkswagen service shops. Then, a school with a playing-field. Then, a boxing club. Their garden between the freeway and the railroad line became an oasis. Their fig tree was stolen while they were in North Port. By the roots. Fernando's mango tree was stolen in the same fashion when he went on an unmarried honeymoon with the dispatcher. Chinese refugees from Vietnam did it, boat people, who had been pulled from the sea. How was it known it was them? Who else would have stolen a tree? Zoíla's father wasn't complaining about anything, but ate less and less. One day, he said to her, "Don't give me any more food. I'm tired, I want to die, I want to rest." There was nothing wrong with him: heart, blood-pressure, cholesterol—all perfect. He just didn't want to go on.

They fished on a jetty extending far into the bay, and shared the fish with pelicans. The pelicans knew them, stood to the side and waited. Grey and white, short legs like ducks, long storklike necks, long thick beaks, baggy throats. They fed their young with those throats and not with breasts. They waited patiently, in a civilized manner, like Americans. A slender white heron would stand at a respectable distance off on the side, his shapely aristocratic beak and head held high on his long delicate neck. He would gaze off into the distance listening to the zephyr, as though this was not about food.

Ben had dextrous hands and feet, but put out a plate which was too small, a knife which was too big, and cut grapefruit lengthwise instead of crosswise. He had trouble finding his car in large parking lots, and had to be read the names of streets he was passing. He didn't notice signals, and several times drove onto a drawbridge as it was being raised. It was hard for them to drive on the increasingly busy freeway. They decided to leave St. Petersburg and to set up a congregation in North Port. They signed Pinellas over to the local Adventists for a house of worship. Benito underwent a prostate operation successfully, but his stomach bothered him. Zoíla was having trouble breathing again. Those frequent hurricanes on the coasts also distressed them. Perhaps after they sold the house in St. Petersburg, they'd buy in Peru? Fernando would leave too. He'd return to the farm in Yurimaguas.

Peru is much larger than on the map. Bolivia and Ecuador, which the Europeans signed away, are all Peru. And large parts of Argentina and Chile. The Cajamarca springs are the deepest in the world, and the most effective. And Titicaca is the deepest lake, no one has sounded its bottom because it doesn't have one. They also wouldn't have found the Palace of Atahualpa, if he hadn't been given fresh fish from the sea passed to him every day from hand to hand, on gold trays. Pizarro who landed on the beach just followed those trays. Atahualpa was a giant. A hundred men were needed to carry his gold chain. The entrance to a tunnel, the longest in the world, was hidden behind a tapestry in the palace. No one knew where it led, because whoever went in never returned. Atahualpa threw his golden chain there so as not to give it to the Spaniards. They handed him a cross and ordered him to kiss it. "What is it?" He threw it to the ground. They ripped him apart with horses. He was very strong. With horses, they ripped apart our Inca. And Velasco de la Vega took our princess and had a son by her, Garcilaso. Young Garcilaso saw the Incas weeping by the walls, asked why they wept and wrote everything down. That's how we know.

Four thousand kinds of potatoes grew in Peru. And *puru-puru* whose thorny flower the Christians called "Passion." The elixir made from it soothes the soul. Its delicate fruit, also called "Passion," prolongs life. And the milky tree of Chuchuacha whose milk—white resin—cures anemia and worms. Just a tiny glass on an empty stomach for ten days, that's all. Peru had plants for everything. And air—mountain air for the lungs, lowland air for asthma and the heart. Peru was the past which, by contrast with Ben's past, still existed. That's why he would go there with Zoíla. But on the phone, once, he said he was sad he'd die so far away. And more and more often, he called across the ocean at dawn to talk to his distant cousins.

A Family

For Piotr, Valentina Nikolayevna, Isaak Markovich and Lena

1. Volkovitsky

Coat-of-arms Lubicz. Cross in horseshoe on shield field of blue, above the shield, a helmet and three ostrich feathers. From a warrior who had fought valiantly against the pagans above the river Drwęca, known at that time, the thirteenth century, as Lubicz. There is also a Lubicz with two crosses in a horseshoe or one in the middle and the other on the arc of the horseshoe, and one which has a cross on the arc of the horseshoe and a six-pointed star inside. Lubicz was also the seal of Brzeziński, Brzozowski, Chojecki, Choromański, Czartoryski, Czerwiński, Kijowski, Lisowski, Łysakowski, Niezabitowski, Piczkowski, Potocki, Rakowski, Rapacki, Romanowicz, Skolimowski, Sulimirski, Szumborski, Zahorski, Zaleski, Żydowicz. Catherine II, discovering a suspiciously large number of gentry on the Polish-Lithuanian lands she had annexed, ordered verification. Papers of the Land Court confirmed that Stepan, son of Olechna, for services in war on behalf of the throne, had received from the Lithuanian prince, Kazimierz Jagiełło, later king of Poland, Tokary in the Grodno area. Of Stepan's descendants, the brothers Łukasz, Marko and Iwan Rusiło Wołkowicki figure in the records of 1598 as the co-owners of Tokary and Wólka, which had been in their possession since 1523 under the rule of the "Polish King Zygmunt I of blessed memory." Iwan Rusiło begot Fiodor and Griszka; Fiodor begot Ivan, Jan and Daniło, and one of Jan's five sons was Mikołaj. The verification had been undertaken scrupulously and unhurriedly, as indicated by the

protocol of *Grodnenskoye Dvoryanskoye Deputatskoye Sobraniye* of
the 25th of July, 1847, in which it is mentioned that Michał
Wołkowicki received the required certificate on the 5th of February,
1820, and Ildefons only on the 22nd of November, 1822. Also pre-
served is the report of the General Staff of the 6th of October, 1886,
which states that Ildefons Wołkowicki, son of Michał, lieutenant-
colonel and *uyezdny vojensky-nachalnik,* decorated with the Order of
Saint Vladimir, Fourth Class with ribbon; St. Anna, Third Class; St.
Anna, Second Class; St. Stanislaus, Second and Third Class, as well
as the Bronze Medal of the 1853–56 War, after forty-six years of
service for the Tsar, retired in 1856. In Rubric VI—Faith: Roman
Catholic. The report mentions his wife Aleksandra Mihaylovna
(daughter of Captain Studyonny), the sons, Ilya and Waldemar
(who having converted to the Orthodox church changed his name
to Vladimir) as well as daughters Anna, Varvara and Maria. The
Catholic and Orthodox Wołkowickis or Volkovitskys did not maintain relations with each other. My great-grandmother, grandmother
and mother, having lived many years in Warsaw, never met our Polish relatives.

Great-Grandmother, Princess Matilda Kudashev, came from a
Tatar family, from Kudash, whose son was Tchepai Mirzha Kudashev. Their princely title is recorded in *Shatskiye Pistsovyje Knigi* in
1649. Alei, great-grandson of Tchepai, christened as Vassily, was
esquire to Tsar Aleksei Mihaylovich, from whom he received
Rakovo in Shatsky District. Colonel Danilo Ivanovich Kudashev
(1760–1845) gave it up to his uncle Fyodor. An illustrious family.
Their portraits hang in the Hermitage—Hall of the Heroes of
1812. Prince Sergei Danilovich (1796–1862), chamberlain and
governor of Kiev, married Princess Matilda Oktavyevna Choiselle-
Goufier, and their son Vladimir (1833–1871) married Olga Nikolayevna Horvat. My great-grandfather Vladimir Ildefonsovich came
to Princess Olga to buy horses for his regiment and created such a
good impression that he received not only horses but a daughter,
Matilda. The marriage produced four sons and three daughters.
Vladimir Ildefonsovich, who had risen to the rank of general, edu-

cated his sons in the Pages' Corps and his daughters at Smolny. The oldest, Aleksandra, finished the Institute and married Piotr Avgustovich Gelwich, an officer who lectured on theory of artillery at the College of the General Staff. A Baltic German, not tall, with pointed, dyed whiskers. In 1912, he solved the problem of an aircraft cannon whose recoil was too strong for an airplane. He did this in a very simple manner: constructed a gun which shot forwards and backwards at the same time—backwards with blank ammunition of course—and both recoils reduced themselves mutually, not affecting the wings or the course of the airplane. My grandmother, ten years younger than Aleksandra, interrupted her studies and went to the front as a Sister of Mercy. The youngest, Miletina, was still a child then. Two hospital trains were filled with young ladies from good families. The one in which Grandmother served bore the name of Tsarina Aleksandra Fyodorovna. The doctors, on the other hand, came from various classes and in this way she met Dr. Ludwig Rapaport of Łódź, who had been educated in Germany. Grandmother, raised as a devout Orthodox, wanted to be married in the church, but the Orthodox church did not allow marriages with Jews. The Lutheran church did, on condition that children would be raised Lutheran. That's why my mother was Lutheran. Doctors weren't killed in the civil war, so this part of the family survived.

Grandmother's brothers fought the Reds. The youngest, Oleg, whom she loved most, perished in central Asia; Rostislav in Ukraine; Yuri in France under romantic circumstances at the hands of his lover—Grandmother did not give me the specific details because I was too young—Vladimir joined Piłsudski. Eight of them stand in a semi-circle. In front, a round table and on it a cup, a statuette with a clock, a horn—all finely decorated. Behind them, a dark wall, shadows of trees. Three are tall, Vladimir the tallest. Four-cornered hats with high rims and sparkling silver eagles; silver zigzags on collars; shapely jodhpurs; glossy boots with spurs or without. Vladimir with upturned moustache, two others with cropped whiskers. Vladimir has high cheek-bones and a short scar between left eye and ear—a centimeter from the temple—his Tatar cheek-bone saved him. Vladimir and another tall one with canes. No sabres. Arms folded behind or in front—the year is 1922, nothing to do. They look at the lens casually, in a gentlemanly manner, Vladimir not at all, and no one is smiling. And here, a close-knit group, the cadre of the Sixteenth Regiment. Vladimir is sitting with the senior officers, the younger ones at their knees leaning on their elbows, the rest stand at the back. "Seniors" and "younger" only in rank, because they are equally shapely and agile, their faces equally hardened, as though all are of the same age. They had galloped through the same fields, the same slaughters and graves— not a trace of youth in their eyes. The third photo on horseback: Uhlan Rzelichowski, Colonel Volkovitsky, Senior Uhlan Rozbut— ranks and names in Russian letters above their heads, and no longer readable names of the horses under the hoofs. After leaving the military, Vladimir settled on an estate in the Grodno District and was killed there in September 1939 by peasants attacking manor houses. He left no one behind, and my grandmother maintained that I was his heir. She knew what that estate was called, but I've forgotten. She thought I looked like Vladimir and it shows in the photos.

Great-Grandmother Matilda also fled to the Polish side, with Miletina. Three women on three sides of a table; screen with delicate oriental patterns in the background; dark dresses up to the neck, hair pinned high. One has tied it up with a bright ribbon, the second has put on a hat in the shape of a halo, the third one nothing. One wears a cameo, the second a cross, the third one nothing. It's not known when or where it is, and it's hard to tell their age from the murky photograph, but the clothing and hairstyle are from before the revolution, and they all seem beautiful. And here, too, neither a smile nor "a pleasant facial expression," they're thinking their own thoughts as if no photographer were there, and each is looking somewhere else: the one with the cross and the halo straight ahead, the one with the ribbon and cameo leans her head toward some memory, the one with no decorations has lowered her eyelids and gazes into herself. I don't know who the other two are, but that third one is Great-Grandmother Matilda.

The Bolsheviks took Gelwich hostage when Yudenich was marching on Petrograd. Yudenich never got there, so they let him go. After the war, they retained him as a lecturer in the same Military College and in the thirties, arrested him together with other senior officers. He was released—either by Yezhov when he took over after Yagoda, or by Beria when he took over after Yezhov—because he proved indispensable to the armaments industry and was transferred to Moscow. He designed cannons and wrote interesting works about the theory of probability, with which theory the artillery is closely allied. He received an apartment on Gorky Street and the Stalin Prize.

After the civil war, Grandmother also found herself in Moscow where Dr. Rapaport was working in a clinic. They lived among the intelligentsia which did not like Bolsheviks. Grandmother used to say how happy everybody was when that maniac Lenin died. In the summer of 1924, she took her five-year-old daughter and went for a cure abroad—to see her mother, sister and brother. The place of the ostensible cure was Sopot. Grandmother was an attractive woman. My mother claimed that Aleksandra was the smartest, Miletina the most talented, and Grandmother the prettiest. In Sopot, Grandmother met a journalist, Wacław Olszewski, who was taking a summer vacation, and wrote to Dr. Rapaport that she wasn't coming back. She settled in Warsaw with that Olszewski who also turned out to be a Jew. I don't remember his real name, I only know that he was forever establishing newspapers which always collapsed. Dr. Rapaport, seeing no reason to stay in Russia, returned to his family in Łódź—that was still possible in the twenties. He became chief surgeon in a Jewish hospital, earned a good salary and saw to his daughter's education. She completed a prestigious Warsaw gymnasium attended by high-brow youth with leftist leanings and met socialists. Grandmother said that she had to air the apartment for hours each time those socialists left. Mother didn't get into Warsaw University because she had a Jewish surname and—also from her father—a prominent nose, so Dr. Rapaport sent her to the Sorbonne. She stayed there with his wealthy friend, Zhenya Rivoche, a Russian Jew, who had made his money buying art from the Bolsheviks. Grandmother immediately went to visit her, embarked on a romance with Zhenya and stayed in Paris which seemed much more attractive to her than Warsaw. At the time, Zhenya's nephew, Georges Barski, a student at the École Polytechnique, wooed my mother. In summer 1939 both came to Poland—Mother for a vacation, Grandmother to set her personal affairs straight—and they did not make it back to France. Mother fled to Lwów, Grandmother stayed in Warsaw.

Grandmother traded in cosmetics she made herself and managed quite well. But in 1944 she was caught and sent to Auschwitz like many other illegal traders. I don't know any specific details because she didn't like to talk about it, only that when she received a little margarine, she wouldn't eat it but used it as a face cream, because in Auschwitz you had to look healthy to survive. Grandfather Ludwik survived the Łódź ghetto where doctors were badly needed. But towards the end of August 1944 when our liberating army stood and watched as Warsaw burned, the Germans gathered trains and deported that last ghetto—over sixty-thousand people—to Auschwitz. Great-Grandmother Matilda died in Warsaw in 1943. Miletina volunteered for labor in Germany. She found herself in Dresden in February 1945 when the famous Allied carpet bombing covered the town and thousands of foreign laborers.

The Volkovitskys did not like Jews. One of Grandmother's brothers, she wouldn't say which, even belonged to the Black Hundred. At the same time all three of her husbands and her son-in-law were Jews. I once asked her why she had spent her life with Jews, and she replied in all seriousness that it was a punishment from God. "For what?" I asked. "For the sins of my father," she said. "What sins?" It turned out that General Volkovitsky had a second family in Warsaw. In Petersburg he lived with Princess Kudashev, his lawful wife, and in Warsaw with a Jewish woman by whom he had three daughters. It all came out into the open when he died in Warsaw in 1905. Grandmother didn't like to speak about it, so I don't know what happened to that branch of our tree. I only know the Russian and the Polish-Tatar past of our family.

Father came from Przemyśl. His father had a metal workshop. His older sister, Syda, was a pianist. Her fiancé studied in Lwów—I don't remember his first or last name. The younger, Irena, was still going to school. Father did not get into Lwów Polytechnic—there were only two places for Jews. He forged metal in his father's workshop. Made a balustrade for a balcony as his craftsman's diploma project. He got in for academic year 1938–39. The other Jew was his friend, Józek Backenroth. At lectures they stood because they didn't want to sit on the so-called "ghetto benches." Jewish students were beaten, several were killed, Syda's fiancé among them.

"On November 18, 1938, the Pan-Polish Youth beat Jews coming out of lectures. A janitor hid several in the laboratory but they were found and slashed with knives—Samuel Proweller died two weeks later in the hospital. On the evening of November 24, four students coming out of the Pharmacology Department were attacked—Karol Zellermayer, stabbed with a knife, died that same night. On May 24, 1939, at the Polytechnic, Markus Landsberg of Zbaraż was wounded with a knife and died two days later in the hospital. Was one of them Syda's fiancé?"

I don't know . . . Two of Father's uncles had gone to Palestine and wrote telling them to flee, but they couldn't because they had built a house and were heavily in debt. They fled east in September, but when the border was drawn at the river San, their house turned out on the Soviet side, so they returned home. In June 1941, the Germans just jumped over the San, and no one escaped them. Grandfather was called Chaim Orenstein, Grandmother's name was Gizella.

Mother wasn't accepted at the Polytechnic in Lwów because she didn't have papers. She crossed the frozen San at night, reached Warsaw and went back to Lwów the same way. After seeing her papers, they said they didn't accept refugees from the West. My father, a rightful citizen of the section of Przemyśl which had become part of the Soviet Union, offered her a fictitious marriage but she refused. She went to Gelwich in Moscow. Gelwich put on his uniform with all rhomboids, took her by the arm and went straight to Pyetrovka. The guard stood to attention. "To the Commissar!" Gelwich commanded. "What do you need, Comrade *Voyenatchalnik?* asked the Commissar. "Register my relation under my apartment on Gorky Street," replied Comrade *Voyenatchalnik.*

The Polytechnic was evacuated to Altay. Father was sent to the Institute of Aviation evacuated from Moscow. Mother entered the Energetics Institute, evacuated from Moscow and returned with this institute to Moscow in 1943. Father completed three years, but did not receive security clearance for a fourth, so he finished aviation in a less secret institute in Tomsk and signed up as a volunteer with the First Polish Air Regiment. He already knew then that no one from his family was alive. Before leaving for the front, he proposed my mother a real marriage and this time she accepted. As soon as they occupied Warsaw, he went to my grandmother's address, but that house was no longer there. He left a card in the ruins. When Grandmother appeared at his base in Dęblin, he reported that he was her daughter's husband, and kept her as a translator because most officers in that regiment either didn't know Russian or Polish.

Father didn't like Russia and would have gladly stayed in Poland where he had been offered a military career, but Mother didn't like Poland and didn't want to go back, so he came with Grandmother to Moscow. Gelwich was locked up again because now attention was directed at a completely different kind of weapon and he was no longer needed. Their apartment on Gorky Street was taken away. Aleksandra sold things and sent parcels to the labor camp, saving his life. They all lived in a communal apartment out of which the police kept chasing Grandmother because she didn't have the right to live in Moscow. An emigré, an aristocrat, the daughter of a tsarist general! There were big problems with Grandmother, and it would have ended badly had it not been for Ilya Erenburg. During his studies at the Aviation Institute, my father had got to know Grisha Gershonzon who was a close relative of the famous Pushkinist, Gershonzon—and through him Erenburg signed what was needed or said a word. It wasn't easy. Erenburg's daughter, Irina, when she met Lena, my wife, thirty years later, remembered the affair.

We lived in a room, fourteen meters square, with brick coal-burning stove and kitchen shared with neighbors, with no bath, no toilet, water brought up from the yard. We had electricity, and, with time, gas was brought in. It was a two-story barracks, a wooden structure filled in with cinders, like all of those on Fourth Vladimirskaya Street (there were several Vladimirskiye Streets) by the road to Vladimir which, for some reason, had been called the Road of Enthusiasts. We lived there ten years, first four of us, and then five when my sister Olga was born. Mother was always busy, Grandmother brought me up.

"How did she stand such conditions?"

With stoic calm. She placed no value on material things, knew from experience how transitory they were, said that the most important thing was what we had in ourselves. She passed her inner resources on to me. What I have is from her.

Father and Mother worked in institutes and on their doctoral dissertations: she in power engineering, he on high-octane airplane fuels. Father, who worked in an environment with a large density of lead, received milk and buttered rolls daily. He drank the milk, but brought the roll for me. The first thing I remember in life is waiting for Father and his buttered roll. When I was four, a mechanic from his regiment arrived, Leon Wyszyński, also a Jew. He had been sent from Poland to the Moscow Military College and was staying at the Metropol Hotel. We went to see him, and the second thing I remember in life is the great Metropol Hotel.

It wasn't bad for me in our barracks with Grandmother who devoted her entire time to me. I was treated like one of the boys in the courtyard and on the street where the *shpana* ruled. Adolescents, I once saw them surround someone and stab him to death with a knife. I was six years old then. Nobody touched me, I was a local. I had nothing to do in school, I skipped grades. In 1949 both Father and Mother lost their jobs and then it was bad for us.

"Was it then that your grandmother decided that God had punished her by a life with Jews?"

Absolutely not. She saw things in different dimensions. After what she had seen during the civil war, in occupied Warsaw and in Auschwitz . . .

Father recalled that he had a house in Przemyśl and he managed to sell it, but Stalin when he heard about it, ordered a conversion of money and nothing was left. Father came down with full-blown TB and could breathe only with one lung. Grandmother went to work in the hospital, after all she had been a Sister of Mercy. She liked the work, but made scarcely enough money to live on. We were saved by a commercial councillor from the Polish embassy who gave Mother a job. Perhaps through Wanda Wasilewska, because Mother knew her and many other people from Lwów who found themselves with the authorities in Poland after the war. Her job involved industrial plants which had been sent to Poland, like "Pobyeda," manufacturing cars renamed "Warszawa" in Poland. Mother, who knew technical terminology in both languages, checked and corrected documentation. It wasn't fascinating work, but paid well. She lost the job in 1956 when Bierut died during a visit to Moscow and the Polish embassy didn't want any more Soviet workers. Father got a new job with thermal treatment of metals which didn't require any security clearance. In 1957 we were given two rooms so that Father, a tuberculoid, could sleep by himself. The third room in the same apartment was occupied by a retired policeman, an anti-Semite. It was a normal, many-storied house in Moscow proper. There I was accosted in the courtyard and called a Jew.

Grandmother's surname was Volkovitskaya, Mother's Rapaport, while Father, I, and my sister were Orensteins. In the Soviet Union, married women could maintain their maiden names, and children could use the surnames of either the father or the mother. The same thing with *natsonalnost*. Children of mixed marriages were eagerly written down as Russians so that there'd be as many Russians as possible. My mother, though a Rapaport, was identified as Russian in the documents. When I finished school and was going to get an identity card, Mother took Grandmother's surname, and then signed me and my sister over to herself. In this way we became Volkovitskys and only Father remained Orenstein. Father didn't object, being pragmatic, he didn't want to make life difficult for his children. But the mathematics teacher whose favorite student I was, held it against me. He came into class, sat at the desk and read us a poem about people who changed their surnames, forsook their identities, were afraid of being themselves, ran away from their own shadow. Mother was outraged. Because I'm myself, I am a Volkovitsky and a Russian. I didn't know my Jewish family, never encountered the Jewish faith or culture. In our home, only Grandmother believed in God—the Russian Orthodox. No Christian holidays were observed in the country, but we did celebrate Easter because it was on Sunday. Everybody baked a cake, painted eggs and drank more than on First of May and the Seventh of November to show that we were Russian. It was a real holiday, the only one observed of free will. Father didn't drink. Mother told me that the only time he'd tried to drink was when he found out what had happened to his family.

I attended a school with a mathematical orientation and there, too, I skipped a grade. In ninth grade I audited classes at the university. I won awards at Math Olympiads, some when I was still Orenstein. I was accepted by the Physics Department at Moscow University thanks to my being Volkovitsky, because they didn't take Jews. I got a degree from the Institute of High Energy, but wasn't accepted for graduate studies because I was a Jew. I went to the Institute of Theoretical and Applied Physics where they did take Jews. It was ever that way: some places took Jews while others didn't. Or sometimes they did and sometimes they didn't, and nobody knew why. But everyone always knew where they did accept and where they didn't. The standards at the Institute of Theoretical and Applied Physics turned out to be higher than at the Institute of High Energy. Because they accepted Jews? Perhaps. During vacations I went to *sovkhozes* to build cow-barns and pig-sties. My college stipend had been fifty rubles but as a carpenter in the students' work group I earned a thousand. As a graduate student I received one hundred and twenty rubles a month, but as a construction worker fifteen hundred. I formed my own work team, transacted private agreements, built *dachas*, moved walls in apartments. In doing so, I found myself in the apartment of my future wife.

I defended my doctoral dissertation on the theory of elementary particles, but didn't get a job because I was a Jew. I wanted to leave like the others, but couldn't because I was Russian. After a time, the head of the laboratory, Professor Ter-Martirosian, said he'd take me on condition that I would promise not to try to leave, because it would endanger him and several other people. It also wasn't easy to make the decision to leave. A friend waited for seven years, on the blacklist, unemployed. I promised.

Aleksandra found Miletina through the Red Cross and brought her to Moscow after the war, but Gelwich was in prison again by then, and she wasn't able to register her. In 1949, Miletina was living in Ashkhabad and made it through that memorable earthquake there. Gelwich kept writing memoranda saying that he had designed a cannon with an unusual explosive force, so after Stalin's death they let him out a little earlier than the others. Before leaving, he demanded his uniform. "You arrested me in uniform, you'll release me in uniform," and wouldn't leave until they gave it to him. This was probably the only time that someone was released from the Gulag in general's uniform. Diakov wrote about it in the first book about the camps which appeared in Russia. Aleksandra again brought Miletina to Moscow. Miletina's nerves were shattered and she never married. Gelwich lay in the hospital for several months and then in the sanatorium of the Ministry of Defense. We visited him there, it was called *Arkhangelskoye*. He'd invented nothing, but wrote those memoranda to get out. Or maybe, after all of this, he just imagined he did in his old age. He died in 1956, and Aleksandra that same year. Miletina stayed in their apartment and worked as a nurse. She wrote fantastical stories for me, and later for my little sister, which she illustrated with even more surreal pictures. Grandmother lost her memory and towards the end of her life didn't remember who she was. The same happened later to Miletina.

Father and Mother went to Poland in 1967. The house in Przemyśl was standing as before. The balustrade Father had made for his diploma still stood on the balcony. But they learned nothing new. A thousand Jews of Przemyśl were killed in Lwów on Janowska Street; sixteen thousand in Bełżec; three-and-a-half thousand in Auschwitz; two thousand were killed on the spot; a group of young people ran into the forest to join the partisans and were murdered there. It's not known where members of Father's family perished. Father received a pension at sixty years of age. Two years later, he was taken to the hospital with TB but died there of a heart attack in his sleep. Mother died five years later, also due to her heart, also on a pension. My sister got a degree in biology but taught chemistry, then worked for a branch of an English chocolate firm and for the American Western Union company. Her husband, a Russian whom she divorced and re-married several times, graduated from the Institute of Aviation.

My grandmother's cousin, Boris Klimov, a geologist, married a Jewish woman before the Revolution, to the outrage of all the Volkovitskys, even though she had herself baptized. Professor Klimov became an associate member of the Academy of Science. They had a magnificent apartment in the center of Moscow, but their daughter, Milena, moved her husband in there, and the son, Slava, moved in his wife. They produced children and the magnificent apartment turned into a horrible *komunal*. Milena's husband, Yura—also a geologist—was a Ukrainian and an implacable anti-Semite. They had three children: Nikita, Boris and Anna. Nikita studied art history and restored paintings. Boris became a physicist. Anna's husband, Andrei, whose mother was Jewish and father Russian, became a religious Jew. When Anna and Andrey filed papers to emigrate to Israel, her anti-Semitic father was fired from his work. Years later, when people were allowed to travel abroad, Milena and Yura went to visit Anna and that old anti-Semite liked Israel so much that he returned as a great friend of Jews. Their son Boris worked with me at the Institute, and it's from him I got our family papers.

2. SHCHORS

He was born in Snovsk, seventy kilometers from Chernihov, the oldest of five brothers and sisters. His father, a Belorussian from the Pinsk swamps, was a railroad driver. The mother's name, Aleksandra, revealed little, but her brother was called Kazimir and her sister, Zosia, which suggested a Polish background. Kazimir, partly a revolutionary, partly a dreamer, tried to build a flying machine, but it fell apart—on the ground. He eluded the police in 1905, but in 1914 they took him to Siberia in shackles. Nikolai went through a four-year parochial school which had a library. He read about the Cossack Sitch, their colonels and *atamans*. He later gave his first regiment the name of Bohun. His mother died of tuberculosis when he was twelve. The father was always on the road, the children had no one to care for them, so he married a second time. The two oldest, Nikolai and Konstantin, he brought to the Army Surgeons' School in Kiev which accepted children of railroad workers free. Nikolai fell in love with medicine there. He didn't want to be a military man, but a physician. After school, he was sent to the Vilna military district and served in a reserve regiment which came under the Tsar's personal command. When war broke out, the Tsar sent his reserve regiment to Poltava and forgot about it. They stayed the whole year in Poltava which had a religious seminary with a well-stocked library. After the Revolution, when it was turned into a rural-technical school, the *Komsomol,* removing inappropriate literature from the library, found a voucher with the name Shchors in one of the books. My mother later found a certificate among his papers. It turned out that while stationed in Poltava, he had taken four courses as an external student in that school. Why? Because it entitled him to get into medical school. That religious seminary is never mentioned in his biography. I come to university, an archivist calls me in one day—a tiny, immaculate, old man. "You're Shchors?" "Yes, Shchors." "Nikolai Aleksandrovich your father?" "Yes, father." He shows me an application. "To the Rector of the Moscow University: I am requesting admission to the Faculty of Medicine when the fighting is over. Nikolai A. Shchors."

Only those of suitable birth could be officers then, but young officers perish quickly in war, and they had to take additional ones from the commoners. He completed the Vilna Military Engineering School, quickly because there was no time, and they sent him to the Pinsk swamps. In the swamps, dug-outs and trenches, he came down with tuberculosis. They kept him at the military hospital in Simferopol for eight months and he returned to Snovsk with a white ticket: unsuitable for military service. His stepmother didn't want him in the house with tuberculosis, and there was no work for him either. When the Reds took power in Snovsk, he had to hide from the Cheka because he was an officer. Uncle Kazimir persuaded the Cheka that Nikolai was not a real officer but one of them. This put him in danger from the other side. His friends came to him one day and said, "Nikolai, you'd better leave, your stepmother's saying that you're a Red bandit." Because an Austrian armored train was approaching Snovsk, he fled with others of military age including Uncle Kazimir and another former exile, Kazimierz Kwiatek, a Pole from Warsaw, with narrow, Tatar eyes. They were heading for Unecha through which the main evacuation was moving, and along the way people joined them. Nikolai was the only officer, so they offered him the command themselves. He led a company, then a battalion, and in Unecha formed a regiment.

At Unecha, Ukraine met Russia and Belorus. My mother, Fruma Rostova, née Haykina, was lying in wait at the Cheka border post for smugglers, who were mostly Jews. She came from nearby Novozybkov. Her father and mother traded in kerosene and both died of tuberculosis. Her brothers got infected with the Revolution, and she caught it from them. Her first love had been Natasha Rostova of *War and Peace,* and she adopted her name. She had lush black hair, blue eyes, delicate features. German soldiers photographed her and sent the prints home as postcards. She saw Shchors—young, handsome, at the head of a regiment—left the Cheka to follow him. She sewed beautifully, made him a uniform. That was September 1918. By November, he had two regiments; in January he took Chernihov; in February Kiev. In March he became the commander of the First Ukrainian Soviet Division. He took Zhitomir and Vinnitsa on the march—on horse and sled—and crushed Petlura's main forces in the region of Sarny, Rovno and Brody. His friend Kwiatek led the Bohun regiment. He established a leadership school. I saw the curriculum: tactics, topography, fortifications and—*tanki.*

"*Tanki?* Gun carts, perhaps? They had no tanks . . ."

Tanki means dances in Ukrainian. Ballroom dances, like in the old officers' school. They had nothing to wear or eat, but an officer had to know how to dance. He set up a medical commune for the wounded and invalids, where they could stay with their families. He was the first to befriend the Germans. He was sent against Czechs, former prisoners-of-war, who had organized an insurrection. He crossed Moscow as one of ten commanders. They stopped there to pay Lenin a visit, but in the book listing all those who paid homage only nine names are to be found, and Shchors was not among them. Why? Because instead of going to the Kremlin and paying tribute to Lenin, he went to the University and applied for medical school. He also stopped in Samara on the Volga, liked it very much and told my mother he would have gladly stayed there forever. He fought Germans, Czechs, Poles, Petlura, White Guard—and tuberculosis. The fever never left him.

That victorious army seemed too independent, and the glittering career of its commander provoked unease among the Bolsheviks who were always afraid of the outstanding. In the summer of 1919, he had Haller and Petlura in front of him, and Denikin in the rear.

He lacked ammunition, clothing, boots and was losing men. As happens in civil war, they went over to the one who had clothing, boots and the advantage. When they lost a fight and had nowhere to go, they returned. But when passing by their village, it was over a fence, into a cottage and again they weren't there. He retook Berdychev with great difficulty, and was defending the Korosten knot to secure the evacuation of Kiev, but the *Voyensoviet* wanted him to break away and relieve Donbas. He didn't do that because it would have meant total retreat and catastrophe. They insisted he move on Kiev, but he knew he had too few forces, and if he went, would lose everything. He was a trained military officer, not a party maniac. They demanded he give them a company of his future officers, the best he had, had trained them himself. And just then he lost the commanders of both brigades: Chernyak by a sniper's bullet in Rovno, Bozhenko by poison in Zhitomir. He could get more men anywhere, but not commanders. They accused him of *partisanshchina* and insubordination. They came so he'd show them his positions. He went with them accompanied by his second-in-command, Dubovoi. A machine gun opened up from a shed and shooting broke out. He got a bullet in the back of his head. They said that he'd turned around to see who was firing, and that's why it was in the back. He was twenty-four years old. Mother was twenty-one.

A problem arose where to bury him. Bozhenko had been buried with honors in Zhitomir. Shortly after, the Petlura army came in, they dug him up, tied him to the tail of a horse and dragged him through town for two days. It was civil war against everyone, dead as well as living. Mother remembered that Samara had greatly appealed to him and no one knew him there. She took him there in a zinc coffin. Her sisters came along, but no one from his family because he was a Red. His brother Konstantin joined *ataman* Skoropadski. Uncle Kazimir was dying, or had died, of tuberculosis in the medical commune in Klintsy. Forty-three days they traveled around. There was no direct road, because civil war was everywhere. They buried him in a cemetery near a metal works—closer to the

working class. When war ended, they returned to put up a grave-
stone but found neither grave nor cemetery—the metal works had
taken everything over. A single tomb remained, in which cleaners
kept brooms and buckets. They dug this way and that, the zinc coffin wasn't there.

I was born within a few months of his death in Klintsy, in the
health clinic he'd established. Mother left me with Dunyasha, a
peasant girl, and went to Moscow, to the enroll at the Workers Department—to learn, learn and learn again, as Lenin prescribed. After that she studied Power Engineering at the Bauman Institute
which had the best specialists. Power engineering, because Lenin
taught that communism was power plus electrification. She was the
first woman at that institute, studied together with Trotsky's son
and with Malenkov. Then she worked in Germany at Siemens and
Schuckers for a year. Volhovskaya, the first Soviet power station, was
her diploma project. She consulted on the Dneprogres, installed
power stations in Novorossyisk and Novosibirsk—all the power stations were her work. In 1937 she became head of the Chelyabinsk
TEC, *Teplo-Elektro-Tsentrala*, of the entire construction, not just in-
stallation. The little river Mius flowed through there. When all
stood ready, there turned out to be only enough water in that river
to reach a sparrow's knee. And a lot of water is needed to cool the
boilers. There were mountain lakes, but these were considered by
the local tribes sacred, untouchable. Under military guard, the level
of the lake was lowered by a meter and a half, and Mother had to
have personal protection, but the power station opened and still
works.

Kwiatek was a high-ranking *voyenachalnik* in Vinnitsa. I went
there for vacations, I was friendly with his Volodia. In 1937,
Kwiatek was summoned to Moscow. He took a suitcase, went to the
station and threw himself under a train, but, unluckily, just had his
leg cut off. They stood him at the wall on his one leg. Dubovoi had
gone insane before he died. In Chelyabinsk they arrested the direc-

tor of the tractor factory; the director of the railroad; the secretary
of the *Gorkom*. Chief engineer Vinogradov, an aristocrat with a foreign education, came to my mother and said, "I'm old and don't
have much to lose, but you'd better leave here." Mother took a business trip to Moscow, and Vinogradov placed me in the hospital for
two weeks of tests. Moscow was a four-day ride. During the journey, Mother lost use of her legs, was paralyzed, couldn't walk. They
wanted to take her off the train, but she wouldn't let them until she
reached Moscow. Hearing that my mother was sick in Moscow,
Vinogradov took me out of the hospital and drove me in a company
car to the station together with Dunyasha who had bundled a few
things together for us. While Mother lay in the hospital, Dunyasha
and I lived with her older sister, Eva, who had finished the Med-
Institute. Mother's brother, Faivel, was arrested at the same time.
They said he was sentenced to ten years without right of correspondence. Years later we learned that they'd shot him immediately—
that's what they meant by "without right of correspondence." Many
months passed before Mother started to walk, but she was saved.

After the arrests, there was a lack of heroes because they all had
turned out to be "enemies of the people." They started dragging out
those who had died in time—before being arrested. They made a
film about Chapayev. But Chapayev meant Russia, and where is
Ukraine? So Stalin says, "Why is there no film about Shchors?"
They entrusted it to the best Ukrainian director, Dovzhenko.
Mother helped choose the material. The actor, Samoylov, greatly resembled Shchors, but shouted about Lenin too much: Lenin told
me this, Lenin told me that, and Lenin hadn't told Shchors anything because he'd never seen him. The film suggested that the Trot-
skyites had pressed Shchors to march on Kiev. And there's no
mention of tuberculosis, or a Jewish wife. He'd been an outstanding
commander, but always wanted to be a physician—to cure, not kill,
and that's the most important thing I can say about him.

When they heard in Kiev that there was to be a film, they wrote
an opera. They always had superb singers. Mother was invited as a
consultant, and because it was vacation, she took me with her. The

Opera had a huge tailoring shop, and while sewing costumes, they decided to take the opportunity of dressing the main hero's wife and daughter who had had nothing to wear for a long time. Staging the opera and sewing dresses required time, and the summer was hot so I was placed in a rest house in Vorzel near Kiev. I stayed there for two periods, and was about to go back, when a student of physics arrived from Dnepropetrovsk. It was Isaak Khalatnikov, who had just been awarded a Stalin stipend. Later, he used to come Moscow, to the famous physicist Landau—and me!

When war broke out, Isaak was taken, together with other alumni of his Mat-Fiz Department to the Military College in Moscow. His parents and sister were sent south, but they quickly realized that this was the wrong direction, and leaving their luggage, squeezed into a train moving east. That saved them. When the Germans reached Moscow, the Military College was evacuated to Penza. The physicists, of whom there were two hundred, didn't have to study long, and were inducted into the anti-aircraft artillery. Isaak found himself among the thirty most gifted who were sent to the defense of Moscow and only they survived. The rest fell at Stalingrad. I had completed two years of biology when the university was evacuated to Tashkent. Mother wouldn't let me go. "I have no one but you," she said, she wanted to keep me with her. We were evacuated with the *nomenklatura* to Kuybyshev, formerly Samara, my father's chosen town. Mother was to set up electrical power installations for the evacuated production plants. There was a shortage of people. Of five aircraft factories, only one had arrived with a crew. You had to drag yourself for two hours in one direction to work, and work a twelve-hour shift.

"Voluntarily?"

What do you mean "voluntarily"? We were workers. Apart from the ration bread, commercial bread was sold in the factory departments. We had money, because we exceeded the quotas—the prewar quotas were very low. I stood at a milling-machine for a year and a half. When I returned to Moscow, biology no longer interested me. There were so many wounded, so many crippled. I took an intensive medical course. In February 1944, in an unheated, un-cleaned *ZAGS* office, Isaak and I were married—and in doing so, we managed to bring his family out of Tashkent where people were dropping from hunger and epidemics. I didn't make it to the front, because I got pregnant.

Isaak was chief of staff and then commander of an anti-aircraft regiment. The war with Germany was ending and he says he is stay-ing in the force, likes it so much. "The army pays," he says, "and what do you get in graduate school, four hundred rubles? You can starve to death." I never interfered in his professional affairs, but this time I had to. I didn't want him to become a military man. And they still needed to go east and fight the Japanese, thousands were falling there too. I went straight to Kapitsa. "You write as his wife," he said, "and I as the head of the Institute." Both letters went where needed, and he was released. So he comes at me: "What have you done? Why are they releasing me from the army?" And I say, "Because you're a scientist, not a soldier."

Together with Landau, he established a theory of quantum flu-ids. Worked with Landau, Abrikosov and Pomeranchuk on princi-ples of quantum electrodynamics, with Lifshitz and Belinsky on relativistic cosmology. Received a National Award. In 1965, estab-lished the Landau Institute of Theoretical Physics. In 1984, was elected to the Academy of Science.

"Why so late? Because he was a Jew?"

Most physicists were Jews. His institute has trained famous scientists. The Americans bought most of them. No money was spared. Why invest in unknown quantities when you've got the ready-made? Isaak accepted a five-year contract in Israel.

In 1949, a commission came from Ukraine, questioned older work-ers and one of them recalled that in the old days he used to climb over the wall with his friends to have a quiet drink in the cemetery, and one day had seen somebody important being brought in a zinc coffin, and some strange family seeing him off. And that he was buried right by that tomb where brushes and buckets were kept now.

Hundreds of letters kept coming in. From soldiers, school-age youth and little children, because they taught the civil war from the fourth grade on. Before, my mother attended to it, after her death it fell to me. "Dear Valentina Nikolayevna, our detachment requests your father's name and we would very much like you to send us photographs, documents or other personal things." I couldn't stand them. My God, if only someone would send *me* something of his, we lost everything escaping from Chelyabinsk.

They erected a solitary obelisk in the field where he was killed. In Kiev, a statue—on horseback, revolver in holster, right hand pointing the way—in a beautiful square where Aleksander, I don't remember which, once stood. Snovsk was renamed Shchors. Every Ukrainian town had a Shchors Street. In Vinnitsa they organized school athletic *Spartakyads* in his name. On the hundredth anniversary of his birth, they invited me to the town of Shchors—still called Shchors—but I was in Israel with Isaak by then and the letter arrived too late. Samara, where he was buried twice, is called Samara again. I don't know whether his statue still stands in Kiev, but I hope they leave the obelisk in that field.

In Moscow, in memory of the liberation from Napoleon, stood the Church of Christ the Redeemer, by the river near the Pushkin Museum established by Professor Tsvetyev, father of the poet Marina. A very valuable collection. The church was large, extensive. It was torn down in the thirties to make room for the Palace of the Soviets with a thirty-meter-high statue of Lenin, but nothing the hell came of it, the foundations moved. The church had stood, but this didn't want to. They spat blood, but couldn't do it. They packed in superfine steel, hundreds of thousands of tons—nothing helped. In 1941, Zhukov ordered the steel retrieved and out of it they made armature for the tanks which wouldn't let Hitler into Moscow. After the war, nothing stood there for a long time, and later they made a huge, heated swimming pool. But the steam was harmful to the valuable paintings in the Museum and the pool had to be filled in.

Now, the Church of Christ the Redeemer has been erected again. The same one as before, from the same plans—and it stands.

3. KHALATNIKOV

My father came from Ruzhin near Berdichev, my mother from somewhere by Molodechno, they met in Dnepropetrovsk. When the *NEP* was brought in, Father set up a fabric shop in partnership with another Jew. When the *NEP* was recalled, he became a *lishenetz*—from *lishenye*—deprived of the right to vote. Which was not such a great loss. I, however, did have the right to an education, and finished school with top scores, gaining me the right to get into higher studies without an entrance exam.

Physics stood at a high level in Dnepropetrovsk where Abram Joffe had opened a branch of his Leningrad Physico-Technical Institute from which nearly all Russian physics came: Kapitsa, Semyonov, Zeldovich, Chariton. Kurchatov was also Joffe's co-worker. In 1939, I received one of the first Stalin stipends for outstanding students. Mother was proud of me and I had enough money to treat girls to chocolates. I traveled to Landau in Moscow, took his exams. In summer 1941, I was to start graduate studies. On Saturday the 21st of June, I got my diploma in Dnepropetrovsk, but on Sunday morning bombs fell and, instead of graduate studies, I had to go to the Moscow Military College. My parents and my younger sister managed to get evacuated to Uzbekistan. Mother's brother went to war and perished in the first weeks near Kiev. Her sister stayed in Dnepropetrovsk. Blonde, light-eyed, she married a Cossack from Kuban and considered herself Ukrainian. Neighbors who considered otherwise gave her away to the Germans.

After four years of anti-aircraft artillery, I no longer felt sure that I could go back to physics, but after the American atomic explosion, Kapitsa easily persuaded the high authorities that physics was more important than artillery, and in September 1945, I came to the Institute of Physical Problems and studied low temperatures, knowing nothing about the *Spets-proyekt*. Meanwhile in January, the *Spets-komitet* was set up with Kapitsa, Kurchatov and with Beria as the head. Beria insisted they follow in the Americans' footsteps. Kapitsa being a scientist, did not want to repeat what others had already done, but to find a new, shorter way and a conflict ensued. Kapitsa wrote to Stalin requesting to be taken off the committee because of the incompetence of its chairman. Kapitsa did not know that in his pocket Beria had a drawing of the bomb with a precise account of dimensions and materials. In order to limit the possibility of a leak, he had shown these details—obtained even before the American test—only to Kurchatov. Kapitsa was right that Beria knew nothing about physics, but Beria knew more about the bomb than he did. He was dismissed not only from the *Spets-komitet* but also from all other positions. Even his institute was taken away from him, and he spent eight years in his *dacha* in Nikolina Gora, under *de facto* house arrest. Kurchatov engaged Chariton. Chariton's father was editor of a newspaper in independent Riga. When our army occupied Latvia, he was immediately arrested. Chariton had a personal in with Beria and with Stalin, but he did not attempt to free his father because that would have implied he was making use of his position for personal ends. Such principles ruled at that level.

In December 1946, Landau informed me that I would be working on the bomb with Liftshitz. We calculated the processes which occur during an explosion together with the coefficient of output, knowing nothing about the information which had been provided by the Intelligence Service. Besides, it wasn't enough to know the dimensions and materials, nor even the method of reaching the critical mass. One had also to know how to ignite it with neutrons. The task we had been assigned demanded such a quantity of calculations that the theoretical department had to be supplemented by an office with thirty girls armed with German electrical calculators from the Mercedes company. It was headed by mathematician Naum Meyman. The equations demanded a lot of work, and we didn't have much time. We couldn't solve them analytically, they required numerical calculations. We managed to discover models which expedited mathematical solutions while preserving the accuracy of the calculations. I worked on both sides, as a physicist and as a mathematician, coordinating the work between Landau and the mathematicians, for whom I prepared equations in a form which wouldn't allow them to know their use—they didn't need that knowledge. In calculating the parameters of ignition—no one among us had worked on it before—I managed to obtain an interpolative formula of such elegance that Landau was enchanted, and as a reward gave me his photograph with a dedication to "Dear Khalat." Our calculations agreed with the results of tests carried out in 1949, and we were showered with prizes. I received only a decoration, but participants on the level of Landau got *dachas* and their children were admitted without examination to institutions of higher learning. Stalin raised the salaries for all scientists without taking into account the dreadful economic situation in the ruined nation. A professor's salary was five or six times higher than the average, the prestige of scientists rose, and young people went in droves to study.

In that year, 1949, Tamm's group made great strides on the hydrogen bomb on the basis of two ideas. The first, Sakharov's, was so ingeniously simple that today it can be explained to high-school students. The second, Ginzburg's, also seems obvious now: why prepare tritium beforehand, when it can be obtained in the very process of explosion? At that time, Landau fell out with Zeldovich because Zeldovich wanted to draw him into additional work, and after that he contacted only Sakharov. We made calculations in the Department of Applied Mathematics under Keldysh simultaneously with Tikhonov's group. The assignments that we received were written in Sakharov's hand on a slip of paper in green-blue ink. All the initial data were there, together with dimensions and construction details—no typist was allowed to see it. The Americans did not know this variant at that time. I received the slip in order to prepare problems for the mathematicians. We hid it very carefully for some two months at the Institute of Fiz-Problems, and then turned it over to Tikhonov's group for further calculations. Suddenly, the sheet disappeared. After a visit from a high ranking security officer, the head of the department committed suicide. Sakharov cited this in his memoirs as an example of the behavior of the time: a man takes his life because a piece of paper vanishes, apparently Sakharov didn't know what the "piece of paper" in question really was. It was impossible to explain what had happened to it. Perhaps it was burned together with the rough drafts which we were under obligation to burn. No other paper ever disappeared.

The hydrogen bomb calculations were much more complex than those for the atom bomb, and it is probably a miracle that we were able to carry them out with our "manual" methods. At the Institute of Fiz-Problems under the direction of Landau, we revolutionized numerical methods for integrating partial differential equations. The biggest problem was the stability of solutions. Tikhonov's mathematicians maintained that there was no such problem, and tried to persuade the high authorities that we had made up non-existent tasks for ourselves. But without taking into account the stability, instead of smooth curves a "sawtooth" arose. At Tikhonov's it was smoothed out by means of curve fitting, but you don't get reliable results that way. For four days, at a conference headed by Keldysh, we maintained that there is a problem and that we had solved it, and Tikhonov's group insisted that there wasn't. In the end, the high authorities ordered us to hand our algorithms over to Tikhonov's department and there they were finally persuaded of the virtues of our propositions, in which not only had we presented the problem, but also ways of getting around it. I don't know how to explain it in lay terms, and I don't know whether it is possible to express in words at all phenomena that occur only in mathematical symbols—that's what mathematics is for. I can only say that it had to do with taking into account the future, and calculating in what is still unidentified, wanted, unknown. Now it is called "invisibles." I can also say that it's a method which allows the conjoining of the unknown future with the past and the present, and that these unseen patterns of unusual elegance allowed us to carry out, in a few months, calculations which would otherwise have taken years. Experts who today solve complicated problems on computers with the help of these "invisibles" are still filled with admiration: "Ah, so you thought it up?"

All the analyses were carried out completely independently in our department. The hydrogen bomb exploded in 1953 was absolutely original, without a single drawing in Beria's pocket. The tests carried out in 1953 turned out to be totally in keeping with our calculations and we were awarded the last Stalin Prizes. Landau never once came to the *Obyekt* and showed no interest in the practical application of his ideas, but his input and accomplishments were of the highest order. For example, the stability problem was solved in the American project by the most famous mathematician, von Neumann. Landau showed no initiative, limited himself to problems which he had to address as a "scientific slave," as was stressed in the recently-disclosed KGB files. He understood that he was taking part in the creation of a dreadful weapon for dreadful people, but after being interrogated in Lubyanka, didn't have the courage to refuse. And the fact that what he did, he did as best as he could, was because he didn't know how to do it any other way. On Stalin's death, he said to me, "That's it. He's no longer here, I'm no longer afraid of him, and I'm not going to do this any more." Kurchatov invited me into his office where Sakharov and Chariton were sitting. They proposed that I take up Landau's assignments. I knew we had already carried out the work and that nothing interesting remained, but I was thirty-three years old and their proposition flattered me, especially because it came from such learned men. It was like sports, it drew you in. When you started something, contributed to it, thought something up, you began to love it.

In 1929, after graduating from the university, Landau received a six-month stipend from Narkompros and went to Niels Bohr in Copenhagen. Then Bohr arranged a Rockefeller fellowship for him and he went on to Zurich, Leipzig, Berlin and Cambridge. When he was abroad, his father, an oil engineer in Baku, got ten years in a concentration camp. Landau worked first in Leningrad and then in Kharkov. After his co-workers Shubnikov, Weissberg and Rozenkevich were arrested, he fled from Kharkov to Moscow to seek protection from Kapitsa. After him, Korets, Lifshits and Pomeranchuk also fled to Moscow.

Korets, part-physicist, part-poet, sought friends in the Institute of Philosophy and Literature where poets studied, but also Shelepin, the future head of the KGB. On April 23, 1938, Korets brought Landau a draft of a leaflet which was to be distributed at the 1st of May parade. Landau edited it in his own hand. In addition to his handwriting, it carried the hallmarks of his clarity and precision of thought: "The nation is drowning in blood—millions of innocent people are in prisons and no one knows when it will be his turn—Stalin's clique has staged a fascist revolution—socialism remains only on the pages of mendacious newspapers—destroying the nation to remain in power, he is turning it into easy prey for bestial German fascism—the only solution is a determined fight against Stalinist and Hitlerian fascism—don't be afraid of NKVD thugs, they only know how to massacre the defenseless, seize unsuspecting innocent people, loot national property and fabricate senseless trials against non-existent conspiracies—organize AWP groups at workplaces—prepare a mass socialist movement—Stalinist fascism rests on our lack of organization." Signed: "The Moscow Committee of the Anti-Fascist Workers Party." Only a few could evaluate and describe the situation as accurately at that time.

On April 28, he was arrested. That same day Kapitsa wrote to Stalin that the twenty-nine-year-old Landau was the most outstanding theoretical physicist in the USSR; that his work on magnetism and quantum theory was cited in the country and abroad; that just a year earlier he had discovered a new source of stellar radiation energy which could explain why the energy of the sun and stars had not been depleted so far; that Bohr and other leading scientists foresaw a great future for his ideas and "it is indisputable, that the loss of Landau to the Institute, as well as to the whole of Soviet and world science will not go unnoticed and will be deeply felt." Kapitsa admitted that Landau had a "nasty character," that he was "argumentative and pugnacious, looked for faults in others, especially in important old people like our academics, and when he found them, liked to annoy, and in this way had made a lot of enemies." But for all his faults, "it is hard to believe that Landau was capable of baseness." Nothing indicates that this letter had any effect on Stalin.

Landau started testifying only in July. On the 3rd of August, he signed a statement in which he admitted that he had edited the anti-Soviet document he was shown, and that he regarded materialistic philosophy as false, and Marxism disastrous to science. That his views were shared by: Gamov (who had not returned from Denmark in 1934); Ivanenko (sentenced in 1935); Bronstein (arrested at the end of 1937); and Frenkel who had publicly come out against Marxism. That as an advocate of "pure science" (Court-clerk's quotation marks) he separated theory from practice. That as head of the theoretical department in Kharkov, he removed subjects which were technical "and, therefore, military in nature," such as the testing of the properties of iodine-gas and of electronic properties of plasma. That as a consequence of his harmful activity and that of his group—Shubnikov, Weissberg, Rozenkevich and Korets—the work of the atomic core laboratory which cost millions was divorced from the practical aims of technology for defense. That in the presence of his students, Lifshitz and Pomeranchuk, he talked about the trials which were regarded in his group as staged settings for accounts with inconvenient people. That Kapitsa and Semyonov also regarded the arrests of scholars for political reasons to be ruinous to science. Also that the socialist nature of the leaflet was a tactical ploy because a capitalist agenda had no chance of success. To the suggestion that it was German intelligence who had given Korets the idea of distributing a seemingly anti-fascist leaflet, he replied that Korets had communicated nothing of the sort to him, and that he'd been exclusively concerned with battle against the party and the government.

"My anti-Soviet activity began in 1931. Being a scientific worker, a scientist, a theoretical physicist, I was hostile to the party's recommendation to implant dialectical materialism which I considered harmful to science and scholarship. These views were shared by the scientific community in which I found myself at the time, including the leading theoretical physicists of Leningrad . . . We mocked dialectical materialism in our conversations . . . We exposed the poverty of dialectical materialism in our lectures. I propagated anti-dialectical views . . . I put down the dialectic aspect of physics . . . In Kharkov at the beginning of 1935, a group of like-minded scientists emerged, composed of: Shubnikov, Rozenkevich and myself . . . Korets also shared our views of dialectical materialism." He wrote that in his own hand as part of an additional "Personal Account."

On the 23rd of September 1938, Bohr wrote to Stalin: "Only a feeling of gratitude for the fruitful collaboration with Soviet scientists in which I had the good fortune to participate for many years, and the enormous impression made on me, during my numerous visits, by the successes and enthusiasm with which scientific knowledge is inspired in the USRR, motivates me to bring to your attention, Sir, the importance of scientific-experimental work of one of the outstanding physicists of the younger generation . . . Professor Landau gained a renowned reputation in the scientific community for his contribution to atomic-physics . . . and contributed decisively to the creation of the school of theoretical physics in the USSR . . . With enormous satisfaction I maintained a close contact with Professor Landau for many years and regularly corresponded with him about scientific problems which interested us both. However, to my deep concern, I have received no further replies to my letters and—as I know—none of the numerous foreign physicists who follow his scientific work with particular interest have had replies from him. I tried to contact him through the Soviet Academy of Sciences, of which I have the honor to be a member, but the reply which I received from its president contains no information about the place of residence, or the fate, of Professor Landau. I am profoundly distressed by this, especially since the recent news of his arrest. I continue to believe that this news is unfounded, but if it is true, I am convinced that a deplorable misunderstanding must have taken place because I cannot imagine that Professor Landau, who had completely given himself up to scientific work and whose forthrightness I value highly, could have done something to justify arrest. Because of the enormous significance that this has for science in the USSR and for international scientific cooperation, I appeal to you, Sir, to look into Professor Landau's case and, if there has been a misunderstanding, to see that this unusually talented and productive scientist can return to his unusually important work for the advancement of mankind."

On the 10th of November 1938, the deputy of *Narkom*, Potiomkin, gave Poskrebyshev a translation of this letter. In the enclosed remarks it was stressed that Bohr conducted experimental studies on splitting the atom, had been to the Soviet Union several times and—according to embassy information—"never spoke out against the USSR, and had always expressed himself very positively about Soviet science and culture." Poskrebyshev, Stalin's personal secretary, lived in our building. When his wife was arrested, Stalin said to him, "Don't worry, we'll find you another." And they did. We often saw her on the balcony.

In December, Landau was served the indictment, which was transmitted to the Prosecutor's Office in January, and in March to the Moscow Military Tribunal. On the 6th of April 1939, Kapitsa wrote to Molotov:

"Working recently on properties of liquid helium at near-absolute zero temperature, I managed to uncover several new phenomena, which will, perhaps, explain one of the most puzzling areas of contemporary physics. I plan to publish parts of this work over the coming month, but in order to do so, I need the assistance of a theoretician. Here in the Soviet Union, Landau has the best knowledge of this theory, but the problem is, he's been under arrest for a year now." Kapitsa stressed that "this is abnormally long for an investigation," and that "during this time, for unknown reasons, both

Soviet and world science has been deprived of Landau's expertise."
He added that, "Landau is frail, and if he starves to death, it will be
a great disgrace to us, the Soviet people," and asked, "could the
NKVD be asked to speed up the Landau's case," and, if not, "would
it not be possible to use Landau for scientific work during his stay
in Butirki Prison, as is apparently done with engineers?"

The head of the NKVD Investigation Department, Kobulov,
personally interrogated Landau. From his remarks dated the 8th of
April, 1939, we learn additionally that in Moscow Landau and Korets had recruited Rumer, to whom Landau spoke about "a need to
act in all possible ways to change the country's regime," and who
had agreed with him that it was necessary "to organize a struggle
against the Soviet regime"; that Landau had initially also named
Kapitsa and Siemyonov as members of the anti-Soviet organization,
and later introduced a correction into the protocol, that he had
merely counted on them, but had not dared to be totally open with
them; that in the end, he had taken back *all* his earlier testimonies,
and when asked why, "was unable to give any coherent explanation," stating however that "no physical means had been used to influence him during the interrogation." Below these remarks,
Kobulov had added that Moysei Abramovich Korets remained in
the Butirki NKVD prison, and Juri Borisovich Rumer "was performing special work in the Moscow institution No. 82." That institution was, of course, a *sharashka* like in *The First Circle*. Rumer
worked in an air force construction office, like Tupolev. The conditions in the *sharashka* were considerably better than in a regular
prison, that's why Kapitsa suggested—as a last resort—putting Landau in some place like that.

On the 26th of April 1939, Kapitsa signed a short letter to
Beria: "Please free arrested professor of physics, Lev Davidovich
Landau, on my personal recognizance. I guarantee the NKVD that
Landau will not conduct any counter-revolutionary activities
against Soviet authorities in my institute, and I will do everything in
my means to ensure that he will not do any counter-revolutionary
work outside the institute. If I notice him making any statements

hostile to Soviet authorities, I will instantly inform the NKVD officials."

On the 28th of April 1939, taking into account that Landau "is an outstanding specialist in the area of theoretical physics, and may prove useful to Soviet science," the captain of State Security, Vizel, made the "decision": "to free the arrested Landau, suspend the investigation, and hand over his case to the archives." Where it remained until 1991.

Stalin probably never saw the leaflet edited by Landau. Poskrebyshev may have seen it, but was afraid to show it to him. Landau really did think about how to overthrow Stalin, but the leaflet was, of course, a provocation. Rumer worked in the *sharashka* until 1956, then became director of the institute in Novosibirsk. Korets returned after eighteen years in the Gulag, but was no longer a physicist, became a historian of science. He claimed that only he, Landau, and one poet from the Institute of Philosophy and Literature, who fell at the front in 1941, knew about the leaflet. Korets's daughter emigrated to Israel and published that poet's name in her memoirs, but there is no evidence against him, and because he was killed in the war, I don't want to name him. Perhaps he had been persuaded it was for the country, for ideals? It's not difficult to convince a poet of something like that.

Landau had been a member of the Academy since 1946. He received two Orders of Lenin, and became a Hero of Socialist Labor. In 1951, he was elected to the Danish Royal Academy of Science; in 1956 to the Dutch one. In 1957 he wanted to go abroad. The CK turned to the KGB. The "File of Academician Landau" of December 19, 1957, mentions that Landau and his father had both been imprisoned in the thirties and that Landau was hiding the fact. On the basis of information from agents, "close acquaintances," and acquired by "operational methods," statements were cited indicating his continued antagonism to "Soviet reality." In 1947 he claimed that "in our country science has been prostituted to a greater degree than abroad," and that there is no "room for scientific individuality" because "the direction of work is dictated from above." He "systematically" denied the superiority of Russian and Soviet science, saying: "I'm an internationalist, and it doesn't matter to me who made this or that discovery." From 1952, he tried to work for the state as little as possible. He said that "one must try by all possible means not to get into the thick of atomic matters, but such a refusal and self-alienation requires extensive caution." In January 1953, he told one of his "close acquaintances": "Were it not for my Fifth Point, I would not be involved at all with the *Spetsproyekt,* only with science with which I am now behind . . . *Spets* work assures me some power, but I've been reduced to the level of scientific slave." The Fifth Point was ethnicity. On November 30, 1956, he said, "How can one believe this? And believe whom? Those thugs?" It was a reference to the Hungarian events. And on December 1, 1956: "If our political system doesn't collapse in a peaceful manner, a third world war is unavoidable . . . thus, a peaceful dismantling of our system is a question of human survival." On January 12, 1957, to member correspondent of the Academy of Sciences, Shalnikov: "Our system is patently fascist and to feed the hope that it can lead to something decent is simply laughable." In a conversation with Meyman: "Lenin was the first fascist." Shalnikov and Meyman are obviously beyond suspicion, the naming of them is their best alibi. The KGB never reveal the names of their true informers, those "close acquaintances." Stalin was dead, and Landau was no longer afraid—wrongly so. Someone from his "closest circle" said that "allowing him to go abroad would be imprudent, because there is no certainty that he'd return." And I think there wasn't.

In 1959, Landau became an honorary member of the British Institute of Physics; in 1960, a foreign member of the Royal Society of Great Britain and the United States Academy of Science. That same year, he was awarded the American F. London Prize and the West German Max Planck Medal. On January 7, 1962, on the way from Moscow to Dubna, his car collided with a truck approaching from the opposite direction. He was not admitted to the Kremlin hospital which had modern foreign equipment, but the best doctors came on their own and did everything they could. After three months, he regained consciousness, but was no longer the same person. Didn't work, lay in bed mostly. In 1962, he was given the Lenin Prize and the Nobel Prize, but he was no longer a scientist. In 1964, I established an institute in his name. In 1984, I was elected to the Academy.

"Why not earlier?"

Theoretical physicists were mostly Jews, and you can't elect just Jews, there has to be a balance . . . Like in physics . . . I never met the leaders. Only Chernyenko, in a way: in 1985, when a new wind was already blowing, I stood in a place of honor among the notables—at his funeral. Poskrebyshev, he knew them—and everything about them. "Everything" in those days meant more than they knew themselves. He knew more than anyone in history. He lived in the same building as we, but we never saw him. A modest, unimposing man, people said. He retired, someone met him in the CK sanatorium. "What are you doing now, comrade, writing your memoirs?" "No, not memoirs!" He nearly got a heart attack.

Landau's files have only now been pulled out—from the Presidential Archives. The KGB would never have revealed them.

4. DAUGHTER OF ISAAK

Stalin ordered the building of Government House in the thirties. Five hundred and five apartments for high-ranking officials, senior military officers and other *nomenklatura,* so he could have them all together in the palm of his hand. Tukachevsky lived there, Dimitrov, Peters, Lysenko, Stakhanov. One splendid elevator at the front, and another at the rear—a black one, of which I was always afraid. I later learned that the black one was used to take arrestees. Dimitrov, as head of the Comintern, suggested which of the foreigners should be finished off, and Lysenko which of the scientists. Peters lived there, also an "internationalist," a Latvian, the chief assistant to Derzhynsky. Stakhanov—who had a huge five-room

apartment with a view of the Kremlin, decorations and honors—
was an alcoholic perpetually intoxicated. I was in class with his
daughter. He had two of them, pretty girls, both drank from seventh grade on.

The first plaque was mounted on the wall when Dimitrov died:
that he lived here from 1935 to 1943, an international hero. When
Stalin died, other plaques appeared—for those who'd only lived until 1936, 1937, 1938. Tombstones, because those were more or less
the dates of their deaths. There was not always a reason to mourn.
Tukachewsky—1937—bravely suppressed a peasant revolt in the
Tambov Oblast, killing insurgents along with their families. Hundreds of plaques were mounted, practically an entire history. Grandmother got one of those vacant apartments, because it was then they
remembered she was the widow of a hero.

I went to the Government School with the children of ministers
and secretaries of the CK who were driven there and back in black
ZIS limousines. The teachers, corrupt hypocrites, obsequious to
those little brats. The principal, a retired KGB man, enough to
make one sick. At the end of 1952, I was put into a black ZIS and
driven to the Kremlin. They looked me over and questioned me and
another girl. We were to hand Stalin flowers at the 1st of May Parade. And probably kiss him. They made the selection six months in
advance. Thank God, he died in March.

I was revolted by the teachers—parrots mouthing stupid, worn-
out slogans and making us repeat them. And by the poems of
praise—it didn't matter to whom or why—they were all the same.
And why do we love Lenin? And why do we love Stalin? Orally, and
in writing. Not Stalin later on, but we continued loving Lenin.
Why? I couldn't understand why. He always disgusted me, even by
his appearance: those mean, sharp, little eyes flashing from all the
walls, there was nowhere to hide from them. I used to run away
from school and play truant with the boys.

I didn't experience shortages, nor know about repressions. I
didn't know my grandmother's brother had been shot in 1938. Her

sister's husband came back from the Gulag, and I didn't know he'd been imprisoned. Such things were hidden from children. "Uncle's gone far away, we don't know when he'll be back."

When I finished tenth grade, my surname was changed to Shchors. Grandmother liked that a lot. I wanted to go into biology, but Jews—Shchors or not Shchors—encountered difficulties at the university in Moscow. Grandmother went with me to Kiev where Shchors stood on horseback opposite the university. But even there I lacked some point to get in. Grandmother went to the CK of Ukraine. "All right, she may study, but in Dnepropetrovsk." Hunger raged in Dnepropetrovsk. I lived at the librarian's. We got up at four in the morning to get pigeons and a few potatoes at the market. I didn't complain, I was learning to live, acquiring experience, but Father went to Kapitsa and after a year, I returned to Moscow—to study medicine. There were two Med-Institutes. One exclusively for the elite, unbelievably corrupt. Kapitsa, an Academician, a laureate, managed to arrange only the other one. It had two departments: general medicine and pediatrics. General medicine ranked higher, but I was accepted into pediatrics, although the grades I brought from Dnepropetrovsk were outstanding. Jews did study medicine, but only those whose parents treated government and CK members, and they all needed more backing than everyone else, without exceptions. The institute fought the "fraudulent theories of Weismanism-Morganism"—although this was already the beginning of the sixties. Genetics? There was no such thing.

I wanted to work in research, so after pediatrics, went to the Rheumatology Institute, submitted my papers, and the head of the cadre says right away, "I would not encourage . . ." The Director of the Institute was a crazed anti-Semite and Jews were "not encouraged." I went into biochemistry then, and involved myself with enzymes, from which Jews were not dissuaded.

I had arguments with my grandmother. I showed her documents, books which were starting to come in from abroad. "Just look, you can agree or not, but at least look." "No, its *anti-*

sovietchina, and if you're going to keep it in the house . . ." "Then what? What?" A girl from Novozybkov, a small Jewish town, what could she have known about in those days? How to sew—she sewed beautifully. Then suddenly the revolution, heroes on horseback. Her personal life was very short. A brief love affair which she surrounded with a halo. She clung desperately to those years and rejected anything which could destroy the memory of those few great moments. She had frozen in time, wouldn't allow anything to be explained to her, couldn't be talked to. With horror, she yelled that during the civil war we'd be on opposite sides. I had to admit she was right about that. Yes, there had been mistakes and transgressions, Stalin might have erred. But not Lenin. Lenin was a saint, simply God. When I said he was the chief bandit, she was ready to kill me—literally. Fortunately, the discussion was taking place forty years after the civil war.

I married a Russian who had a room in a *komunal* on Leninsky Prospect. One kitchen, one bathroom, one toilet, and a family in each room—eleven people. So I said, "Let's sign up for a cooperative." But they admitted you into the cooperative only if you had less than five square meters a person. So I signed myself out from Grandmother's in the Government House, and my husband went to sign me into his *komunal.* The woman behind the desk looked through the documents. "Where did you find yourself such a wife? Shchors, but—daughter of Isaak . . ."

On vacation in Yalta, I met Ira Braude of the extra-mural Krupskaya Pedagogical Institute. People not accepted elsewhere studied there: the poet Oleg Chukhontsev; the director, Polonsky; prose-writer Voynovich; and Ira's first husband, Kamil Ikramov. His father, first secretary of Uzbekistan, had been shot, his mother was Jewish, he, himself, also was imprisoned for many years. Ira, touched by his fate, married him, even though Voynovich was already in love with her then. This was after the trial of Daniel and Sinyavsky, when the great divide arose: some sided with the accusations, others with the accused, the third were silent. We listened to foreign radio for twenty-four hours a day, to the commentaries of Anatol Goldberg, we were brought up on those commentaries. Galich had a song: "Silent is comrade Goldberg, silent the BBC, only Song of Solveig sounds over land and sea." Because, of course, they jammed them, if not with Grieg then with Tchaikovsky. We read *samizdat* at night. I didn't hesitate even for a moment. At the Voynoviches', I got to know people like Grigorenko, Irina Erenburg. When Stalin murdered the Jewish anti-Fascist Committee, he confiscated all materials about the Holocaust on Soviet territory, about collaboration on the part of local people, and the hatred encountered by the Jews who returned. Irina Erenburg hid documents she'd found in her father's archives, and later donated them for the *Black Book*.

Voynovich was summoned to the "Metropol," the KGB had rooms in hotels for all kinds of meetings. They gave him a cigarette. He got palpitations, nausea, dizziness. They both hid with me. I was divorced then, and Ira pregnant. We were afraid for Voynovich. A letter from Andropov to the Politburo was discovered in the archives "considering the matter of the writer Vladimir Voynovich," in which Andropov informs that Voynovich is attempting to set up a chapter of the International Pen-Club, and if he does not desist from this activity, "special means" will be applied. Why did he write that? To get tacit approval for those "special means." My father was afraid, made me scenes, but they didn't summon me, or threaten me, didn't even try to recruit me. My name protected me on this occasion. They had enough problems with other well-known names like Yakir, Litvinov, Ikramov, or Antonov-Ovseyenko, whose son was imprisoned twice for seven years. They didn't want another scandal.

Those who could were leaving. Marrying Jews, manipulating documents. I went to the airport with the Voynoviches, Irina Erenburg saw them off, too. It was hard for me when they left, and when Vladimov left, and Aksyonov; when Galicz died in Paris as a result of a very suspicious electric shock. I was suffocating, wanted to leave as well, but I couldn't do it to my father because I would have ruined his academic career—and he, being a Jew, had enough problems without that.

Petya had faith when all those changes started, I didn't. For me, those who held party positions and occupied themselves "professionally" with that nonsense had to be mentally retarded. It had to be some kind of genetic, or psychological defect, because could a reasonably normal person choose a career like that? Each of their ceremonies, each speech, each quotation from their "works" was obviously pathological. And the Institute of Marxism-Leninism: thousands, tens of thousands of buffoons! They studied, they analyzed, they couldn't have been psychologically sound. Those things were simply unreadable.

"Perhaps they considered it simply a business which provided a career, privileges, power."

A black business, the blackest: death, generations of broken lives, nowhere have so many crimes been committed. I can understand people who joined for a position, a few privileges and conveniences—millions did that. My mother worked at the KGB polyclinic where every doctor had to be a member of the party, a non-member couldn't cure a KGB man . . . Father had to join the party because he was a commander in the war. They wanted me as well, because of my name, but I couldn't. For me, it would have been like treading in shit. Some could, all right, I can understand it, but not muck around in it—professionally!

That's why when Gorbachev came, I said right away, don't get excited, nothing will come of it. Same with Yeltsin. People don't change from one year to the next. Lenin stood at the Institute. I went to the director, "Aren't you ashamed? You, a decent man, a well-known scholar?" And he says, "That section has been leased to another institute, nothing can be done." Or take that corpse in the square in the middle of Moscow. No one's going to move him. So many crimes, and was anyone punished? Because they are still around and protect one another. As long as they're there, nothing'll come of it. So many crimes and no punishment, what kind of future can come of it?

They never let Petya go abroad because he's a Jew. It didn't matter that it said "Russian" in his papers. All at once they let him go to Japan for three months. He came back a different person. He earned more in those three months than he had throughout his whole life, so we made a trip to America. In New York, a friend brought a car to us at the airport, and we drove through sixteen states. Petya gave lectures, we visited friends along the way—I became infatuated with America. When we reached Seattle, on the other side of the continent, I took Petya to the Jewish Community. "We're Jews, they discriminate against us, don't let us live decently, may they go to hell, I don't want my children to grow up there." A woman from Kiev spoke with us, very nice, polite, advised us on what we should do. Everything was fine with Petya's papers, but then she saw my name: "Shchors . . . ?" She went and didn't come back. A woman from Kiev. We returned to New York, gave our friend his car back.

A rabbi came from Jerusalem to Moscow twice a year and decided who was Jewish and who wasn't. I went twice, explained. It turned out not to be so simple. My grandmother who participated in the Revolution as a young girl had taken the name Rostova, because pseudonyms were fashionable with the revolutionaries, and Jewish names were not. Later she signed Rostova-Shchors and that's how it remained in her documents. When she gave birth in Klintsy, far from any registry, she sent Dunyasha, a peasant girl. Dunyasha, a good soul, nursed my mother and me, devoted her whole life to our family, but what did she know? That father was Shchors, and mother Rostova. No ethnicity, no religion. And a Ukrainian, she didn't understand Russian well. I explained that my grandmother was Jewish and her real name Haykina. A secretary came in, her family was from Novozybkov. "Shchors? Everything's fine," she told the rabbi, "everybody knows there that Shchors's wife was a Jew from Novozybkov." But the Jerusalem rabbi, an earnest man, had to have it on paper. They wrote to Novozybkov, but the Jewish documents in Novozybkov had perished along with the Jews, so my mother isn't a Jew and neither am I.

I didn't want any aid, I wrote that Petya and I could easily get jobs and support ourselves without anyone's help, but nothing came of it. Party activists, dregs of society, informers, fictitious marriages on fraudulent papers, all those were leaving. In Moscow you could get anything for money now. A former wife of an Academician who'd never lacked for anything, sold her luxurious apartment and brought out her entire wealth, and she received welfare, medicare and a subsidized apartment as a "refugee" here. I won't go to Jewish organizations any more. I'm not Jewish, so be it.

Petya, as an outstanding scientist, received the status of an "alien with extraordinary abilities." I also got a very good contract. My daughter Ksenya studies in Chicago—genetics! Old Lysenko is turning over in his grave. My sister who studied languages settled in Switzerland with her husband, a Russian businessman. Petya receives invitations to international conferences. Scientists from America, France, Germany, Israel—but mostly Russian names. It's a little sad.

Our son, Alyosha, asked when it'll be his turn to tell a story. I told him, "Your life will be so undramatic that no one will be interested." That's why we left.

FOR THE BEST IN PAPERBACKS, LOOK FOR THE

In every corner of the world, on every subject under the sun, Penguin represents quality and variety—the very best in publishing today.

For complete information about books available from Penguin—including Penguin Classics, Penguin Compass, and Puffins—and how to order them, write to us at the appropriate address below. Please note that for copyright reasons the selection of books varies from country to country.

In the United States: Please write to *Penguin Putnam Inc., P.O. Box 12289 Dept. B, Newark, New Jersey 07101-5289* or call *1-800-788-6262.*

In the United Kingdom: Please write to *Dept. EP, Penguin Books Ltd, Bath Road, Harmondsworth, West Drayton, Middlesex UB7 0DA.*

In Canada: Please write to *Penguin Books Canada Ltd, 10 Alcorn Avenue, Suite 300, Toronto, Ontario M4V 3B2.*

In Australia: Please write to *Penguin Books Australia Ltd, P.O. Box 257, Ringwood, Victoria 3134.*

In New Zealand: Please write to *Penguin Books (NZ) Ltd, Private Bag 102902, North Shore Mail Centre, Auckland 10.*

In India: Please write to *Penguin Books India Pvt Ltd, 11 Panchsheel Shopping Centre, Panchsheel Park, New Delhi 110 017.*

In the Netherlands: Please write to *Penguin Books Netherlands bv, Postbus 3507, NL-1001 AH Amsterdam.*

In Germany: Please write to *Penguin Books Deutschland GmbH, Metzlerstrasse 26, 60594 Frankfurt am Main.*

In Spain: Please write to *Penguin Books S. A., Bravo Murillo 19, 1° B, 28015 Madrid.*

In Italy: Please write to *Penguin Italia s.r.l., Via Benedetto Croce 2, 20094 Corsico, Milano.*

In France: Please write to *Penguin France, Le Carré Wilson, 62 rue Benjamin Baillaud, 31500 Toulouse.*

In Japan: Please write to *Penguin Books Japan Ltd, Kaneko Building, 2-3-25 Koraku, Bunkyo-Ku, Tokyo 112.*

In South Africa: Please write to *Penguin Books South Africa (Pty) Ltd, Private Bag X14, Parkview, 2122 Johannesburg.*